**Signs, Songs, and Memory in the Andes**

*Figure 1.* Tape recording a song by the hearth, the tropical forest, Ecuador. (Photos are by author unless otherwise specified.)

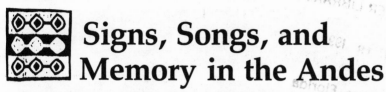

# Signs, Songs, and Memory in the Andes
## Translating Quechua Language and Culture

BY REGINA HARRISON

UNIVERSITY OF TEXAS PRESS   AUSTIN

Copyright © 1989 by University of Texas Press
All rights reserved
Printed in the United States of America
First edition, 1989
Requests for permission to reproduce material from this work should be
sent to Permissions, University of Texas Press, Box 7819, Austin, TX
78713-7819.

The paper used in this publication meets the minimum requirements of
American National Standard for Information Sciences—Permanence of
Paper for Printed Library Materials, ANSI Z39.48-1984. ∞

Library of Congress Cataloging-in-Publication Data

Harrison, Regina, [date]
    Signs, songs, and memory in the Andes : translating Quechua
language and culture / by Regina Harrison. — 1st ed.
        p.   cm.
    Bibliography: p.
    Includes index.
    ISBN 0-292-77627-6. — ISBN 0-292-77628-4 (pbk.)
    1. Quechua poetry.   2. Quechua poetry—Translating.   3. Quechua
Indians—Social life and customs.   4. Indians of South America—
Andes Region—Social life and customs.   I. Title.
PM6308.6.H37   1989
898'.3—dc19                                                        89-30889
                                                                          CIP

*For my mother, and in memory of my father and sister*

**La irrealidad de lo mirado**
**Da realidad a la mirada**
**O. Paz**

# Contents

## Illustrations

### Maps

### Figures

# Acknowledgments

THIS BOOK is filled with words and photographs of Quichua-speaking people who welcomed me, a complete stranger, into their homes and communities over fifteen years ago. Their patience and their generosity have allowed me to enter their lives and to transcribe their thoughts and their songs. My first lessons in Quichua were repeated, again and again, by Felipe Shihuango in the Ecuadoran *selva,* 1974. Several months later, now somewhat conversant, I studied the highland dialect with Carlos Conterón in a bilingual program directed by Louisa Stark. Louisa Stark and Donald Dilworth provided names of likely singers in the community of Colta-Monjas, near Riobamba, and I set off for that village. There, Rosa Muyu Sayai and her family fed me, sheltered me, and chased the *cuys* away from my sleeping bag. Juan Remache hiked with me to fields where women and men harvested grain, and he introduced me to Lorenzo Chimbolema, Manuel Maji, Antonio Llallico, and Manuel Banda Hernández. Gunter Schulze generously loaned me song texts he collected in this community, and Sylvia Forman later clarified issues of women's roles and inheritance patterns for me. Louisa Stark and Pieter Muysken also guided my way to the community of Saraguro as a source of traditional songs. There Juan Manuel Cartuche accompanied me, my tape recorder slung over his shoulder, in my quest for songs; Balbina Shunaula and Alegría Shunaula also were invaluable companions and teachers.

To my friend Elena López Andi in the Pastaza province I owe my fluency in Quichua and my understanding of lowland Quichua culture; she spoke to me of myths, histories, and life stories while we interpreted the songs, coiled clay for ceramics, and wove a carrying bag together. A model Quichua woman, she weeds her garden plots without fail, and she always serves abundant *chicha* in thin-walled, painted *mokawa* bowls. Alonso Andi and Carlos Calapucha immeasurably encouraged my comprehension of language and culture with their animated telling of tales late in the afternoons. Ted Macdonald shared with me his knowledge of lowland Quichua communities, as did Lloyd and Linda Rogers. The women of the community and nearby settlements encouraged the project of collecting and interpreting songs: Rosa Shihuango, Graciela Grefa, Paula Aguinda, América Santi, Vicenta Andi, Corina Dahua, María Tanguila, Maruja Vargas, Sirena Tanguila, Paula Tanguila, Catalina Calapucha, Clara Mamallacta, Francisca López Shihuango, and Ospina Rosalita Santi. Carmen Chuquín, linguist and educator, helped unravel the intricacies of the dialects and the song texts, upon my return to the United States.

The fieldwork and the library research were originally funded with a generous fellowship for two years from the Social Science Research Council and the American Council of Learned Societies. Arq. Hernán Crespo Toral graciously provided an affiliation in Ecuador with the Instituto Nacional de Antropología e Historia, and P. Julián Bravo, S. J., opened wide the doors to the Biblioteca Ecuatoriana Aureliano Espinosa Pólit in Cotocollao. The National Endowment for the Humanities has substantially increased the scope of the study through several grants: one award allowed me to return and tape commentary to the women's songs in the summer of 1980, another bountiful fellowship for 1982–1983 freed me from the responsibilities of teaching so that I could continue writing and research, and a third award, a Summer Institute at the Newberry Library, enriched my understanding of the colonial period. The Schmutz Faculty Research Fund of Bates College allowed me to travel again to Peru and Ecuador in 1982. Thomas Hedley Reynolds, President of Bates College, authorized the President's Discretionary Fund for Faculty and Curricular Research to release funds to defray costs of publication. Recently, an award from the Latin American Studies Program at Cornell University allowed me access to the rich lode of Quechua materials in the library, as well as providing hours of conversation with Andean specialists Billie Jean Isbell, John V. Murra, and Mercedes López-Baralt. I am very grateful for the support I have received.

I also thank those scholars who shaped my skills of analysis while I studied at the University of Illinois. Martha Paley de Francescato continues to mentor me, intellectually and spiritually, as a result of a friendship which began in her class of the Latin American short story. Merlin Forster encouraged me to write (and rewrite) a dissertation which explores the contribution of Quichua to Latin American literature. Donald Lathrap's meticulously crafted lectures and examinations allowed me to appreciate the depth of South American culture history and the discipline of anthropology. R. T. Zuidema always enthusiastically disseminated his knowledge of structuralism, his reading of the colonial dictionaries, and his slides of Andean *keros*. Frank Salomon's copious notes of praise and criticism also are present in many aspects of my research. Norman and Sibbey Whitten patiently offered advice and information about living and studying in a tropical forest environment. Rodolfo Cerrón Palomino, in his office down the hall, often helped me explore Quechua texts written by José María Arguedas.

Many people have read early drafts or final versions of this book. Rolena Adorno often put aside her own research and graciously accepted the task of reading each transformation of the manuscript. Her complex and exacting commentary has enriched the content and the organization of *Signs, Songs, and Memory in the Andes*. In terms of *ayni*, I also come up on the owing side with Richard Chase Smith, whose politics, passion, and knowledge have long inspired me. He should be able to see some of his thoughts reflected here in these pages. Bruce Mannheim, as a reader for the University of Texas Press, guided my writing with both specific and theoretical suggestions, as did the detailed report from the other, anonymous reader for the Press. To Lawrence Carpenter, a *diusilupagi*, for helping me with the transcriptions of the Quechua and Quichua texts. Certain people appear in the footnotes and parentheses who should be acknowledged for their reading of specific chapters: Kathy Waldron, Ann Megyesi, Sharon Kinsman, Christine Franquemont, David Boruchoff, Frank Salomon, Irene Silverblatt, Sherry Ortner, and Julio Ortega. I take responsibility, however, for all errors of fact and interpretation. In addition, I thank John McCleary for coming up with the title and Gene Bell for tracking down the quotation from Borges. The solitariness of writing has been dispelled with greetings from many friends who manage to live lives filled with laughter and academic discourse: Alison Weber, Paula Matthews, Maureen Ahern, Fred Padula, Sara Castro-Klarén, John Ackerman, Danny Danforth, Kathleen Sullivan, Jim Leamon, Marjorie Agosín, Richard Williamson, and Laurie Donnelly.

A number of people have helped to prepare the manuscript. Sylvia Hawks typed patiently, deciphering my handwriting and transforming it into hundreds of pages of more readable computer script. The Interlibrary Loan staff of the George and Helen Ladd Library at Bates College helped gather articles from faraway sources. Joanna B. Day facilitated the reproduction of diagrams. Sean and Robin Honan aided in the compilation of the bibliography; Sean also deserves thanks for proofreading the entire manuscript. Peter Scarpaci and

Beth Carvette are responsible for the care with which my photographs are reproduced; Ted Macdonald also granted me permission to use several of his photographs.

Parts of Chapter 3 appeared previously in *From Oral to Written Expression: Native Andean Chronicles of the Colonial Period*, edited by Rolena Adorno (Syracuse: Foreign and Comparative Studies Publications/Latin American Series, 1982). Parts of Chapter 5 were published in *Cuadernos Hispanoamericanos* 417 (March 1985). David P. Williams I thank for the use of his poem, "In Praise of the Potato," originally published in the *Atlantic Monthly*, March 1987. "Papa tarpui" was first published in *La sangre de los cerros/Urkukunapa yawarnin* (Lima: Centro Peruano de Estudios Sociales/Universidad Nacional Mayor de San Marcos/Mosca Azul Editores, 1987).

Many people who should be acknowledged remain unnamed, but wholly remembered, for sharing with me their intimate thoughts, the poetry of their songs, and the poetry of their lives. *A tantos (y por tanto), gracias.*

# The Orthography of Quechua and Quichua

IN THIS book I use *Quichua* to refer to the Ecuadoran varieties of the native language. *Quechua*, on the other hand, designates the dialects spoken in Peru. Also, in some chapters, *Quechua* is an inclusive term and refers to all the varieties of this language spoken by millions of people.

The orthography for *Quechua* follows the Official Alphabet of 1975, revised in 1983 by the First Workshop for the Writing System of Quechua and Aymara (I Taller de Escritura en Quechua y Aimara).

| labial | alveolar | palatal | velar | post-velar | | | |
|--------|----------|---------|-------|------------|---|---|---|
| ph | th | chh | kh | qh | | | |
| p | t | ch | k | q | | | |
| p' | t' | ch' | k' | q' | i | a | u |
| | s | sh | h | | | | |
| m | n | ñ | | | | | |
| | l | ll | | | | | |
| w | r | y | | | | | |

*m, n, s, w* represent sounds traditionally represented by these letters

*sh* represents a sound like that in the English word *ship*

*p, t, ch, ñ, l, ll, r, y* represent sounds like those letters in Spanish

*k* represents a sound like that in English *sky*

*q* represents a post-velar stop, far back in the mouth

*qh* represents a sound like the initial consonant in English *cat*, but further back in the mouth

*ph, th, chh, kh* represent sounds like those represented in English when initial in a word: *pie, that, chair, kill*

*p', t', ch', k', q'* represent glottalized consonants, which sound like a suction or a click after the consonant

*h* represents a sound similar to the English *h*

*i* represents a sound ranging from the Spanish *i* to *e*

*a* represents a sound like Spanish *a*

*u* represents a sound ranging from the Spanish *u* to *o*

The orthography for *Quichua* has not been standardized according to the language itself. The system which I use to represent the sounds of Ecuadoran highland and lowland dialects is a composite Ecuadoran alphabet. Different dialects have different configurations of the graphemes below:

| *labial* | *alveolar* | *palatal alveolar* | *palatal* | *velar* | | | |
|---|---|---|---|---|---|---|---|
| ph | th | tyh | chh | kh | | | |
| p | t | ty | ch | k | i | a | u |
| (b) | (d) | | | (g) | | | |
| f | s | | sh | j | | | |
| v | z | | zh | | | | |
| | ts | | | | | | |
| m | n | | ñ | | | | |
| | l | | ll | | | | |
| | r | | (rr) | | | | |
| w | | | y | | | | |

*m*, *n*, *s*, *w* represent sounds traditionally represented by those letters

*p*, *t*, *ch*, *ñ*, *l*, *ll*, *r*, *y* represent sounds like those letters in Spanish

*z* represents a voiced alveolar fricative like that in English *zinc*

*k* represents a sound like that in English *sky*

*sh* represents a sound like that in English *ship*

*ph*, *th*, *chh*, *kh* represent sounds like those represented in English when initial in a word: *pie*, *that*, *chair*, *kill*

*f*, *v* are bilabial fricatives

(b), (d), (g), (rr) are used to represent sounds showing influence of Spanish

*ts* represents the sound in the English word *cats*

*zh* represents the sound in the English word *rouge*

*ty*, *tyh* represent sounds that have no English or Spanish equivalents

*j* represents a sound similar to English *h*

*i* represents a sound ranging from the Spanish *i* to *e*

*a* represents a sound like Spanish *a*

*u* represents a sound ranging from the Spanish *u* to *o*

These two alphabets are utilized in the writing of the song texts I tape recorded and the songs I have reconstructed. The specific alphabet preferred by each author, however, is cited in quotations from studies of Quechua and previously published Quechua texts.

My explanation of the graphemes is derived from a system in Hardman (1981) and Carpenter (personal communication). Representations of phonemes for specific dialects may be found in studies by Cerrón Palomino (1987), Taylor (1980a), Isbell (1978), Howard-Malverde (1981), Whitten (1976), Cole (1982), Stark (1975), and Stark et al. (1973).

**Signs, Songs, and Memory in the Andes**

# Introduction

I BALANCE carefully as I walk on the single tree trunk which serves as a narrow bridge over the fast-flowing stream below. My toes turn inward, grasping the smooth bark, just as my Indian friend ahead has taught me. We step off the bridge onto the cushioned floor of the tropical forest and turn down a path to her garden. Today she will show me thirty-five kinds of manioc, a starchy root tuber which she cultivates in a cleared-off space of the jungle. I will try to remember all their names by jotting them down in a spiral notebook. She will laugh at me when, days later, I have forgotten how to identify manioc, even though *I* am the one who knows how to write.

I am caught up in our different ways of living and thinking the first time that Sisa, my Quichua-speaking[1] woman friend, helps me transcribe the songs other women have sung for us (and for the tape recorder). I am mired in the thought of how I prize my own way of doing things. In the midst of our listening and writing down the song, I interrupt to ask, "OK, but what did she sing *right before* she mentions that monkey with yellow-colored hands?" I know how to say the words in Quichua and they flow freely, but what I've said cannot be literally translated. Directions—*right before* or *right after*—only have value in my system of written notation. For Sisa, songs are not verse lines, rhyme, stanzas centered on a white page. For her, a song is an emotional response voiced in a wide range of musical tones. My system of signs, dictated by the alphabet, is devoid of meaning for her.

Transcribing more songs with sixteen-year-old Felipe is easier, for he is bilingual and literate. He patiently watches as I write down the words of the song, occasionally pressing the pause button when I cannot write fast enough. Suddenly, though, he jumps up from the tape recorder, grabbing his rifle and peering intently out of the house. I am frightened, but he gestures calmly, "Be silent"; he is

stalking a bird whose call he recognizes. We will both laugh, min-
utes later, when we realize that the bird only exists, imprisoned for-
ever, on the tape.

   This book evolves from a sustained effort to understand the indige-
nous people with whom I lived in the tropical forests and Andean
mountains of Ecuador. Understanding, of course, means learning
Quichua, the language spoken by the descendants of the Inca Empire
as well as many people in the tropical forest. At first, I approached
the task as a mere problem in translation. Pineapples, monkeys, avo-
cados, a canoe, little sticks used when steaming manioc in the bot-
tom of a pot all appeared miraculously before me if I simply uttered
the words I had memorized in Quichua. Yet, as I learned Quichua
syntax and incorporated more forms in my speech, I came to know
that complex translation could only come about with an immersion
in the thought patterns of culture. I worked hard at overcoming a
resistance to abandon a part of myself which, only then, would allow
me to integrate these people into my frame of reference.
   Still, I know that the cultural distance between us is considerable.
Centuries of plant domestication have brought forth a classification
system in the tropical forest which uses leaf shape, tuber color, soil
environment, taste, and growing time in a manner which seems hap-
hazard to me. On the other hand, centuries of writing allow me to
reproduce sounds on paper, signs that are unintelligible to my woman
friend who gardens and sings. Felipe, bilingual, understands both
these systems yet is misled by the technological reproduction of a
bird's song. And I, the one who taped the original, never even heard
the bird sing until Felipe jumped up and searched for it. Intent upon
translating the words sung by women, fulfilling the outline of my
research proposal, I stuck to my preconceived role of interpreter.
The chapters of this book chronicle a process which allowed me to
go beyond my initial translation of Quichua words to English and to
begin the comprehension of other categories and other knowledge
which defied the rigid methodology prized in my world.
   Years later, after studying some colonial Quechua-Spanish manu-
scripts and thinking more about these experiences, I came to fear
that I had crossed over, translated, this other world perhaps too well.
It came about as my college students and I were hiking the Inca Trail
from Cuzco to Machu Picchu. On the fourth day, we finally arrived
at the spot where I had said there was a magnificent view of the
ruins. Yet, when we got to that scenic overlook, all was shrouded.
The clouds covered everything below us. I lightheartedly recited an
Incan prayer to Inti, Father Sun, in my Ecuadoran dialect:

Inti yayalla
uyayayri
chay puyuta paskapay
kambak churi kaypi tiyanchi
kambak llaktalla rikungapak
uyayayri

The students who stood with me at Inti Punku, the Doorway to the Sun, barely understood my words. Our Quechua-speaking guides, however, knew that I was begging the sun to lift the cloud cover hiding our view of Machu Picchu:

Father Sun, dear one,
please listen to me.
Open up those clouds.
Your children are here
to see your sacred place.
Please listen to me.

My own levity changed to silence as right then the mist parted, ever so briefly, allowing time for each of us to snap a picture from this vantage point. When the mist settled over the stones again, our guides (four Quechua Indians) approached me: "How had I learned to speak, to live, in a manner that I could be heard by the heavens?" An atmospheric occurrence, a coincidence, had thrust upon me the awkward role of cultural mediator. I endeavored to translate back to them, in Quechua, a version of their own knowledge, gleaned from reading the few extant ancient ritual poems and their analysis by a handful of scholars. Here the process was more complicated. I was not snared in the trap of explaining my own cultural systems, such as writing, but instead served as a cultural broker, returning to our Quechua-speaking guides knowledge that I myself had obtained secondhand.

Later on, I thought about how little was known of the first interpreters of culture who, alongside Pizarro, began the difficult process of explaining patterns of Andean life. With limited vocabulary, they attempted to decrease the cultural distance of gods, gold, and existence. Unfortunately, today little remains of their efforts. There are some ascerbic commentaries by the Inca Garcilaso, brief texts by the Spanish conquistadores mentioning a *lengua* (interpreter), and archival papers recording their deaths. This encounter of my own in Peru thrust me back into the moment of conquest, forcing me to question the nature of how things were said in Quechua, the meaning of specific words in specific situations, and in instances their transformation in the mouths of Iberian priests and newly titled landholders. I saw that, although the pronunciation remained intact, meaning was altered so that *virakocha* became synonymous with "Spanish master" as well as retaining its ancient meaning of a supreme, perhaps invisible spiritual force.

My concern for my position as translator, in its broadest sense, often weighed me down with footnotes and intricate explanations of the Quechua songs, both ancient and modern. However, to translate fully would be to recapture the exuberance, the sheer energy in the telling of the songs, the myths, the personal narratives. The Quechua language has many ways of saying "to talk," "to utter commands," "to gossip," "to speak eloquently." Some of these meanings we share, theoretically, although our own culture has turned away from an oral tradition to one of visual images and technology.

In these pages, the selection of historical texts, linguistic analyses, stories, and songs should not overshadow the personal enthusiasm of the "telling of the tale" in a manner that does not alienate the "other," that very human person who may wear a poncho or a necklace of jaguar teeth. In the process of understanding the Quechua-speakers' system of values we may come to embrace the mystery of our own selves, which we often neglect in the pursuit of our own revered objectivity. "Sing, sing your own song," my Quichua-speaking friend coaxed me after she explained her visit with her song mentor, the *ukumbi* snake-woman. Her careful teaching, combined with my hours in the libraries away from the tropical forest, enables me now to sing those words with some measure of their profound significance.

### The Translation of Culture: Imaging between Languages

The anguish and the pleasure of translating words and thoughts from one culture to another are the subject of this book. Today in the Andean region of South America, millions of people speak Quechua; they are descendants and transmitters of millenarian civilizations, reduced today through historical circumstances to a life of subsistence as very poor peasant farmers. Their songs, beautiful in their own right for their melodies alone, also articulate indigenous cultural values and allow us to enter their world. My translations of these songs and other texts in this book attempt to preserve a native voice and to convey the underlying Quechua cultural expression, as free as possible from the distortion of my own cultural biases. In this book, the original Quechua text and the English translation are

*Figure 2.* The Volcano Sangay of the Andean Highlands as seen from the headwaters of the Amazon, Ecuador. Photo by Regina Harrison/Ted Macdonald.

placed side by side on the same page. Fortunate are those who can read both the Quechua and English versions. For me, as translator, the two versions of the song continue to interact on the written page. The Quechua words resonate with what I have learned by living in the indigenous communities. With potato farmers and herders at elevations of 11,000 feet and with slash-and-burn farmers/hunters at 1,000 feet, I have searched for songs. Translating the words sung in Quechua into English, my own language, I am obliged to contemplate my well-defined world of cultural assumptions.

Although both texts are printed in this volume, I know that there are few readers who are prepared linguistically to pronounce and interpret the ancient and modern words of the Andean Indians. My privileged reading of both texts is coupled with a weighty responsibility to translate and fashion an image of the Quechua-speaking Indians which allows for the integrity of their culture. The task of translation—to convey the diversity, the style, and the presence of the Quechua-speaking peoples—colors the texts I have written as poems and interpretations.

The act of translation is more than an esthetic or a linguistic rewording of one text into another; the transposition of Quechua words to English also involves statements of an ethical nature. The choice of words to translate Quechua must reflect the reality of the Quechua-speaking peoples, who endure and survive in a postcolonial society which devalues their linguistic expression and their cultural ethos. Spanish, the language imposed by the colonial regime, is accorded the highest status in daily interaction, government proclamations, instructions to fill out bureaucratic forms, street signs, and shops where Indians now buy household necessities. Quechua is spoken by many people in Indian fields and homes, in the churches of provincial parishes, and in scheduled radio programs, but it is always marked by its designation as a language of the illiterate masses. In translating Quechua to English, I worry that the language of the Indians may once more be pushed from the center of the world to the periphery. In that white margin of space where Quechua leaves off and English begins, entire worlds shift and revolve, are relinquished or regained. In the transposition of words, is Quechua once again subsumed, marginalized, and enveloped by an imperious English text?

Another ethical concern inherent in translation occurs in the portrayal of cultural values. Some of the songs I taped and transcribed offer alternative visions of sexuality and gender which may titillate or offend some readers. I am concerned about my participation in constructing a text that might reaffirm common prejudices that these people are "savages" or "uncivilized." I attempted to free my own translations and commentary of judgmental conceptions in a desire to liberate the reader as well.

The issue of confidentiality likewise has influenced the writing of this book. My decision to give pseudonyms to the singers in these pages may be interpreted as a paternalistic gesture or as a means by which I emphasize my own presence and usurp the "authorship" of the people who have sung the songs. My decision is motivated by a desire to protect a relationship of trust which evolved between the individuals in the Andes and myself. This choice is particularly acute in the songs where a snake-woman specifies that the singer learn the song, sing it in times of need, and never reveal it word for word to anyone. I deeply appreciate the singer's sharing of the song with me. It is a gift given freely that attests to our ongoing friendship. Although I publish the song and the interpretation with her permission, I nevertheless am uneasy about entrusting its secrets and its message to people we do not know. The end result, the neatly ordered and numbered lines of the song translations, often belies the struggle with these issues that are a large part of translating culture.

The act of translating images of a people who live, dance, sing, and work in the varied climatic zones of Ecuador and Peru is also accompanied by a translator's responsibility to the Quechua oral tradition.

The musical notes sung by an individual today harmonize with many other lyrical texts that were written down over three centuries ago. These few ancient texts, which survive embedded in long, hand-written manuscripts, provide a means to assess the structural formation of Quechua lyric expression as well as to establish the semantic parameters of words which are still in use today. However, translation of these colonial texts is hampered by the absence of well-founded philological reconstructions of the originals. The phonemes of the previously unwritten Quechua language were heard differently by each Indian or Iberian scribe who worked at preserving the oral tradition in the colonial period. Philological reconstruction of the texts has now begun and will eventually eliminate the linguistic confusion as to what was intended in the original texts.

I mention these difficulties in several chapters, but I do not attempt to resolve these complex linguistic problems. Instead, I write to summarize the conceptual constructs existent in the colonial period—Incaic and indigenous as well as Hispanic—when priests were gathering material for their grammars, dictionaries, and religious tracts. I translate these texts with reference to cultural continuities and semantic dislocations which come about through the interaction of Hispanic and Quechua peoples in four centuries of contact.

These priests and conquerors also struggled with this issue of imaging between languages. These colonial writers, compelled to describe the New World for a European audience, translated these American signs of life using comparisons of likeness and difference or with recourse to a third term. The flora, fauna, and human customs took on meaning only when likened to "those of Spain" or, in another vein, catalogued as "different from ours." These methods of interpretation (or modes of translation) have profound significance, as Antonello Gerbi suggests:

> This constant reference to *our* animal and vegetable species, as if to an unvarying paradigm, contains an implicit and categorical Europeocentrism that is of crucial importance both because of the value judgments which it prompts and dictates and because it leads on to the assimilation and absorption in an undifferentiated exoticism of whatever is *different* from what we know, of a generic "differentness" in which the specific characteristics of each single exotic thing become confused and submerged. (Gerbi 1985: 5–6)

In this book of translations of culture, I write not only to identify what is similar to our own world but also to describe what is different in Quechua configurations of culture. Emphasis on similarity exalts a humanness which allows for "commensurability" (Lakoff 1987: 322–324) in translation, for both cultures experience life with the same intensity. Commonalities which link us to Quechua-speaking poets are evident in the songs of this book: the anguish of unanswered prayers, the sorrow at the death of a child, the pride in one's work, and the yearning of sexual desire. Aided by the methodology of linguistics and anthropology, we learn to understand these songs and overcome cultural obstacles. However, there are many other songs than these which I have taped, transcribed, selected, and translated for this book. They continue to defy analysis and translation, and they are not included here. They exist for those who sing them, alive, vibrant, and mysterious, beyond the intrusion of the translator.

# 1. *The Dimensions of Quechua Language and Culture*

THE REALISTIC figure of the Otavalan Indian catches my eye. Rarely is a lifelike Indian depicted in advertisements in Ecuador. Usually a stern, depersonalized Inca face is the only Indian symbol widely used to sell bags of flour or attract tourists to a restaurant. But this billboard (Figure 3) accurately portrays all the identifying characteristics (shoes, pants, poncho) worn by members of the indigenous community to the north of Quito. I smile as I see what he is promoting—a trip to Europe on Iberia Airlines.[1] A good choice: I have seen Otavalans peddle their scarves, wall hangings, and sweaters on the street corners of New York City. Yet this Indian is not depicted as a street vendor. His poncho opens slightly so that his hand steadies the golf clubs which balance on his shoulder. A quick glance at this advertisement leads me to wonder: Are things looking up for the Indians of Ecuador? What does this billboard mean?

However, what I think this billboard means may be very different from what an Ecuadoran or an Indian assumes it means. The same sign—the poncho-clad Indian with golf clubs—"translates" differently, depending on the code of culture which defines it. Of course, an advertiser, in this case Iberia Airlines, would prefer that one message is read in the billboard, for "in advertising the signification of the image is undoubtedly intentional; the signifieds of the advertising message are formed *a priori* by certain attributes of the product and these signifieds have to be transmitted as clearly as possible" (Barthes 1977: 33). However, with the image in this example, the signifieds (what this image means) can vary considerably.

Barthes's essay "Rhetoric of the Image" is an aid to describe what we see and to outline the rich cultural associations we bring to our viewing. Although the image message and the linguistic message of the advertising enter our consciousness at the same time, we separate them out to perceive the structure of the billboard. The first

*Figure 3.* Billboard advertisement for Iberia Airlines in Quito, Ecuador: "I've come back from Europe on Iberia Airlines. When are you traveling?" By permission of Iberia Airlines.

process is to identify the visual iconic message which describes "real" entities. In this drawing, the male Indian most definitely is a member of the Otavalan ethnic group in Ecuador (Figure 4). People from Otavalo wear their native dress; the men wear blue ponchos, which distinguish them from other indigenous groups who may wear red or black ponchos. The white cotton pants cropped at mid-calf also are indicators of indigenous origins, though some of the younger male Indians from Otavalo now wear long white jeans. The shoes of cotton fabric and rubber soles and the broad, brown felt hat are made in Otavalo. Yet, other than clothing, Indianness is obscured somewhat because, from this angle, the distinctive thick, shiny braid is not depicted; we see instead a set of golf clubs in a leather bag slung over his shoulder. The literal message denotes a cultural contradiction. Indians do not usually play golf nor are they members of country clubs.

In proceeding this far in our analysis, we leave the identification of details and enter a study of interpretation. These very signs are grouped in a manner which contributes to symbolic meaning. Here, at this stage, the sign-reader must know something about the cultural configurations of Ecuador. Why choose an Indian? Why an In-

*Figure 4.* Close-up of Otavalan Indian on the billboard for Iberia Airlines.

dian from Otavalo? Why the golf clubs? If we could eavesdrop on a conversation in Ecuador where Indians are discussed, this is what we might overhear: "Ecuador's problem is a race problem. . . . The Indians are lazy. . . . Sometimes they cut their hair and work, but not often. There are no poor people in Ecuador—there are only Indians. They are uneducated and unhealthy" (Theroux 1979: 286). This typical conversation, reported in Paul Theroux's *The Old Patagonian Express*, alludes to the symbolic importance of what is depicted in the billboard drawing. This Indian presumes to leave behind his lower-class status by carrying golf clubs of the elites.

The choice of an Otavalan is not arbitrary, for this group is one of the most prosperous indigenous communities in the country. The 45,000 Otavalans are well known for their high-quality weavings sold all over Ecuador and in many foreign countries. This group is accorded high status within the category of "Indian" by "white" Ecuadorans; their cropped pants and cloth shoes are spotlessly white and their hair is neatly braided in contrast to other Indians who are considered "dirty" and, therefore, inferior.[2] The "hidden" braid and the golf clubs signify an Indian who has moved even closer to the dominant paradigm of European "whiteness," prized in Ecuador.

The linguistic message of an advertisement often guides our interpretation of the visual signs. This message, coded in Spanish, occupies significant space on the billboard:

| | |
|---|---|
| Vengo de Europa por | I've come back from |
| Iberia | Europe on Iberia |
| | Airlines. |
| cuando viaja Ud.? | When are you traveling? |

The coded message clearly states that the Indian figure has just returned from Europe and asks the sign-reader when he/she is going abroad. However, from within the confines of Ecuadoran culture, this message is laden with ambiguity and conflict. There is an implicit challenge to the reader in having an Indian state that *he* has come back from the Grand Tour, while the non-Indian middle-class or upper-class Ecuadoran reader is made aware that he/she has stayed home. The message provokes and may backfire because of the tensions found in interethnic relations in Ecuador. When "Indian" is most often accompanied by the adjective "dirty" as an insult in Ecuador, this billboard may be less persuasive and more provocative in its message. According to Barthes, the linguistic message often helps anchor the meaning of a variance of terms; here it connotes another message than that of an Indian traveling to Europe. Although parallels may be drawn between golf clubs and Western civilization as a positive connotation, an Ecuadoran reading this message sees a confrontation of cultural stereotypes.

As a North American, my reading of this sign was conditioned by my own cultural expectations. Seeing an Indian in advertisements in the United States is not such a rarity as in Ecuador. The Indian symbol has been used in ad campaigns to halt ecological destruction[3] and to discourage ethnic stereotyping to sell Jewish rye bread. The native depicted is strong, muscular, and packaged as a palatable consumer image. The depiction of South American Indians in U.S. advertisements is very different. A glossy pamphlet distributed with a Sunday newspaper describes an imaginary trip to Peru.[4] In realistic terms, the Peruvian Indians are photographed with tourists wearing the latest Western fashions (Figure 5). The attitude of the U.S. tourists is paternalistic; they drape their arms around the shoulders of the petite, female inhabitants of the Andes, identifiable by their native dress. The tourists' downward gaze directs our assessment of meaning in the advertisement. Their cultural superiority is affirmed by their height and their leisure clothes. The caption, "They talk to the animals," further diminishes the human presence of the "friendly natives" and reduces them to exist merely as a part of the Andean scenery.

## The Quechua Language: A Sign of Cultural Identity

The advertisements depict three different images of Indianness in the mountainous regions of Ecuador and Peru: a poncho, a saucer-shaped hat, a bowler hat with flowers, and braids. All are signs of ethnicity, as Indians in most regional centers in the Andes are identified by their dress as well as by their language. In Ecuador, the colors of the ponchos reflect geographical area: blue in Otavalo, black with purple stripes in Saraguro, a densely woven red poncho in Riobamba. In Peru, some Indian communities are differentiated by abstract patterns woven in the ponchos or a variety of hats; each design or hat reveals a distinct place of origin up and down the Andes. In the eastern slopes of the Andes in both Ecuador and Peru, however, identity is less a function of everyday clothing. Indigenous men in the tropical forest now wear permanent press trousers, and the women sew up brightly colored dresses made of factory-produced cloth. Language, in these circumstances, becomes a better key to ethnic identity. The Quechua language, as an indicator of cultural

They talk to the animals.

Sweats by EBE striped jersey. $22
Sweats by EBE twill pants. $31

Catalina striped knit woven top. $28
and woven short, $24
Gold Toe socks, $3.50 and $4.50

Friendly natives bring
mama vicuña and
family for a big group picture.

*Figure 5.* Advertisement for Jordan Marsh: "They talk to the animals." By permission of Jordan Marsh Company.

affiliation, often remains even after a long braid is snipped off or the flouncing skirts of orange-and-red-colored homespun wool are shed for a close-fitting skirt made of stretchy nylon cloth.

Over eight million people speak the Quechua language today, in spite of its identification with the less prestigious members of the society, the Indians of the rural sector. Although Quechua is rarely used in the technical professional sphere or in official publications, those who speak the language prefer Quechua to Spanish for expression of emotions or esthetic description (Albó 1979: 273). There exists strong native loyalty to the Quechua language even though it is stigmatized within the society. A bilingual, rated by others, is seen as "stronger, more sincere, less arrogant, more ambitious, [and] smarter" when he or she speaks Quechua (Wölck 1973: 138). However, because Spanish is the prestige language in the Andes, Indians are encouraged to forsake Quechua. Gregorio Condori Mamani, a monolingual Quechua speaker, tells of his experiences when he served in the Peruvian army many years ago:

> Chhaynallataq mana simiyoq haykunki, mana simillayoqtaq lloqsimunki, apenas castellanoman simi t'okhashaq. Cuartelpin chay tenientekuna, capitankuna, mana munaqkuchu runa simi rimanaykuta.
> —¡Indios, carajo! ¡Castellano!—neqkun.
> Chhaynatan a pura patada castellanota rimacheq kasunkiku clasekuna.
> (Condori Mamani 1977: 45)

> Up until that time [entering the army] I didn't speak Spanish and I scarcely left there speaking Spanish; I almost spoke some Spanish at the end. The lieutenants and the captains didn't want us to speak in Quechua (*runa simi*).
> "Indians, dammit! Spanish!" they used to say.
> With that, they make you speak Spanish in classes.

However, there have been periods of increased recognition of *runa simi* (Quechua) within Peruvian society. For instance, in 1975, General Velasco Alvarado declared Quechua the second official language of Peru. In a press conference, an indigenous leader who was present at the official ceremony summed up the meaning of this legislation in his statement, originally in Quechua: "We would have been pleased to have our language a required school subject, but now General Velasco has given us more. Quechua is just as worthy as Spanish. Now the judges will mete out justice to us, the doctors will cure us more skillfully, and teachers will learn to respect the dignity of our children, because they will have to learn Quechua" ("Peru: *k'ausak'rak'mi kani*" 1975: 175). Unfortunately, the fanfare of proclamations diminished; after a brief promotion of bilingual school programs and the publication of magazines and newspapers in Quechua, the language resumed its status of second-class citizen.

The words of Gregorio Condori Mamani and the proclamation of General Alvarado both refer to the same language, Quechua. However, Condori Mamani uses indigenous nomenclature for designating the native language, *runa simi*. The diversity of labels contradicts a common attribution of Quechua as a single monolithic language. It is not; there are regional differences in syntactic structures, vocabularies, and the number of loan words accepted into the native language. Andean linguists distinguish at least eleven dialects of

Quechua based on analysis of phonetic constructions, geographical boundaries, intergroup communication, and cultural identity.

Linguistic models enhance our understanding of the scope of the language and its variation. Alfredo Torero's theory (1974), most generally accepted, defines two major language groups, Quechua I and Quechua II. The language called Quechua I is found in the Lima area and in the *montaña* (the eastern slopes of the Andes); Quechua II is spoken in the remaining areas of the northern coast of Peru, Cuzco, and southern Peru, as well as in the countries of Colombia, Ecuador, Bolivia, Argentina, Chile, and Brazil. These two major language groups are further divided into three dialects of Ecuador (map 1) and eight dialects of Peru (map 2), according to a study by Rodolfo Cerrón Palomino. Although some linguists claim that these dialects are not mutually intelligible, Cerrón Palomino's research suggests that sociocultural factors, not the linguistic structures themselves, are the obstacles to understanding between dialects (1987: 229).

The geographic sweep of the language evident on maps 1 and 2 attests to the march of advancing armies and interregional trading which spread the language in the pre-Incaic and Incaic periods. Diffusion of Quechua was also brought about by the Catholic Church and Spanish bureaucrats, who used the language to proselytize and collect taxes. Many colonial chroniclers at first referred to the Quechua I dialect as "standard Quechua," but as the years went by the Cuzco dialect (Quechua II) assumed more and more prestige. In the many dictionaries and catechisms printed in Lima, the Cuzco dialect is prized and the other Quechua dialects often are characterized as "imperfect and barbarous" (*Doctrina christiana* [1584] 1985: 167).

Some of the linguistic plurality is evident in the spelling of the language. In Peru, people refer to Quechua (spelled with an *e*), while in Ecuador everyone clearly enunciates the word Quichua, with an *i*. Historical documents, written after the Spanish invasion in the sixteenth century, show the language first referred to as Quichua, but by 1616 the spelling Quechua was used more frequently in the early dictionaries printed in Lima and abroad.[5] This orthographic preference to represent the sounds of the language was begun by the Spanish priests and officials, who were the first to record the unwritten native language. This confusion in orthography persists to the present day: "In general, chaos reigns. Parker [a linguist] has even said that there are perhaps more alphabets than authors, since several use various ones" (Albó 1979: 275).

The orthographic disarray was partially resolved for Peru and Bolivia in 1954 when a standardized phonemic alphabet was agreed

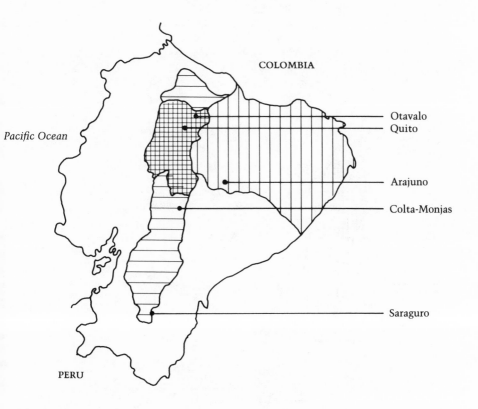

COLOMBIA

Pacific Ocean

Otavalo
Quito

Arajuno

Colta-Monjas

Saraguro

PERU

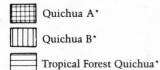 Quichua A*

Quichua B*

Tropical Forest Quichua*

*Quechua is written Quichua in Ecuador.

*Map 1.* The Quechua II dialects of Ecuador. Sites referred to in the text are indicated. After Cerrón Palomino 1987 : 55.

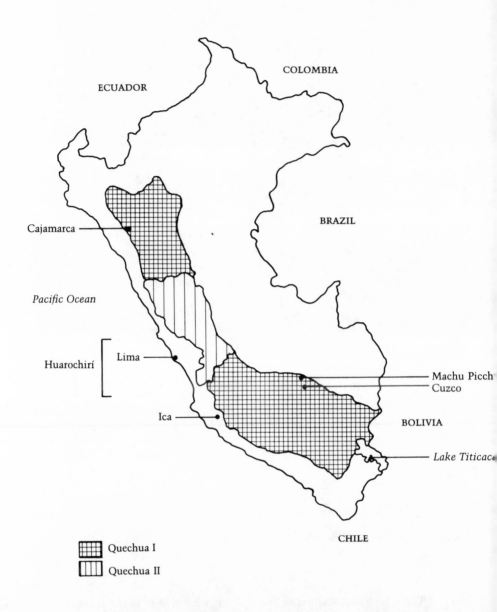

Map 2. The Quechua I and Quechua II dialects of Peru. Sites referred to in the text are indicated. After Cerrón Palomino 1987:63.

upon by linguists of those two countries. In 1975, however, another official alphabet was established in Peru which has subsequently been revised in the First Workshop on Writing Systems for Quechua and Aymara (1983) (Montoya, Montoya, and Montoya 1987: 685). Similarly, in Ecuador, choice of writing systems is a political issue and still hotly debated. In 1975, for example, Consuelo Yáñez and Fausto Jara proposed a system which contained *k*, *y*, and *w* to represent certain sounds. Their alphabet, according to Luis O. Montaluisa (1980), was criticized by "revolutionaries" who opposed the orthography for ideological reasons:

> —La "k," la "y" y la "w" son letras gringas.
> —La "k," la "y" y la "w" no son letras quichuas.
> —Emplean la "k," la "y" y la "w" para hacer que consumamos más wiskey y tabacos king. (Ibid.: 128)

> —The *k*, the *y*, and the *w* are gringo letters.
> —The *k*, the *y*, and the *w* are not Quichua letters.
> —They use the *k*, the *y*, and the *w* in order to make us consume more whiskey and "king" tobacco.

This disagreement, voiced in 1975, has been repeated in numerous other sessions where Quichua speakers—Indians and linguists—have been brought together to resolve differences of opinion. In 1980, at meetings which encouraged indigenous participation in the debate, representatives of Indian communities voted to allow speakers of each dialect to determine their own form of writing the language: "Hay que respetar el derecho que cada comuna indígena tenga su propia escritura y método de acuerdo a sus problemas y necesidades" (The rights of each indigenous community must be respected; [each should] have its own writing system and method according to its own problems and needs) (ibid.: 132).

The writing of *runa simi* (Quechua) in this book similarly reflects decisions on my part to respect dialectical differences as well as national preferences. I use Quechua to refer to the language in Peru and to the language in general in its most extensive spread. Quichua, as a label, describes the dialectical and cultural differences found in Ecuador. In transcribing songs and texts from the two countries, the orthography varies to respect each country's preference. The ritual prayers written down by Santacruz Pachacuti Yamqui (chapters 3 and 4) conform to the dialect of southern Peru. In the same manner, I differentiate the dialects spoken in the central Andes of Ecuador from the dialect spoken in the lowland areas (chapters 5 and 6).

**Songs: Personal and Collective Memory**

The writing of Quechua of necessity conforms to the signs of the alphabet brought by the Spanish invaders; in a like manner the songs have also been classified and analyzed with a comparison to European standards. Although many scholars over the centuries have attempted to distinguish genres and formal versification of Quechua poetry, much of the analysis stems from a European tradition, with expectations of what poetry should be. Jesús Lara, a respected scholar of the literature of the Quechua people, in his *La poesía quechua* ([1947] 1979: 70–92) defines eight genres of poetry which he finds mentioned in the colonial texts: the *jailli* (a hymn), *arawi* (love song), *wawaki* (amorous song in dialogue), *taki* (a generic, thematic song), *wayñu* (less subjective than the *arawi*), *qhashwa* (festival song), *aranway* (humorous song), and the *wanka* (an elegy). The basis of the classification is either by content (funereal, victory song, dynastic history) or by a criterion of choral participation.[6] Lara admits that few of the chronicles transcribe lyrics exemplifying each genre; he supplements his study by using modern examples to illustrate each genre type.

When we look closely at the few surviving texts from the early colonial period written by Quechua-speaking natives or priests who have learned the language, we encounter additional problems other than the definition of song genres. The older manuscripts written by Felipe Guaman Poma de Ayala and Joan de Santacruz Pachacuti Yamqui Salcamaygua use no line breaks but instead transcribe the *oraciones* (prayers) as prose. Their contemporary, the mestizo Inca Garcilaso, who wrote in Spain, assimilated to the stylistics of Spanish versification; his short Quechua poem is broken into four brief lines ([1609] 1963: pt. 1, bk. 2, chap. 27, 79). Decisions as to where one line ends and another begins are arbitrary with the lyrics found in the older manuscripts; with the more modern Quichua songs in this book, I have based the lines on the breath groups heard in the tapes of the singers. In addition, often an internal rhythm marks the poetry of the song; Quechua discourse and poetry are laden with repetitions of words which are exactly the same or show evidence of slight change in syntactic and semantic structure in the many affixes of the language.

The songs which are translated in these chapters represent the survival of the oral tradition in the Andes and the lowlands of Ecuador and Peru. The songs vary in their voice and their structure; in their content they share themes with some of the songs mentioned

*Figure 6.* Singing while harvesting grain in the Andean community of Colta-Monjas in Ecuador.

in the oldest Quechua manuscripts. As an example of ancient Quechua poetry, I analyze the ruler Manco Capac's lyric address to a deity he cannot see, a god who does not answer. His rhetorical questions plead for a sign from the heavens; his descriptions abound with the symbols of hierarchy in the growing empire. Manco Capac mentions the trappings of royal authority and questions who will be his successor. There is one solitary voice and no chorus in this dense, verb-laden statement, which relies upon our knowledge of Incaic cultural patterns to interpret it well. The contemporary funeral song from Ecuador (chapter 4) is seductive in its apparent simplicity; a Quichua interlocutor speaks with birds, animals, and plants. Its links with seventeenth-century Peruvian myths attest to the existence of a vital Andean oral tradition. Both versions (myth and song) treat oppositions: the ancient myth contrasts the coast and the highlands, while the contemporary song is more centered on birth and death.

The agricultural harvest songs maintain an ancient Andean song pattern, where indigenous workers (male and female) set the pace of the task by singing a lively chorus (Figure 6). "Jaway, Jaway," sing women and men as they pile the long sheaves of grain in the central

Andes of Ecuador (chapter 5). The male lead singer, called a *paki*, inflames old rivalries between Andean villages in his songs or entertains the workers with lyric commentary on amorous interludes. The singing is communal and public and the songs are passed down from generation to generation by men who have the strength to sing and work from dawn to dusk.

The chronicles often mention melancholic love songs, called *arawi*, as a song genre among Quechua speakers. The expression of personal emotions by women in songs of the lowlands and highlands of Ecuador is colored with verbs and phrases of both physical and spiritual strength (chapters 5 and 6). Instead of lamenting the absence of the lover, for instance, the women singer intones lyrics which glorify her powers for bringing the lover back into her presence. Primarily, this female power is expressed using the word *supay*, as in an oft-repeated phrase, "Andi warmi supayga" (Andi woman spirit strength), in one song. Here the word recovers some of its original depth of "power which can be associated with good or evil." This contemporary meaning in the highly individual songs of the women recovers the traditional pre-Hispanic essence of this Quechua concept of *supay*, which the Spanish altered to only mean "devil." It is significant that through the medium of song, and outside the reach of Hispanic culture, this more ancient meaning has been maintained.

Yet not all the songs suggest the persistence of Andean value systems in centuries of commingling with an imposed, more prestigious Spanish culture. One harvest song from Ecuador addresses the problem of maintaining cultural identity for Quichua speakers, especially after they have entered into the processes of the school systems in the Andes. Although admission of indigenous persons to the educational system serves, on the one hand, to facilitate greater access to the Spanish-speaking enclaves of society, schooling can also serve to encourage separation from one's ethnic group. Learning to read and write may be the only way to change status in an oppressive system, yet it is accompanied by the risk of severing ties with the indigenous community. A song I collected in Colta-Monjas, in the central Andes of Ecuador, describes the dislocation which can occur when Indian children graduate from primary and secondary schools. In this harvest song the protagonist, a young boy, learns how to write and signs his name with a flourish. His education enables him to work for *hacendados* and politicians; he begins to earn a lot of money and he is successful, according to the commentary revealed in song. Yet this success causes him later to reject his own people so he can hang around with the *buena gente* (mestizo middle-class folks) in his Andean town:[7]

| Quechua | | English |
|---------|---|---------|
| Uyarilla | | Listen, |
| doña María | | lady María. |
| maytagarilla | | Where in the world |
| kambak wawaka? | | is your child? |
| *iscuila*llamun | 5 | In grade school. |
| yaykukun ninka | | He is enrolling, they say, |
| *colegio*llamun | | in high school. |
| yaykukun ninka | | He is enrolling, they say. |
| mana *valilla* | | He's not worth anything |
| walindanguka | 10 | [his penis hanging down]. |
| uksha chumbiwan | | With a belt of straw |
| chumbillishkaka | | he has kept his pants up. |
| *buena litra*ta | | Good handwriting |
| japishpa ninka | | he's got, they say. |
| *buena firma*ta | 15 | An impressive signature |
| japishpa ninka | | he's got, they say. |
| *amuku*nawan | | With all the big bosses |
| rimakun ninka | | he is talking, they say. |
| *doctor*kunawan | | With all the doctors |
| *parla*kun ninka | 20 | he is talking, they say. |
| *saludak*pipish | | When one says hello to him |
| manashi *parlan* | | he doesn't speak. |
| *saludak*pipish | | When one says hello to him |
| manashi riman | | he doesn't say anything. |
| *saludak*pipish | 25 | When one says hello to him |
| mana chaskinka | | he doesn't receive our hello. |
| *saludak*pipish | | When one says hello to him |
| mana rimanka | | he doesn't speak. |
| alli *suerti*ta | | A lot of good luck |
| charikushkaka | 30 | he has already held for himself. |
| *gobernadur*ta | | From the governor |
| ña *gana*grinka | | he begins to earn money. |
| chasna purina | | Acting like that |
| layachu karka | | he became a "white." |
| chasna kawsana | 35 | Living like that |
| layachu karka | | he became a "white." |
| *amu*kunata | | From the *hacendados* |
| ña *gana*grinka | | he begins to earn money. |
| jatunkunata | | From the big bosses |
| ña *gana*grinka | 40 | he begins to earn money. |
| kunanka jatun | | Now a great man |
| tiyarigrinka | | he's getting to be. |
| kunanka jatun | | Now a great man |

| tiyarigrinka | | he's getting to be. |
| deputadurka | 45 | As a political representative |
| ganagripanka | | he begins to earn money. |
| alli sueldota | | A good salary |
| ganagripanka | | he begins to earn. |

The song criticizes one Indian boy's success when that success is accompanied by a denial of his ethnic heritage. He no longer bothers to say hello to the people of his ethnic group; he is busy cultivating friendships with the non-Indians of the middle class. The degree of separation from his ethnic group is indicated clearly in his refusing to speak Quichua on the streets in a greeting of familiarity. There is also critical mention of his ultimate transformation: "layachu karka" ([he turned into] a white man). While there is a small measure of ethnic pride that this young boy could attain wealth and status, the song also conveys a plea for maintaining strong ties with the community and with indigenous cultural patterns.

This song, a lesson about the virtues of cultural continuity, at the same time provides a text which attests to the vitality of Quechua as a language of communication. A number of loan words from Spanish (italicized in the song text) are easily incorporated into the phrasing of the harvest song. To halt extinction of the language, efforts must be made to infuse Quechua with a new vitality which allows for scientific and intellectual expression, allowing it to compete with a power structure fashioned by a legacy of colonialism.[8]

## Textualizing the Other: Translating Our Selves

The matter of equivalents and cultural boundaries interfered with cultural understanding of the peoples of indigenous America. As we see in the first chapter of this book, language systems clashed, alongside the cannons and the slingshots, with the arrival of the Spanish in the Andes. Often, the zeal to convert the Amerindians to the rigorous hierarchies of Catholicism intentionally obliterated the subtleties of the native discourse regarding their own belief system. From the moment of conquest an intent to "civilize" the indigenous populations was in effect, which almost always meant the assimilation of the Indians to the normative Hispanic forms of life: "Colonialism and imperialism propose to and impose on the world one discourse, one form of conscience, and one science. Thus restricted, the world and reality appear as the only dimension worthy of being known. . . . All other forms of nature and society are denied, ignored, rejected and made imperceptible" (Varese 1982: 30).

Our knowledge of the Quechua past comes to us filtered through theological and historical perspectives common to the Spanish invaders of the sixteenth century. As the Quechua peoples had no system of writing, the descriptions of their achievements and failures reflect a selectivity of observation which reveals more about Hispanic cultural consciousness than a faithful accounting of the features of Andean civilization. In the colonial manuscripts, ethnocentricity is pervasive; for instance, corn, a New World food substance, is repeatedly referred to as wheat, the Old World crop. Similarly, even invisible beings, the Indian spirits and devils, lose their unique cultural value and are viewed with a European eye. It is the Spanish versions of the Andean civilizations which have endured, bound and archived, facilitated by the European system of writing.

In the texts of proselytization—in the catechisms and in the confessionals—we glimpse the native peoples subjugated by a dominant Spanish text which attempts to reorient nonconforming Amerindian thought. The Hispanic attempts to differentiate a Christian viewpoint from an Amerindian concept often provide a glimpse of the disparity of thought. However, although the Christian theology is phrased in Spanish and accurately reflects Catholic dogma, in translating these very concepts to Quechua, the priest-translators were forced to convert the Indians using their Quechua terminology for gods and spirits, nouns that deviated from Catholic teachings. For example, the priest-translators often described the indigenous heavens in a manner to convince their converts that these entities were not sacred deities: "P. [regunta] Pues el Sol, la Luna, Estrellas, Luzero, Rayo, no son Dios? R. [esponso] Nada de esso es Dios mas son hechura de Dios q̃ hizo el cielo y la tierra y todo lo que ay en ellos, para el bien del hombre" (Question. Then the sun, the moon, the stars, the morning and evening star, the thunder, are they not God? Answer. None of these [things] are God; rather, they are made by God who created the heavens and the earth and everything in them, for the good of humankind) (*Doctrina christiana* [1584] 1985: 47). The list is considerably enlarged when this question is translated into Quechua by the same priests. They include a fuller range of deities sacred to Andean peoples: "Ma chayca. Inti, Quilla, coyllurcuna, chasca coyllur, choque ylla, huaca, villcacuna, orcocuna, cay caycunaca manachu Dios?" (Now this. The Sun, the Moon, the morning star, the evening star, the lightning, the *huaca* spirits, the [sacred] plants, the hills, are they not God?) (ibid.).

This expansive translation is part of a conscious decision to not render Christian theology "word for word," in spite of the sacredness of the Divine Text, the Word of God. Although the Church fathers are concerned about an "authentic translation" of the texts, they also are careful to explain that the Quechua and Aymara passages in the catechisms will be phrased in terms of a general sense of the concepts, not a narrow translation (ibid.: 167). In the "Epistle on Translation," the authors and translators state that they have reached an agreement on one approved version after a lengthy process:

> . . . este Sancto Concilio Provincial [manda] . . . que ninguno use otra traduction, ni enmiende ni añada en esta, cosa alguna. Por que aun que ouiesse cosas, q̃ por ventura se pudieran dezir mejor de otra suerte (que forçozo es que aya siẽpre en esto de traductiõ diuersas opiniones) pero hase juzgado, y lo es menos inconveniente, que se passe por alguna menos perfection que tenga por ventura la traduction: que no da lugar, a que aya variedad y discordias, como en las traductiones de la Sancta Scriptura saludablemente lo ha proveydo la Yglesia catholica. (Ibid.: 17)

> . . . this Holy Provincial Council [prohibits] . . . the use of any other translation and corrections and editions to this translation. Even though there may be some things that can be said better in another way (it is unavoidable that many diverse opinions [abound in questions] of translation) but it has been decided, and it is much more convenient, that [we live with] less perfection than a translation which is [done] by chance: that this does not happen, that there not be different versions and discord, [but a version given] like in the translations of the Sacred Bible which the Catholic Church has wisely provided.

A special section (*Anotaciones* [Notes]) follows the translations of the Christian doctrine and the two catechisms; it is designed to explicate the more difficult concepts of the faith in translation. Entries include interjections (*Anau*, "a way of expressing pain"), nouns (*Choque illa*, "lightning"), verbs (*Cuscachay*, "to equal, to pair up, to even up, to adjust"), as well as cultural explanations (*Llamacunahina*, "like llamas, a word which serves for animals in general, for the Quechua speakers do not have this concept") (ibid.: 172–174).

The notes and glosses written in the first Church-approved translation of 1584 help to explain the Amerindian world to the priests who would set out to seek converts; the explanations are written to include a learned person in the act of reading. No less important were the *Confession Manuals (Confessionario)*, printed a year later (1585), which aided the penitent in recollecting the sins of the past:

All confession manuals contain the unconditional demand that
all sins be revealed. Over and over again, the convert is urged
to tell all. To account for one's sins is to recount not simply
sinful acts but all the clusters of desire that inform those acts
and so obstruct the full insertion of the individual into the cir-
cuit of divine desire. (Rafael 1988: 101)

The priest, exercising his Catholic duties, assisted the penitent in
this act of memory and confession. The manuals, constructed with a
question and answer format, allowed the priest to direct attention to
the Ten Commandments as he probed the conscience of the convert.
These questions, based on the Laws of Moses, assume a particular
Andean cast as the process of cultural translation enters into the dis-
cussion. The Sixth Commandment, "No fornicarás" (Thou shalt not
fornicate), reveals priestly interest in mechanisms by which sexual
liaisons are achieved in Quechua-speaking communities: "(15) Has
usado del *huacanqui* para alcançar mugeres? (16) Has ydo al hechi-
zero, o a la *guaca* a pedir remedio, o bebedizo para que te quieran las
mugeres?" ([15] Have you used *huacanqui* to obtain women? [16]
Have you asked a *guaca* to give you a potion or a drink so that
women fall for you?) (*Confessionario* [1585] 1985: 219). These pru-
rient questions are supplemented by others which illustrate even
better the Spanish abhorrence of other sexual practices observed in
the Andes: "(21) Has usado del peccado nefando con alguna persona?
(22) Has usado de bestialidad con algun animal?" [21] Have you prac-
ticed the heinous sex act with another person? [22] Have you en-
gaged in bestial acts with an animal?) (ibid.: 220).[9] Of all the sexual
sins, these latter two are the worst in the long list, as we read in the
sermon on the Sixth Commandment:

Sobre todos estos peccados es el peccado que llamamos nefando, y so-
domia que es peccar hombre con hombre, o con muger no por el lugar
natural, y sobre todo esto es aun peccar con bestias, con ovejas o perras,
o yeguas, que esta es grandisima abominacion. (*Tercero cathecismo* [1585]
1985: 651)

[Ranked] above all these sins is the sin that we call heinous, or
sodomy, which is to sin with another man or with a woman in
an unnatural [bodily opening] and above all this is the sin of
[having sex] with animals, with sheep or bitches or mares, all
of which is truly an abomination.

The sermon vividly describes the Iberian disgust when encountering sexual practices which differed from their own Catholic teachings; the confessions and the supplementary discussions portray the native population as knowledgeable in these matters. A close reading of the last text may illustrate less of the Amerindian world and more of a European mentality; all the animals mentioned are of Old World origin and had been brought recently to the Andes. Sexual acts performed with sheep, female dogs, and mares may be more easily imaginable by the inquiring priest than bestial copulation with the fauna particular to the Andean environment. Thus, Spanish observation of an "alien" world was made more familiar by the inclusion of domestic, barnyard animals.

Andean Indians frequently discuss the topic of sexuality openly and graphically. Billie Jean Isbell's research on riddles in the highlands of Peru (Isbell and Roncalla Fernández 1977) gives us new insights into sexual relations in Quechua. In her translation of the riddles, she is careful to describe the context in an explicit manner, and she exhibits no moral censure of the practice of *vida michay*, where large groups of teenagers engage in sexual activity. Other translators, however, may avoid a sexual topic altogether in their translation; Enrique Ballón notes that the Spanish translation of an Aguaruna text omits the direct bodily references to sodomy which appear in the myth and only names the act in Latin phrases inserted into the Spanish translation (Ballón Aguirre 1986: 486).

When we translate "alien" texts we are faced with a responsibility to convey the essence of another society's words without making them sound peculiar: "Clearly, by the style of translation chosen one can make alien peoples seem as peculiar as one likes" (Crick 1976: 160). The skill of the translator, as Walter Benjamin ([1955] 1969) suggests, is to approach that essential "untranslatability" in the original text and convey, not its informational content, but an additional measure of differentness which makes that society *not* like our own. Translating in this mode takes us beyond the matter of semantic equivalence to a realm of unfamiliar cultural values. Translating these different "forms of life," starting from the simplistic dictionary definitions, can serve to have us see the extent to which our rewording of a cultural utterance reveals our society's relationship to the people who have spoken the words which we write down.

Often there is little space in our language system to accommodate the alien mode of expression. Its rigidity is manifested in the difficulty of curbing a tendency for the English translation to dominate the "weaker" voice of the (often) illiterate culture which utters the original text (Asad 1986: 158–159). The linguist and the cultural interpreter, therefore, have an ethical task, as Talal Asad so eloquently suggests, to present, as authentically as possible, the coherent meaning of the cultural acts belonging to another society. The process should not encourage the "textualizing" of other cultures with diagrammatic ideograms as answers to complex cultural questions. Rather, he urges us as translators and readers of other people's words to examine our own participatory role in the process of creating a representation of the people of this nonliterate society. The quality of that alien speech, articulated by an individual and a society, must not be muffled in our own desire to translate those words to our literate tradition, which operates with its own set of codes.

The songs in the sixth chapter of this book present the translator with the most difficult of tasks because the subject matter is not easily discussed in our technologically oriented society. The themes of love, love magic, and movements of the beloved through space and time in the tropical forest conflict with our more rational discussions of sexual energy. Men and women may speak of an "attraction," "real chemistry" occurring between people in love, yet these explanations for events in Western societies depend precisely on technology and scientific principles ("electricity," "a spark"). Talk of magic also is tainted with Western conceptions of witchcraft; these conceptions often carry a negative semantic value. This same conceptual premise about witchcraft, for instance, may not exist in the alien culture; labels used in our culture may have little relevance for the culture we wish to study:

> Great violence must be done to the conceptual structures of another culture in speaking of witchcraft if it lacks those environing categories which defined it in our own. Where the conceptual field is so different we could not reasonably expect to find the same phenomenon, and so the same term should not be used twice. (Crick 1976: 112)

The impasse of cultural barriers has led some translators to invent new vocabulary which averts implanting a negative value on a neutral term.

In the tropical forest, a love potion, a powder which is gathered from ground-up plants or a boa's head (*simayuka*), explains the mysterious forces which inflame sexual passion. Women sing about this force in their songs; in fact, the songs become a kind of love potion themselves and allow the singer to attain her goal of sexual union.

This belief system may seem far removed from our own feelings about love and sex. Yet, as Denis de Rougement states, talk of love potions was common in the twelfth century to excuse the "fascinating violence" of passions condemned by the Church. The romances of chivalry featured love potions sipped by mistake so that the lovers were freed, "willy-nilly," from a "visible connexion with human responsibility" (Rougement [1940] 1974: 48).

When we read Quichua songs of amorous encounters, we are more resistant to them in a way that does not occur when we read the songs in the early chapters. The distance that separates us chronologically from the older texts of the seventeenth century allows us to accept androgynous gods, animals that talk to each other, and spirits that move about. These songs do not challenge our conceptualization of the world; they are seen as quaint and anachronistic. On the other hand, the songs of sexual liaisons with hallucinogenic imagery are being sung at this moment, even as we discuss them. The translation of this particular belief system about attraction and persuasion presents us with "other" highly charged notions of sexuality and union.

The woman who dips her thumb in *simayuka* and then passes the love potion on to her lover in the drink she offers similarly shares with us her own belief system, which is less involved with ideas of self and personal fulfillment. Her seduction of a lover functions as part of a complex system based on the co-existence of two powerful constructs (call them, perhaps, male force and female force). These forces exist in conflict, to be sure, but there is also provision for a space, symbolized by *tinkuy*, where the divisions cease and there is commingling of energy.

For some societies other than our own, the conceptualization of the contradictions and oppositions is a natural, normal manner of viewing the world. Things are not statically described but are seen as things in movement which recombine to make new wholes in meaningful juxtaposition. In the release of energy, a transference of forces, all things are acted upon and, in turn, all things act. Thought in the tropical forest as expressed in song recognizes transference of power from rock, to water, to woman, who then, through *simayuka* and song, releases this energy again to unify with her the masculine forces in her life. The images which abound in the song text are not causally related; the splashing of the water in the river and the bathing of the snake-woman do not explain but *are* the belief system. The plastic image is the very essence of the logic in a society which does not value syllogisms but, instead, intuitive understanding, dream patterns, and the power of song.

This complex reality, a version that we of another culture have a difficult time accepting, if accepted would enrich our own existence.

A challenge to our ethnocentric way of seeing the world may lead to a view of the interconnectedness of phenomena. We are not unaware of these alternative realities in their common manifestation, the dream. But, although we remember the images, they only acquire value in psychological analysis and are not the stuff of our ordinary talk.

The Quechua texts in this book describe a means of linking our rational, analytical world with one which is phrased in other metaphors, other ideologies. In pursuing the essential meaning of the texts we transcend the boundaries of mere translation of pre-Hispanic and contemporary lyrics. The human utterance embedded in the texts—sorrowful, questioning, assertive, and provocative—seeks more than a "translational equivalence." The presence of the word, translated, ultimately seeks to transform us and create a more conscious awareness of ourselves and others.

# 2. Translation and the Problematics of Cultural Categories

WORDS RIVALED swords as an instrument of conquest in the Americas. With words, the whole warring enterprise was justified by the Spanish, who subdued the natives for Christian purposes. Discourse, legalistic and theological, served to shape events in a particular Spanish syntax and Spanish grammar.

A curious document from 1512, the *Requerimiento* (Requirement), reveals the primacy of language to empower one nation to accomplish the subjugation of others. This piece of legislation, in use until 1542, was read to the native peoples of the Americas before the Spanish marched into battle.[1] Its words proclaim meaningful communication between the Spanish and the heathen; yet the *Requerimiento* sets out to explain the Petrine theory of the papacy and the right of the pope to donate the territories of the New World to the Spanish monarchs. The natives were also told that one God, living and eternal, had created one man and one woman from whose progeny the entire earth was populated. They were exhorted to examine the documents and thereupon reach a decision to serve the royal house:

> Wherefore, as best we can, we ask and require you that you
> consider what we have said to you, and that you take the time
> that shall be necessary to understand and deliberate upon it,
> and that you acknowledge the Church as the Ruler and Supe-
> rior of the whole world (*por Señora y Superiora del universo
> mundo*), and the high priest called Pope, and in his name the
> King and the Queen Doña Juana our lords. . . . (Helps 1900: 266)

If the heathen chose not to heed the words, these warring representatives of the royal house of Spain were given license to enslave men, women, and children, seize their worldly goods, and "do all harm and damage" as was necessary under the circumstances.

Las Casas, a defender of the Indians in the colonial period, did not know whether to laugh or cry at the absurdity of this discourse. The modern reader, on the other hand, more easily decodes this message through an understanding of the doctrine of a "just war" waged against the infidel. The author of the *Requerimiento*, Palacio Rubios, was an authority on the issue of "just wars," and he was careful to construct a conclusion to the document which relieved their highnesses and their cavaliers from liability for any deaths and losses. This linguistic act was duly witnessed by those present; a notary was to record in writing that he had seen it read: "And that we have said this to you and made this Requisition, we request the notary here present to give us his testimony in writing, and we ask the rest who are present that they should be witnesses of this Requisition" (ibid.: 266–267). Often, however, the sonorous proclamation was read at great distances from its intended audience: on board a ship far from shore, in a deserted village, or shouted at trees and rocks a league away from the nearest settlement (Hanke 1949: 33–34). Occasionally, the natives actually were gathered to hear the document read to them.

In Peru, the Inca leader Atahualpa heard the friar Valverde read excerpts of the document moments before he was fired upon (Hemming 1970: 41). Several colonial chroniclers recount the scene for us; some writers even record Atahualpa's reaction to the unique Hispanic document. Agustín de Zárate, for one, gives a vivid account of the reading of the *Requerimiento* to Atahualpa in 1532. Zárate begins with his memory of the text of the *Requerimiento*: God, in the person of the Trinity, created the heavens and the earth, then Adam and Eve and a Savior to counteract the effects of original sin. He then recalls that at that moment Atahualpa was told how Saint Peter and the popes divided up the world, and that Don Carlos would offer peace and justice if Atahualpa wished to accept baptism. If not, the Spanish would use force "cruda guerra á fuego y sangre, con la lanza en la mano" (a cruel war of fire and blood, armed with lances) ([1555] 1862: 476).[2]

Whereas the reading of the *Requerimiento* provoked Raleigh to refute its theological assumptions and moved other historians to focus on the "comicity" of the document (Hanke 1938: 25–34), Atahualpa responded to it from his own perspective. His discourse illuminates Incaic values; his questions highlight indigenous categories of thought, which clash with those presented by the Spanish and the interpreters. First, Zárate states, Atahualpa took great care to explain his rightful possession of his forefathers' land, given to Huascar, whom he had conquered recently. Since he knew that to be the case, how could Saint Peter give it to some other ruler: "no sabía él cómo San Pedro las podía dar a nadie" (he couldn't understand how Saint Peter could give the lands away to anyone [else]) (Zárate [1555] 1862: 476). Of Jesus Christ the Savior he knew even less, for he knew that the sun made everything grow, that the earth was their mother, that *huacas* exist, and Pachacamá created everything on earth. What was Spain? He knew nothing about it and he had not seen it; therefore, how could he ascertain the truth of the matter? The Incaic leader was less concerned about theological debates; rather, he focused on possession of land in his empire and the possible existence of a country across the sea.

Although it is officially recorded that the conquered heathen "understood" the translation of the *Requerimiento,* from the narrated account of Atahualpa's queries we see that understanding is hampered by one's own cultural frame of reference. The Spanish monarchs created a document which would legitimize their right to conquer. Their discourse reflects this purpose; the key phrase which appeases the factions on either side of the debate about a "just war" hinges on the Indian surrender. As reported by a Spanish eyewitness, Atahualpa revealed his concern for other issues, reflective of his own world, which are not addressed by the Spanish. In the passage reported by Zárate, we see Atahualpa beginning a discussion of property (land and tribute), a likely theme after his victory over Huascar. Only secondarily does the Incan leader raise issues of religious discourse. His need to "understand" the document went beyond a matter of translation; the Iberian discourse did not fit well into an indigenous Andean format.

The *Requerimiento* was read again in a ceremony in Cuzco, when Manco was crowned Inca in 1533. Sáncho's *Relación* describes another instance when the proclamation was read to the Indians, translated word for word by an interpreter. He dutifully notes that when the Incaic leaders were asked if they understood, they all said that it was well understood (Sáncho [1543] 1988: 72).

## Language as a Conceptual Category

Language, in the sixteenth century as well as the twentieth, bears significant sociocultural indices. In addition to modes of dress, forms of worship, and precious metals, language was a medium for classifying this New World. There was acceptance of, and later rejection of, the Quechua language; the oscillation in attitude often reflected a political turn of events in both Spain and the colonies. The focus on language, lexicon, and interpretation was of paramount interest to those Europeans who brought to America their cultural baggage founded in ancient Greek texts. Foremost in this line of thought is the definition of "barbarian" as "babbler," a designation for those persons who do not speak a prestige language.

This foundation is evident in the origins of the word *barbaros*, which, in Hellenist Greece, stood for those who could not speak Greek. Language, given this context, is a symptom of larger concerns, illustrative of a relationship between intelligible speech and reason. Those humans unable to use language (Greek, in this instance) could not be expected to reason in a manner which enabled them to communicate meaningfully. Deprived of this privileged speech, humankind could not be distinguished from animals. Greeks, by fortune of their birth, were included in the closed world of the *oikumene* (the Greek family of man), a superior linguistic and intellectual world as defined from their own perspective (Pagden 1982: 16). This linguistic theory of *logos* subtly permeates the Europocentric assessment of the reasoning capacity of the native Americans who were encountered on distant shores.

Many societies share this mode of differentiation wherein the speaker's group is deemed "human" and all other outsiders are the equivalent of "nonhuman." The Quechua language also expressly refers to this distinction in the term the natives use for their own language, *runa simi*, the speech of the People. People included within this classification of ethnicity (*runa*) specifically are called humans while others are called *auca* (foreigners), with the connotation of savage.

In matters of race and ethnicity, Greek thought differed from the Quechua. "Barbarian," as used by the Greeks, was a cultural definition rather than one of race; a human became civilized in learning the means of controlling his or her own behavior to the extent that the individual then joined a moral and political community (the *polis*). The Christian adoption of this belief allowed for the conversion of the "barbarian," which admitted the former "outsiders" into the true spiritual and cultural community of humankind (ibid.: 18). The harmonious existence in the civil community was tied closely to human ability to communicate by means of language, *communicatio* (ibid.: 20–21). A code of law governed human behavior in the civilized *polis*, while the *barbari* were seen as those who lived in disharmony, outside the law. Often the *barbari* were depicted as "wild" men in European literature and art; their hairy bodies, scanty clothing, and wooded surroundings clearly set them apart from the Christian believer who, by virtue of faith, was the standard with which to evaluate sociopolitical functions.

When Nebrija wrote the first Spanish grammar in 1492, he included a section titled *barbarismo* (barbarism), a "vice" which is an intolerable pronunciation or orthography of a word. He defines the etymology of the concept, which, as we have noted, comes to us from Classical sources:

> . . . los griegos llamaron barbaros a todos los otros, sacando a si mesmos; a cuia semejança los latinos llamaron barbaras a todas las otras naciones, sacando a si mesmos y alos griegos. I por que los peregrinos y estranjeros, que ellos llamaron barbaros, corrompian su lengua cuando querrian hablar en ella, llamaron barbarismo aquel vicio que cometian en una palabra. (Nebrija [1492] 1926: 123)

> . . . the Greeks called everyone except themselves barbarians; the Romans, following their example, called all other nations barbarians except themselves and the Greeks. And because travelers and foreigners, whom they called barbarians, corrupted their language when they tried to speak it, they called a barbarism that "vice" that is committed within a word.

One means of transforming the barbarian into a human being was through language, of course. There was some difficulty in this pursuit, for, in the opinion of most men of the Church, the impoverished Indian tongues fell short of *locutio* (reasoned discourse). Many missionaries noted the absence of one word for God and the absence of words to describe abstract and universal notions. Lexicons served as an index of civilization; language indicated the operations of the human mind, and the lack of terminology for basic concepts created a controversy regarding language policy in the colonies of the New World. We see this ideology reflected in the writings of José de Acosta: ". . . las mismas palabras y vocablos, según el filósofo [Aristóteles], son señales inmediatas de los conceptos y pensamientos de los hombres; y lo uno y lo otro (digo las letras y las voces) se ordenaron para dar a entender las cosas . . ." (. . . according to the philosopher [Aristotle], even words and vowels are immediate signs of concepts and thoughts of humankind; and both [letters and sounds] are given order so that [we] can understand things . . .) (Acosta [1588] 1954: bk. 6, chap. 4, 185).

On the other hand, many clerics recorded their reaction to the richness of the power of expression and precision granted to the speakers of the native languages. Friar Santo Tomás, writer of the first Quechua grammar, is more appreciative in his comparison of Quechua to the languages of Spain and Rome: "Y breuemente, carecen los Indios de todos los vocablos delas cosas que no tenian ni seusauan en aquellas tierras, como assi mismo nosotros no tenemos terminos de las que no ay en la nuestra y ay en otras" (And briefly the Indians lack all those words about things that they do not have or they do not use in their land, just as we ourselves do not have terminology for things that are not in our land but are in other lands) (Santo Tomás [1560] 1951: 15).

Analysis of the properties of language grew in importance with the expansion of the Spanish Empire in the fifteenth and sixteenth centuries. The publication of Nebrija's *Gramática de la lengua castellana* (Grammar of the Spanish language) in 1492 legitimized Spanish as an "agent of empire" and favorably described Spanish as derived from the well-ordered grammatical principles of Latin. Thus, Spanish, a vernacular language, increasingly assumed a place formerly reserved for the prestigious classical languages in the discourse of royal decrees and religious doctrine. In the sixteenth century, Spanish, now grammatically codified in its similarity to Latin, became a model with which Spaniards evaluated the language and thoughts of the indigenous people in the New World.[3]

The prejudice and the awe with which the Iberian officials and clergy conceptualized the Quechua languge are reflected in legislation enacted to address the problem of teaching the Catholic doctrine.[4] Which language more persuasively led the Indians to join the Christian community? Was Quechua capable of revealing the essence of Christianity so that Indians could be converted? Or would conversion be better accomplished by first teaching Spanish to Quechua speakers? The archbishop of Lima in 1545 resolved the issue by teaching the children in Spanish yet instructing the adults in their own language, because the "old ones" would not learn Spanish so readily (Armas Medina 1953: 88). However, several years later, a royal decree issued by Charles V forbade indoctrination in Quechua because the native languages were not capable of expressing well, and with decorum, the Catholic articles of faith:

> Habiendo hecho particular exâmen sobre si aun en la mas perfecta lengua de los Indios se pueden explicar bien, y con propriedad los Misterios de nuestra Santa Fe Católica, se ha reconocido, que no es posible

sin cometer grandes disonancias, é imperfecciones. . . . (*Recopilación*
[1550] 1943: 193)

Having accomplished a specific investigation as to whether,
even in the most perfect of the Indian languages, one can well
explicate with propriety the Mysteries of our Holy Catholic
Faith, we have concluded that it is not possible to do so with-
out committing great dissonance and imperfections. . . .

The text of this oft-cited decree also highlights a further reason
for the shift in language policy: there are simply too many languages
for a chair to be established in each one so that the clergy could be-
come proficient speakers: ". . . y aunque están fundadas Cátedras,
donde sean enseñados los Sacerdotes, que hubieren de doctrinar á los
Indios, no es remedio bastante, por ser mucha la variedad de len-
guas" (. . . and even if chairs could be endowed so that the priests
who were to indoctrinate the Indians could be taught, it is not a good
solution because of the great number of languages) (ibid.). At the
time this decree promoting the study of Spanish was written (1550),
sixty schools dedicated to this task already had been founded in
Peru; a *colegio* (secondary school) had been set up in Ecuador in ad-
dition to numerous primary schools to teach the reading and writing
of Spanish (Armas Medina 1953: 390). At no time were Indians to be
forced to attend Spanish classes; the Eighteenth Law of the Indies
states that the learning of Spanish is "voluntary" for those who
willingly come forward (*Recopilación* [1550] 1943: 193).

Scholarly interest in Quechua did not diminish, nevertheless, dur-
ing this time period. The publication of Friar Santo Tomás's Quechua
lexicon and grammar in 1560 attests to a continued examination of
the human capacities of the conquered Andeans as revealed through
their language. This analysis of Quechua grammar regularized the
study of the native language, for the student could now learn Que-
chua in terms of the structural models of Spanish and Latin. Santo
Tomás's publication was utilized throughout Peru; many priests had
complained about teaching doctrine by means of an interpreter or
preaching in Spanish. We note a change in attitude when a royal or-
dinance (1578), in fact, is disseminated which requires every priest
to know the native language of the mission where he is assigned to
preach; competence in the native language is to be documented by a
certificate from a university professor, a specialist in the indigenous
tongue (Burrus 1979: 167). The creation of chairs in Quechua (Lima,
1580; Quito, 1581) allowed for an assessment of the linguistic skills

of the religious who intended to administer to the Indians (ibid.: 167; Hartmann 1977: 21). The Catholic congregation of the Third Council in Lima in 1582–1583 sought to promote more profound understanding of Christian doctrine by teaching Indians in their own language:

> Y así, cada uno ha de ser de tal manera instruído que entienda la doctrina, el español en romance y el indio también en su lengua, pues de otra suerte, por muy bien que recite las cosas de Dios, con todo eso se quedará sin fruto su entendimiento. . . . Por tanto, ningún indio sea de oy más compelido a aprender en latín las oraciones o cartilla, pues les basta (y aun les es muy mejor) saber lo y dezirlo en su lengua. (Tercer Concilio Limense [1582–1583] 1982: 63)

> And thus, each person should be taught in such a way that he understands the doctrine—the Spaniard in Spanish and the Indian in his own language. By any other means, even if he can recite well everything about God, in spite of all this his understanding [of it] will not bear fruit. For this reason, no Indian from this day forth is obliged to learn the creed in Latin because it is enough (indeed it is better) that he know it and recite it in his own language.

This shift in language policy diverges greatly from the decree issued scarcely thirty years before that stated that translation of Christian concepts caused "dissonance and imperfections" of doctrine. The Church in Lima advocated conversion designed to increase native comprehension of Catholicism, not mere rote learning and recital. The "Epístola sobre la traducción" (Epistle on translation) in the Quechua-Aymara catechism of 1584 again links preaching in the native tongue to providing a deeper understanding of Christianity: ". . . no basta proveer de doctrina a los Indios sino se da orden cómo se les diga en su lengua para que la perciban" (. . . it is not sufficient that the doctrine is provided for the Indians; instead, it is imperative that one tell them about it in their language so that they perceive it) (*Doctrina christiana* [1584] 1985: 16). However, the same authors of the catechism of 1584 still intend to maintain tight control of how religion is explicated to the natives. Capacity to speak Quechua must be accompanied by an encompassing knowledge of Christian doctrine to translate accurately: "Y aùnque ay algunos expertos en la lengua: ay empero pocos que lo sean juntamente en letras sagradas" (Although there are some experts in the [Indian] language, there are few who are also experts in sacred Scripture) (ibid.). To avoid error in the interpretation of Scripture, future translations would have to be approved by religious authorities before these cate- chisms and creeds were published. These sanctioned translations be- came the basis for conversions which appealed to indigenous powers of reason. Instead of exposure to an overwhelming surplus of termi- nology to describe Christianity, allegedly offered by a well-meaning interpreter, there were guidelines for specific terms to be employed in converting the Indians.

**Interpreter: A Serious Case of "traduttore traditore"**

The eventual acceptance of Quechua as a language for conversion enabled the Catholic priests to speak directly to the natives using approved religious terminology prescribed by the Church. In the latter half of the sixteenth century, religious discourse was standard- ized and a dependence on interpreters was discouraged. The perils which can befall one in the task of cultural interpretation are vividly illustrated in the life stories of two translators who served the Span- ish in the early days of the invasion. Both served as mediators in ne- gotiations—spiritual and commercial—between the Spanish and the natives in the Americas. The *lengua,* as the interpreter was often called, was entrusted to avoid certain errors and misunderstandings and to act as a "cultural broker" in this moment of trauma. In the conquest of Peru, the two most frequently mentioned interpreters are Felipillo and Martín, both of whom Pizarro probably encoun- tered in his trip of 1526–1527 near Tumbez. Both young boys ac- companied Pizarro back to Spain in 1529, and it is said that the two Quechua speakers succeeded in mastering the Spanish language (Lockhart 1972: 449–450). During the dramatic moment of the sei- zure of Atahualpa, however, it is unclear which of the two was there as a *lengua.* Most chroniclers mention the presence of just one inter- preter. However, two sources claim that Martín did the translation, whereas Cieza de León asserts that it was Felipillo.

One account claims that Martín was sent out with Hernando de Soto for the initial encounter with the "great lord," Atahualpa. In this account, it appears that the Inca did not acknowledge the presence of the Spaniard. Atahualpa kept his eyes downcast, even when de Soto approached so close that his horse's nostrils stirred the fringe on the Inca's forehead. The following morning, Hernando de Aldana, who spoke some Quechua, was sent as a messenger to hasten Atahualpa's arrival before nightfall. Later, during the fateful meeting, however, it is remembered only that an anomymous "young boy" strode out with the priest, don Vicente Valverde, to speak with the Incan ruler (Hemming 1970: 34–42).

The eyewitness accounts reported by Estete, Mena, and Cieza de León, among others, attempted to convey in language actually what transpired in those vital moments in Cajamarca. The variance in the accounts, including who served as interpreter at this moment, underlies a greater concern for the roles of the Spanish actors than the indigenous ones. Here, when even the breath of a horse can be remembered, we note in the same passage that the name of the Indian translator is forgotten.

Although we do not know for certain whether Martín or Felipillo served as an interpreter in the capture of Atahualpa, the details of their lives from that moment on are more easily followed. It is recorded that Martín was to receive 10,000 pesos for his service at Cajamarca. Although Pizarro never paid him, Martín rose to great stature as an *encomendero* in Lima, the possessor of a Spanish coat of arms and the title of interpreter general. Felipillo did not fare as well due to his allegiance to various factions of rival Spaniards and indigenous chieftains (Lockhart 1972: 452).

Both *lenguas*, at first applauded by the Spanish, later fell into disrepute. Upon reflection of the events at Cajamarca, the Spanish king was critical of the cruel slaying of Atahualpa, "since he was a monarch, and particularly as it was done in the name of justice . . ." (Hemming 1970: 81). To justify their acts in the eyes of Charles V, the Spanish subjects in Peru blamed the execution on a misinterpretation by their loyal indigenous *lenguas*. The Spaniards claimed that they were misled by distorted testimony which the *lenguas* gathered from Atahualpa's soldiers, who said that a sizable Incan army had gathered to overcome them. The Spanish allowed the two interpreters to become scapegoats for Pizarro's "panicky decision" to kill Atahualpa. Public opinion was critical also of their shifting political loyalties in the times of great unrest. Thus, Felipillo was garroted by Almagro in Chile, where he confessed to inciting Indians against the Spanish in 1536 (ibid.: 82). Martín, now don Martín, also was stripped of his property and *encomienda* due to his support of Pizarro in the uprising of 1550. He died on his way to Spain to lodge a protest (Lockhart 1968: 214).

Many years after the Conquest, the mestizo chronicler, the Inca Garcilaso, devoted much attention to assessing the faulty translations of the interpreter Felipillo. He was influenced by the writings of the priest Blas Valera, who likewise emphasized the value of accurate translations. In Felipillo's case, it was not just his inadequate knowledge of Spanish which caused errors but an inability to trans-

late Incaic concepts (*las razones*): "La falta de Felipillo no solamente
fué en las palabras que no supo decir en español, mas también en
las razones, que por haber sido algo larga la relación del Inca no
pudo tomarlas todas en la memoria y así hizo falta en ambas cosas"
(Felipillo's problem was not just that he did not know how to say the
words in Spanish but also because he did not understand the logic
[*las razones*]; the Inca's account of history had been so long that he
could not hold it all in his memory and thus he failed on both ac-
counts) (Garcilaso de la Vega [1617] 1963: pt. 2, bk. 1, chap. 20, 44).
Atahualpa, Garcilaso states, criticized Felipillo harshly in the early
meeting with Hernando de Soto: "Por lo cual el Inca, penando por su
mala interpretación, dijo: '¿Qué anda éste tartamudeando de una
palabra en otra y de un yerro en otro, hablando como mudo?'" (Be-
cause of this, the Inca, lamenting the poor translation, said, "What is
this man up to stuttering from one word to the next and from one
error on to the next, speaking like a mute?") (ibid.: chap. 19, 43).[5]

   The Inca Garcilaso is most critical of Felipillo's inept translations
of Catholic doctrine: "Y aunque era bautizado, había sido sin nin-
guna enseñanza de la religión cristiana, ni noticia de Cristo nuestro
Señor, con total ignorancia del credo apostólico (And even though he
was baptized, he had little knowledge of Christianity, nor the exis-
tence of Christ our Lord, and was in complete ignorance about the
Apostle's Creed) (ibid.: chap. 23, 48). Most notably, Garcilaso in-
forms us, he did a particularly bad translation of the concept of the
Trinity, because he did not understand perfectly the Catholic sym-
bol and because he drew upon his own Incaic tradition of the *quipu*
(counting knots):

> Tal y tan aventajado fué el primer intérprete que tuvo el Perú; y
> llegando a su interpretación es de saber que la hizo mala y de contrario
> sentido, no porque lo quisiese hacer maliciosamente, sino porque no
> entendía lo que interpretaba, y que lo decía como un papagayo, y por
> decir Dios Trino y Uno, dijo Dios tres y uno son cuatro, sumando los
> números por darse a entender. Consta esto por la tradición de los
> quipus, que son los ñudos anales de Cassamarca, donde pasó el hecho, y
> no pudo decirlo de otra manera . . . (Ibid.)

> In such a way and in such a manner was the first interpreter of
> Peru so blessed; and in regards to his interpretation we must
> admit that it was poor and inaccurate, not because he intended
> maliciously to do it; rather, he didn't understand what he inter-
> preted and it came out like a parrot said it. In attempting to
> relate God Three in One, he said God three and one are four,

adding the numbers up as a means of being understood. This comes out of the tradition of the *quipu*, the knotted yearly accounts of Cajamarca, the city where this all took place, and he could not help himself . . .

Thus, in the exchange between Felipillo and Atahualpa, we again confront the issue of translation. Felipillo shatters the illusion of the Trinity ("three and one are four") because of his faulty understanding of this article of faith. Atahualpa, understanding little of his recitation, becomes confused, angry, and hastens his own death. Both Atahualpa and Felipillo became victims of translation; neither one understood the Spanish discourse well enough to transmit or receive it.

John Hemming (1970: 558) clearly states that this false story of translation arose in the 1550s and was repeated by colonial historians (Zárate, López de Gómara, Cabello de Balboa) and in recent histories by Prescott, Means, and Valcárcel. Our interest is not so much one of assessing blame; rather, this erroneous story and its exaggerated importance serve to discuss the difficulties of translation. The concept of the Trinity is a particularly good example to analyze, for the Trinity, "Dios tres y uno" (God three and one), is an image very difficult to convey in any language. As Anthony Pagden notes, it is a concept based on a paradox (1982: 182). Felipillo may be somewhat pardoned if we recall that José de Acosta, writing his *De procuranda indorum salute* of 1588, doubted that the Trinity could be understood even by learned scholars: ". . . el misterio de la Trinidad, que es difícil aun para los de grande y agudo ingenio" (. . . it is a concept difficult even for those of a large and sharp mind) ([1588] 1954: bk. 5, chap. 4, 552). This Jesuit priest furthermore states that there are many who cannot understand the distinction of persons and the unity of the essence—not only in Ethiopia and the Indies but in Spain and even the royal courts of Italy (ibid.: chap. 6, 555). Ultimately, for Acosta, the matter of the Trinity becomes one of belief, and it is the duty of the believer to profess this truth according to his abilities (ibid.: chap. 5, 553–554).

## The Trinity, Shrines, Devils: Dictionary Definitions

Indigenous comprehension of the Trinity in the colonial period could have been facilitated somewhat by the existence of a pre-Hispanic deity represented by three statues. Acosta writes about three statues of the sun called *Apu-inti* (father), *Churi-inti* (son), *Inti-guaqui* (brother) and another deity called Tangatanga, who was described as "one in three" (cited in Gisbert 1980: 88). In the iconographic representations of the colonial churches, Teresa Gisbert has found a colonial painting of a three-headed figure, each head with the face of the young Christ, joined to one body in an effort to represent the Christian Trinity (ibid.: fig. 85). In other colonial depictions, the Trinity is composed of three individual figures, all in the image of a thirty-three-year-old Christ, dressed all alike (ibid.: fig. 87) or each bearing a symbol to distinguish each member of the Trinity (ibid.: fig. 24).

A visual "translation" of the Trinity as three persons may have been more effective than the verbal description of the doctrine presented in the sermons. In the *Tercero cathecismo* (1585), the priests "translated" the concept for the Indian converts:

> Confessamos los Christianos, que este Dios es uno, y juntamente es tres.
> Es un Dios, un Señor, un poder, un ser, y no tres Dioses, ni tres Señores,
> y juntamente es Padre, y Hijo, y Spiritu Santo, que son tres personas.
> Como son tres personas? Porque el Padre no es el Hijo, ni el Spu
> Sancto, y el Hijo no es el Padre y el Spiritu Sancto. Y el Spiritu Sancto
> no es el Padre, ni el Hijo. (*Tercero cathecismo* [1585] 1985: 410)

> We Christians confess that this God is one and at the same
> time three. [God] is one God, one Lord, one power, one be-
> ing and is not three Gods, nor three Lords, and all together is
> God the Father, the Son, and the Holy Ghost, who are three
> persons. How can they be three persons? Because the Father is
> not the Son nor the Holy Ghost and the Son is not the Father
> and the Holy Ghost. And the Holy Ghost is not the Father, nor
> the Son.

The Quechua and Aymara versions of this sermon follow exactly the text of the Spanish format; the lesson is made more familiar by the usage of the Quechua terms *yaya* (father) and *churi* (son), but, in an attempt to clarify matters, God and the Holy Ghost are described with Spanish nomenclature in the long passages written in Quechua and Aymara.[6]

As we might expect, the notion of the Holy Ghost is the most difficult concept of the Trinity to express. As even learned Spanish speakers have difficulty with this concept, we can detect much effort expended in the Quechua dictionaries to describe this noncorporeal manifestation. Santo Tomás, in his early dictionary, uses *çamay* to describe "spirit" ([1560] 1951: 133). González Holguín depends on a circumlocution of "something like an angel" to convey the meaning (cited in Urbano 1980: 116). This latter definition specifically refers to a lack of bodily substance; "no ay sayanin" (no bodily substance) is specifically attributed to God the Father and the Holy Ghost in the lexical entry. But this emphasis on the non-human characteristic of the Father and Holy Ghost eventually led to misleading comparisons with Andean spiritual beings who also pertained to a specific category of Andean thought. In the end, the Spanish priests introduced the Spanish word *espíritu* (spirit) to distinguish their own Christian apparitions from those of the Quechua, as we saw in the *Tercero cathecismo.*[7]

Spanish attempts to teach native peoples the definition of the Holy Spirit and the sacredness of the Trinity forced a confrontation with the Andean cosmology and entities such as *huaca* (shrine) and *supay* (spirit beings). The Inca Garcilaso makes much of Felipillo's misconception about the Trinity; his text also is full of comments criticizing the shallow knowledge of Quechua concepts among Spanish priests and scholars.[8] As a native Quechua speaker himself, the Inca Garcilaso is competent to judge their familiarity with the language. His frustration in his attempts to translate the semantic clusters from one language to the other often provides us with vivid descriptions, as this one of *huaca*:

> Quiere decir cosa sagrada, como eran todas aquellas en que el demonio les hablaba: esto es, los ídolos, las peñas, piedras grandes o árboles en que el enemigo entraba para hacerles creer que era Dios. . . . También dan el mismo nombre a todas aquellas cosas que en hermosura o excelencia se aventajan de las otras de su especie, como una rosa, manzana, o camuesa o cualquiera otra fruta que sea mayor y más hermosa que todas las de su árbol . . . Por el contrario, llaman *huaca* a las cosas muy feas y monstruosas, que causan horror y asombro . . . También llaman *huaca* a las cosas que salen de su curso natural. . . . (Garcilaso de la Vega [1609] 1963: pt. 1, bk. 2, chap. 4, 47)

It means something sacred, like all those things that the devil talked to them about; that is, the idols, the cliffs, large rocks and trees which had the devil inside to make them believe that he was God. . . . Also they call *huaca* all those things that in beauty or in excellence stand out from others of the same species, like a rose, an apple, or a *camuesa* or any kind of fruit that is larger or more beautiful than all the rest from that tree . . . On the other hand, they also call *huaca* ugly and monstrous things, those that cause fright and surprise . . . Also things that depart from their normal state are called *huaca* . . .

In the Inca Garcilaso's definition, *huaca* is distinct from concepts governed by the absolutes of a Manichaean universe; the Incan *huaca* could be seen as both a good and a bad force. To the Spanish, who attributed all evil to the forces of Satan, the ambivalence was incomprehensible and rarely appears in their texts. In their zeal to uproot idolatry, the Spanish priests may have felt vastly outnumbered in their religious conquest. Trees and mountains, certain stones, springs, snakes, and many other things were all called *huaca* according to the indigenous informants.

In contemporary research *huaca* is generally understood to delimit a sacred space or is a sacred object which was revered as the founding spirit or the protector spirit (Taylor 1980a: 12), or it refers to sacred beings materialized in hills, waters, caves, stones, ancestor mummies (Stern 1982: 14). More importantly, as R. T. Zuidema has shown, the concept of *huaca* was essential to the classification of sociopolitical units in the Inca Empire; each *huaca* represented an Incaic unit. Cristóbal de Molina is said to have made a listing of 328 *huacas* in the environs of Cuzco, a list found in a chronicle by Bernabé Cobo (Zuidema 1982: 427–430).

To understand the *huaca* functioning within a sociopolitical unit, one can study the structure of empire as represented by the spatial configuration of the capital, Cuzco. The city was divided into four quarters and each quarter was the residence of three principal *ayllus* (a group made up of several families who claimed a common ancestor). The city was further divided in half; the northern half was called upper Cuzco (Hanan) and the lower half, in the south, was lower Cuzco (Hurin). Each of the 328 *huacas* was cared for by one *ayllu*; there were celebrations and rituals necessary to maintain each shrine (Zuidema 1978a: 348).

Conceptually, each *huaca* was envisioned as being part of a line (*ceque*) which radiated from the center of Cuzco (ibid.). These lines, marked by real objects in the city, helped to define the sacred spaces in Cuzco (Figure 7). The conception was a fluid one which took into account the expansion of the Incaic territory. If the Inca wished to transfer a group of people, he would give them a new *huaca* of origin to carry with them to the new place. "The consecration of the new *huaca* was carried out by transferring the interest of worship from the original *huaca* to the new one. If the *huaca* was a well of water, this was done by ceremonially carrying water in a beaker from the old *huaca* to the new" (Zuidema 1982: 446).

*Huaca* was an important concept for the Spanish to comprehend because, in a cultural translation, the word indicated the presence of Lucifer. Europe, at the time of the Conquest, was busily engaged in

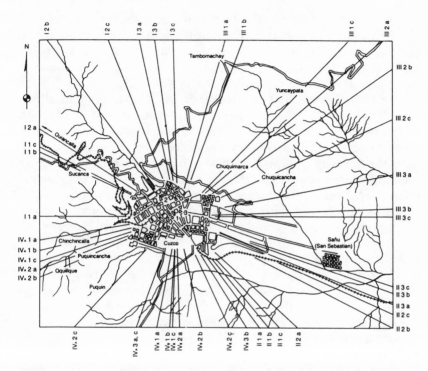

*Figure 7*. The layout of the *ceque* lines in the environs of Cuzco, Peru. From Zuidema 1977:252 (Fig. 15.7), by permission of University of Texas Press and R. T. Zuidema.

activities to purge the world of the menace of Satan, the Lord of Misrule. Ferreting out his presence in the New World, where he supposedly had a freer hand to pollute the world, was an arduous task for the Spanish men of the Church. Especially troublesome to the Spanish clergy was an understanding of the plethora of names which referred to the presence of devils in the New World. While *huaca* in general represented evil beings, there are also specific names of spirits, such as *chapiñuñu* and *achacalla* (Santacruz Pachacuti Yamqui [1613] 1927: 128). Yet eventually the early lexicographers dropped the specific usage and referred to the whole lot of Andean devils with one general term, *supay*, as the century progressed.

This definition of *supay* as devil was not present in the early dictionaries. An entry by Santo Tomás mentions "*çupay:* angel, bueno, o malo, demonio" (angel, good or bad, devil) ([1560] 1951: 279; Taylor 1980b: 49). The distinction between angel or devil was made through preceding the noun with a qualifying adjective *alli* (good) or *mana alli* (bad); *alliçupay* would be understood as "angel." The original form, *çupay*, was "morally neutral"; only in its modified form did it refer to a spirit capable of causing harm or bestowing favors (Silverblatt 1982: 42). Thirty-eight years later, in González Holguín's dictionary, one finds *çupay* defined solely as devil, with no mention of angel. The restriction of the semantic potential further illustrates the Spanish reconfiguration of Andean ideology to match their own patterns of envisioning the world. Although Quechua speakers lacked a concept similar to their own religious cosmos, the Spanish appropriated this term and restricted it to signify the black forces of evil. In a similar time period, we see a Quechua speaker and writer, Guaman Poma, promoting the singular definition as well: "Eran diablos y así decían *zupay*, que por tal le conocian por *supay*" (They were devils and thus they called them *zupay*, as such they knew them as *supay*) ([1615] 1980: 234). *Alli supay*, the Quechua word for a "good" spirit, was not used by the Spanish; instead, they aligned their own language with the positive connotation and used the Spanish, *angel*. Thus, the lines were further drawn in the theological battle; the Indians were associated with the devil through retaining the Quechua word *supay*, whereas the heavenly host of angels was described only in Spanish.

The abundant *huacas* and the *supays* in themselves represented a great threat to the recently formed Spanish colonies. Their very presence threatened a newly founded order of allegiance to Spain and to Christianity, as the subjugated indigenous people continued to consult with them and listen to their discourse. The Amerindians, for their part, observed that the new gods brought in by the Spanish— the *huacas* of the Spanish, for instance—were never offered food to eat. These figures, seen by indigenous eyes, were mere "painted and gilded sticks, deaf and dumb, who didn't speak or answer whoever asked them questions" (Rostworowski 1983: 11). Thus, the confrontation of the two systems reveals fundamental differences in the two categories of spiritual beings: the Christian panoply was more of an abstract concept, while the Amerindian spirits demanded foodstuffs and coca from their believers. Mindful of these distinctions, the indigenous people were "converted," which often meant that the Christian god(s) were accorded a place in a pantheon of Andean deities. In so doing, the natives followed an old pattern of accommodation, where local gods of the conquered people were worshipped alongside those of the conquerors. Thus, the world order was restored and maintained; *huacas*, *supays*, and later *espíritus* all had a specific function in regulating this world of political society and its mirror image, the other world beyond.

## Semantic Spatialization and Equilibrium: Andean Cultural Categories

The historical events which led to an assessment of the "other" often defined the geographical sites, native plants, or humans in the terminology of the victor; therefore, we have seen that it is the ideology of the Trinity which is diffused, not the organizational principle of the *huacas*. The semantic imprecision of terms such as *huaca* and *supay* in translation to Spanish would argue that the language of the victor avoids the problem of accuracy. As J. M. Lotman has stated in his analysis of culture, the dominant culture provides the norm and its "language becomes the metalanguage of that cultural typology" (1975: 97).⁹ Those features which do not coincide with the "chosen" group often appear "not as other types of organization but as non-organization. They are characterized not by the presence of other features, but by the absence of features of structure" (ibid.).

Spatial models often serve as the basic model for diagramming the organization of culture. As Lotman argues, ". . . world view invariably acquires features of spatial characteristics. This very construction of a world order is invariably conceived on the basis of some spatial structure which organizes all its other levels" (ibid.: 101). In the case of the Greeks, we glimpsed one model based on a we/they distinction. To the Greeks and the Romans, the dominant organizational principle was language; those who spoke Greek were rational and worthy of communicative acts, while others were labeled barbarians.

A corresponding analysis of Inca culture, by means of material objects and semantics, similarly leads to a discovery of basic systematization operative in the Andes. Much emphasis was placed on spatial representation: "Concern with spatial relations is characteristic of Incan insistence" (Ascher and Ascher 1981: 43). The spatial organization of Cuzco, determined by *ayllus, huacas,* and *ceques,* is indicative of a complex schemata worthy of an advanced civilization. However, lying underneath this pattern is a basic generative metaphor, one of symmetry and balance.

This attention to "equilibrium" is correctly emphasized by Raúl Porras Barrenechea, who notes that Quechua speakers persistently distinguish objects which are not well matched or "equal" (1952: xxviii). Reference to Incaic divisions of symmetry and balance reveal an elaborate system which features a number of semantic items: *yanantin, chacu, chulla, pacta,* and *tincuni.* All contain reference to elements of balance, order, and equilibrium: *yanantin* and *pacta* describe the perfect match of paired objects, while *chacu* and *chulla* note deviance from the ideal of a matched pair. A glance at the dictionary entries of González Holguín ([1608] 1952) illuminates this concept:

> yanantin yanantillan: dos cosas hermanadas (two things which are related) (364)
> pacta: cosa ygual justa o que esta pareja (something that is exactly the same or forms part of a pair) (272)
> chacu: lo desygual que en pareja con otro (something that does not match in a pair, paired with another object) (91)
> chulla: una cosa sin compañera entre cosas pareadas (something without a mate compared to matched up pairs) (119)

Explanations of *chulla* in its most simple state may mean the unmatched quality of one glove present out of a pair of gloves or a person having the use of one eye when the ideal would be two eyes. The explanation of "unmatched" or "unpaired" often presented an enigma when the example included is "like a *candelabro* or a wine vessel for the mass (*vinajera*)" (ibid.: 119). What was meant here is that these objects had no "mate"; they were made for solitary usage, which was not seemly in Incaic esthetics or philosophy.

*Tincuni*, another key word in Quechua, illustrates another spatial concept, often between matched items or providing unification of the deviant. It has two uses of a single meaning: literally, to meet up with, to run into (*encontrarse, topar*), and a more symbolic one, "ser contrarios, o competir" (to be enemies or to compete) (ibid.: 342). In spatial representation, this concept may be seen as a designated area in between two perfectly matched entities, the eyes: *ñauiptincun* (the space in between two eyes that divides them) (ibid.: 342). It also is used to designate the place where two rivers come together, *tincukmayo* ("junta de dos ríos") (ibid.). Notations in Guaman Poma's writings help us to go beyond the dictionary to begin to understand a more encompassing cultural category. The joining of two rivers is a designated symbolic space where the widow and other relatives of the deceased spouse go to wash their bodies and their clothes within five days of the death and again after one year (Guaman Poma [1615] 1980: 272, 732). Part of the ceremony which takes place in this juncture is a divination ritual, where the widow enters an enclosure and comes out quickly or slowly, denoting the length of her life (ibid.).

González Holguín transcribes a Quechua phrase which aids our more complete understanding of *tinkuy*: "yana huan yurak huan tin-

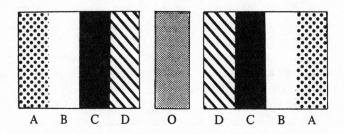

A    B    C    D    O    D    C    B    A

*Figure 8.* Colored bands of mirrored oppositions in an Andean weaving. From Cereceda 1978 : 1021 (Fig. 2), by permission of *Annales: Economies— Sociétés—Civilisations.*

cun" ( "lo negro es contrario de lo blanco" [blackness is the opposite of whiteness]) ([1608] 1952: 342–343). We may unravel its meaning, literally, with a study of woven bags by Verónica Cereceda (1978). Her analysis of the Andean bags concretely illustrates the concepts used by the Quechua speakers, although her informants principally speak Aymara. Cereceda perceives a preference for symmetry in the colored bands; a vertical axis orients the weaving so that the bands on the cloth are seen as mirror oppositions and the colors are arranged in a specific order (Figure 8). The concept of pairedness is privileged; weavers often call one side of the sack *chulla.* The traditional meaning which we note in González Holguín persists; Cereceda states that "l'expression implique qu'il fait partie d'une paire, et qu'il lui manque son partenaire" (the expression implies that one part of an [equal] pair is lacking and that it is lacking its partner) (ibid.: 1021).

As an aid to understanding the meaning of *tinkuy,* we see that a similar concept is expressed in Aymara using the word *allka.* Weavers called attention to this domain in the weavings, an area where opposites joined together. Often *allka* is described as a black line, but, more importantly, it denotes a significant boundary for transition where shades of one color turn into shading of another color: "L'*allka* conjoint les deux termes opposés et complémentaires d'un même phénomène: le blanc et le noir dans le domaine des couleurs naturelles, l'ombre et la lumière sur le plan cosmologique (la nuit et le jour, le féminin et le masculin, etc.)" (*Allka* joins the two opposing and complementary terms in the same phenomenon: white and black in the domain of natural colors, dark and light in the cosmological scheme [night and day, feminine and masculine, etc.])

(ibid.: 1025). This line—an Aymaran *tinkuy*—limits the boundaries of color, frames the design of the weavings, and demarcates spatial relationships between opposites.

The spatial symbolism which occurs on an alpaca carrying bag is apparent also in the festival celebrations called *tinkuy*. A pan-Andean phenomenon, *tinkuy* consists of a ritual battle between groups of men (and often groups of women) which may result in deaths. Tristan Platt (1976) has described a *tinkuy* among the Machas, north of Potosí, where two moieties (kin groups) line up facing each other, women fighting women and men fighting men. These ritual battles maintain intact the ancient Andean preference for dualism (the moieties *hanan* and *urin*) and recognition of antagonistic oppositions, which are mitigated in the confrontation of ritual. The oppositions represented by the battling participants are diverse: Harris (1978) states that the structure is based on the tension of endogamous marriage; Cereceda (1978) reads it as an agricultural rite; while Hopkins (1982), who summarizes all studies of this ritual, links *tinkuy* to a dialectical conjunction of opposing forces from which regeneration and fertility flow forth in the Andes (1982: 183).

In discussions of equilibrium and measure, three other words also stand out as primary cultural categories for Andean societies: *ayni*, *mita*, and *mink'a*. *Ayni*, as glossed by González Holguín, means "to work some more for someone else just as he/she works for me," "aynilla manta llamcapuni" ([1608] 1952: 40). In this sense, *ayni* represents the Andean concept of reciprocity among equals, where labor is not contracted but (theoretically) exchanged as a service to another, who owes a similar service in return as well. Implicit is an understanding that the same type of work will be performed.

Labor also was distributed by a mechanism known as *mita*, where individuals were required to work in the mines, for example, as a service to the state. Here, as Bruce Mannheim correctly observes (1986c: 269), the principle is not one of symmetry but of asymmetry, a response to a governmental "tax" on a community. However, inherent in this type of work is a taking of turns, for *mita* work is cyclical and all persons will accomplish what is expected of them in this "social contract": *mittaruna* (people of the mita), "los que siruen su vez" (those that take their turn) (González Holguín [1608] 1952: 243). It is significant that one of the variants of *mita* is *mittachiccuni*, "hazer que me siruan por su vez" (to insist that they serve me at their turn) (ibid.), denoting an adherence to the principle of distributive periods of work.

*Mink'a* represents yet one more type of labor in the Andes. Usually, this word denotes a communal participation in a public works project, such as cleaning an irrigation ditch, clearing a soccer field, or building a road. In contemporary usage, as studied by Dumézil and Urbain, the same concept of reciprocity is included but with a distinction that a different type of work may be substituted (Dumézil 1955: 9; Urbain 1980: 78). González Holguín's definition of *minccani* as "to rent a person," "alquilar persona" ([1608] 1952: 240), in the seventeenth century then alludes to a crumbling of Andean values which were not based originally on monetary exchange. However, other entries in the dictionary may illuminate another type of exchange for spiritual goods: "mincacuni o miccani humucta," "llamar hechizeros para sus necessidades" (to call shamans for specific reasons) (ibid.).

One of these "reasons" (*necessidades*) may be to rectify certain disparities in *ayni* relationships. In the seventeenth-century dictionary entry (ibid.: 40), *aynini* is defined as "to compensate or repay in kind" (literally, "the same money," "en la misma moneda"). Here, we must not look at forms of monetary exchange but rely more closely on another definition of *aynicamayoc* as *vengador* (one who takes vengeance) (ibid.). This, along with reference to *mittachiccuni* (to make sure that they serve me when it is their turn), presents us with a forceful ethos which insists on a balanced and reciprocal exchange in an ideal system based on trust and kinship. *Tinkuy*, with hand-to-hand combat, further provides release for inequity in a system which privileges balanced equality.

Our understanding of Andean cultural categories is hampered often by the systematization of our own cultural experiences. It is difficult to understand Quechua coupling of opposition and reciprocity in *ayni* because we do not participate in a system where "reciprocity is constituted in everyday practices, in the seemingly trivial details of etiquette, and—as we have seen—in the tacit undersides of Quechua lexicon and grammar" (Mannheim 1986c: 270).

When we look beyond the dictionary and actually observe the practice of reciprocity in the daily interaction, we remain baffled. Our observation would say that certain market exchanges in the Andes are "uneconomic," as Stephen Brush comments (1977: 110). Why would one full saddlebag of maize be exchanged for two full saddlebags of potatoes when the cash value would dictate that one full saddlebag of maize is worth only one and one-half saddlebags of potatoes? When a sheep is worth .350 *soles* and one sack of maize is worth .140 *soles*, why is the exchange set up so that one sack of maize is equivalent to one sheep? (ibid.). In an attempt to comprehend the disparate rates, Brush offers many explanations of supply and demand, market conditions, and crop failure, yet settles on the hypothesis of reciprocity as the most satisfactory. In these exchanges the profit motive does not reign supreme; instead, the "mutual needs of the two households are satisfied. It is not discussed in terms of profit but rather as a process serving a common need" (ibid.: 112). Mental accounts are kept and, theoretically, these exchanges balance out over the years in a system of trust (*confianza*).

As George Lakoff and Mark Johnson (1980) have well established, exchange (and labor) in our industrialized societies is viewed in a different manner. The phrase, "time is money," as they demonstrate, reveals the manner in which a metaphorical concept characterizes our entire system. We use phrases such as "you're running out of time," "I've invested a lot of time in her," and "thank you for your time" because the way we are paid for work (by the week, hour, year) makes time itself a valuable commodity. Thus this metaphor based on money leads to extensions into a whole system where time is "spent, wasted, budgeted, invested wisely or poorly, saved, or squandered" (ibid.: 8).

These same researchers uncover other layers of meaning which are particular to Western industrial societies in discussing "labor is a resource" and "time is a resource." In our society labor (a substance) merges with an abstract concept (time) because they are both "culturally grounded in our experience with natural resources" (ibid.: 65). Because the natural resource is produced by *labor*, which can be assigned a value per unit, then *time* acquires value in the system, for it also can be quantified and used up in the same manner.

Our everyday usage of these words may hide from us the very premises which structure our world. In the phrase "time is money," we now see that our society values purposeful activity over inactivity, that work is not play, and that the human interaction in the exchange of labor is negated. Our analysis of Incaic structural categories can reveal another system where labor is measured in terms of contribution to community and not accumulated in stacks of coins and colored bills. We can never grasp the equation one sack of maize equals one sheep if we do not pause to understand the way in which meaningful units are fashioned out of cultural experience. In each chapter which follows we examine these meaningful units— seeing, understanding, complementarity, male-female, and love—as categories defined by Quechua speakers in their songs and in their lives. In the process, we search for commonalities of experience as well as divergences to reach a mutual understanding, a full cultural translation.

# 3. Script and Sketch: A Semiotics of Knowledge in Santacruz Pachacuti Yamqui's Relación

> Writing . . . was and is the most momentous of all human tech-
> nological inventions. It is not a mere appendage to speech. Be-
> cause it moves speech from the oral-aural to a new sensory
> world, that of vision, it transforms speech and thought as well.
> (Ong 1982: 85)

THE WRITING system brought by the Spanish ex-
plorers to the Amerindians in the New World was a mea-
sure of the distance which separated the two cultural
entities. Because the Spanish knew how to write, they
questioned the very nature of the peoples they encountered who had
no such script for transmitting their culture. The Quechua speakers
likewise, viewing the pieces of paper dispatched by the Castilian
conquerors, concluded that their Iberian lords possessed a magical
means of communication.

The indigenous chroniclers who wrote down the events of the
Conquest in their own words heighten our understanding of the
chasm between culture systems. The references to books and writ-
ing come to the surface in the historical texts against a background
of dependence on the oral-aural transmission. One of the major colo-
nial indigenous writers, Felipe Guaman Poma de Ayala, in describ-
ing the meeting of the priest Valverde and Atahualpa, privileges the
printed Word, the Book. While Spanish narratives of the Conquest
emphasize Atahualpa's inability to *open* the Christian breviary, the
indigenous writers focus on other gestures. Guaman Poma describes
Atahualpa's attempts to "listen" to the pages of the breviary once it
is handed over to him:

Y dixo *Atagualpa:* "Dámelo a mí el libro para que me lo diga." Y ancí se
la dio y lo tomó en las manos, comensó a oxear las ojas del dicho libro.

Y dize el dicho *Ynga:* "¡Qué, cómo no me lo dize? ¡Ni me habla a mí el
dicho libro!" (Guaman Poma [1615] 1980: 357)

And Atahualpa said: "Give me the book so it can speak to me."
And thus he gave it to him and he held it in his hands and he
began to leaf through the pages of the aforesaid book. And the
Inca said: "What, why doesn't this book talk to me? This book
isn't saying anything to me!"

The author of another Quechua testimony, Titu Cusi Yupanqui,
when narrating this scene is also perplexed by the events.[1] He de-
scribes a "letter or a book or I don't know what" being shown to his
uncle Atahualpa: ". . . le mostraron al dho. mi tió una carta ó libro, o
nó se qué diçiendo aquella era la *quillca* de Dios y del rrey" ( . . .
they showed my uncle a letter or a book or something, I don't know
what, saying that it was the writings of God or of the king) (Titu
Cusi [1570] 1973: 16). In both versions, the book is summarily dis-
missed when Atahualpa throws it to the ground in frustration.

Other Andean observations reveal a prolonged curiosity regarding
the Spanish writing system. Atahualpa, once he is jailed, begs to be
taught how to "listen" to these texts. The alphabet, seen through in-
digenous eyes, assumes magical properties. Titu Cusi, in describing
the Spanish, mentions their ability to "speak by means of white
cloths and to name several of us by name without anyone having
told anyone. [They do this] merely by looking at the cloth in front of
them" (y aún nosotros los habemos visto por nuéstros ojos á solas
hablar en paños blancos y nombrar a algunos de nosotros por nuestros
nombres sin se lo deçir naidie, no más de por mirar al paño que
tienen delante) (ibid.: 20).[2] Guaman Poma, after describing how the
Spanish and their horses are accustomed to eating gold, also states
that "day and night each one speaks with his papers, *quilca*" ([1615]
1980: 353).

Letters, sent from one Spaniard to another, were seen as "spies"
who were able to comment on what happened in the conquered do-
main, according to the Inca Garcilaso. In the *Comentarios reales*
(Royal commentaries), he relates a humorous anecdote describing
the indigenous misunderstanding of the writing system in the colo-
nial period.[3] He mentions how an overseer, who lived outside of
Lima, sent ten melons loaded on the backs of the Indians to the land-
owner, Antonio Solar. The overseer also gave the Indians a letter to
carry, and he warned them not to eat the melons as the letter would
certainly report on their actions. The two Indians, anxious to taste

the Castilian melons, paused in their travels to sample the fruit. Before biting into a melon, however, they contemplated the role of the letter: " . . . si comemos alguno lo dirá esta carta" ( . . . if we eat any [of them] this letter will tell [on us]) (Garcilaso de la Vega [1609] 1963: pt. 1, bk. 9, chap. 29, 371). Their solution was to gobble up the melons far out of sight of the letter: "Buen remedio; echemos la carta detrás de aquel paredón, y como no nos vea comer, no podrá decir nada" (A good solution: let's throw the letter behind that wall and since it cannot see us eat [the melons], it will not be able to say anything) (ibid.).

The transmission of anecdotes and alternative visions of the Conquest are the by-product themselves of the indigenous mastery of the European writing system. Yet instruction in the writing system also meant acceptance of the dominant language system, Spanish, as well. The texts which survive are mostly written in Spanish, with the exception of one notable Quechua manuscript from Huarochirí. Words penned by an indigenous hand reflect subtle changes in value systems as the Amerindian author accommodated his thoughts in terms of Spanish grammar and syntax.

### Santacruz Pachacuti Yamqui's Visual and Verbal Text

Joan de Santacruz Pachacuti Yamqui Salcamaygua's text, attributed to the beginning of the seventeenth century, is a document of cultural assimilation and cultural difference. His *Relación de las antigüedades deste reyno del Pirú*, as the title indicates, is mostly written in Spanish yet liberally sprinkled with Quechua (and some Aymara phrases at times) when he serves as interpreter of complex Andean concepts. Little is known of Santacruz Pachacuti Yamqui except what he tells us in an extensive genealogy replete with topographical references:

> Yo Don Joan de Santacruz Pachacuti Yamqui Salcamaygua, cristiano por la gracia de Dios Nuestro Señor, natural de los pueblos de Sanctiago de Hananguaygua y Huringuaiguacanchi de Orcusuyo, entre Canas y Canchis de Collasuyo, hijo legítimo de Don Diego Felipe Condorcanqui. . . .
> ([1613] 1927: 127)

I, Don Joan de Santacruz Pachacuti Yamqui Salcamaygua, a Christian by the grace of God Our Father, an Indian from Santiago de Hananguaygua y Huringuaiguacanchi de Orcusuyo, be-

tween Canas and Canchis de Collasuyo, the acknowledged son
of Don Diego Felipe Condorcanqui. . . .

We may conjecture, as does Zuidema, that Santacruz Pachacuti
Yamqui spoke Aymara (in addition to Quechua and Spanish), for he
lived in a town halfway between Cuzco and Lake Titicaca (Zuidema
and Quispe 1973: 365–366).

Reading Santacruz Pachacuti Yamqui's manuscript one could infer
that the Incaic civilization already possessed a writing system of
sorts. Unlike the Inca Garcilaso and Guaman Poma, he does not
comment on the absence of writing in the Andes. Instead, he men-
tions certain pre-Hispanic *capítulos* (chapters) and a mysterious *li-
bro grande* (large book) which was brought to the Cuzco palace by a
messenger ([1613] 1927: 133, 188). A sign of his assimilation to the
Hispanic cultural system as well as the written discourse is the
pious *incapit* which begins his manuscript; "Jesús-María" and a
hand-drawn cross show his knowledge of the religion imposed by
the Spanish. The *explicit* "Que Dios Nuestro Señor sea alabado por
siempre jamás" (May God Our Lord be forever praised) provides the
appropriate Christian framework to close his long history of the An-
dean peoples.

The oscillation between one cultural code and another—Spanish
and Andean—is evident in Santacruz Pachacuti Yamqui's recourse
to drawing, not writing, the belief system of his own culture. Here,
words fail to convey the image of the cosmos, and he abandons the
European script. Other times within the text we detect his attention
to visual stimuli, even while he writes. The ambivalence found in
his paragraphs and illustrations reflects the two systems of power
and canons of values—Iberian and Amerindian—which shape the
creation of his text.

His written descriptions of Incaic societal rankings are heavily de-
pendent upon reference to a visual code. Throughout the text he
mentions the symbolic meaning of the signs of office, a nonverbal
code for designating rank:

> . . . el dicho Pachacutiyngayupangui sienta con su hijo Topayngayupangui,
> y Amaro Ttopaynga, todos tres con iguales *tiyanas* de *ruua*, hechas de
> oro; todos los tres bien vestidos con sus *capacllaottos* y *mascapachas*,
> y el viejo con su ceptro de *suntor paucar*, hecha de oro, el y
> Topayngayupangui con su ceptro de *ttopayauri*, y el otro sin ceptro, solo
> con *chambis*, pequeños de oro. (Ibid.: 194)

. . . the aforesaid Pachacutiyngayupangui sits with his son
Topayngayupangui, and Amaro Ttopaynga, all three sitting on
their royal seats, made of gold; all three are dressed up in their
royal woven headbands and their royal fringe, and the old [king]
held his scepter and royal standard, made of gold, he and
Topayngayupangui with his scepter of gold, and the other one
without a scepter, only a royal war club, made of gold.

Thus, these individuals are not seen by Santacruz Pachacuti Yamqui
as idiosyncratic personalities; instead, he emphasizes the iconic val-
ues of the *suntor paucar*, the *ttopayauri*, and the *chambi*s.

Similarly, his view of the transfer of power from Incaic rulers to
Spanish leaders is laden with a schema of symbolic mapping which
reveals a conceptual iconicity. A description of Pizarro and the priest
Valverde when they confront Atahualpa becomes a symbolic tableau
vivant amidst the clamor of conquest:

. . . y el Marques con sus canas y barbas largas representaba la persona
del Emperador Don Carlos V, y el padre Fray Vicente con su mitra y
capa, representaba la persona de San Pedro, pontifice romano, no como
Santo Tomas, hecho pobre; y el dicho ynga con sus andas de plumerias
ricas, con el vestido mas rico, con su *suntorpaucar* en la mano, como rey,
con sus insignias reales de *capac unancha*; y los naturales gran alegria, y
tantos españoles! (Ibid.: 235)

. . . and the count with his gray hair and his long beard repre-
sented the royal person of the Emperor Charles V, and the
priest Friar Vicente [Valverde] with his miter and his cape, rep-
resented the figure of Saint Peter, the Roman pontiff, not like
Saint Thomas, who was poor; and the aforementioned Inca
with his litter covered with luxurious feathers, with his finest
woven garments, with his royal standard in his hand, like a
king, with his royal insignias of *capac unancha*; and the na-
tives [with] such great joy, and so many Spaniards!

Each person in Santacruz Pachacuti Yamqui's vision is symbolically
representative of a higher and more powerful being. Pizarro stands in
for a distant Charles V, while the Spanish friar in his miter and cape
embodies the legendary qualities of Saint Peter. Santacruz Pachacuti
Yamqui's recourse to this symbolic manner of thinking is not neces-
sarily the product of recently acquired concepts of Christianity.

Although he emphasizes the liturgical significance of Valverde's pointed miter and cape, he lavishes more attention on those symbols he knows best from his Andean heritage. He mentions the royal litter, the ornate garments and royal plumage, the *suntorpaucar*, and the royal insignia instead of describing the individual characteristics of the Incan ruler. These icons portray the essence of Andean ideological thought and occupy more authorial space in the text. In contrast, the reference to Pizarro reveals less comprehension of the vast Iberian political system. Pizarro is described nakedly bereft of symbolic trappings; with his "gray hair and his long beard" he does not possess full stature alongside the image-laden Atahualpa.

Santacruz Pachacuti Yamqui is disposed to write in this fashion because of his exposure to the *tocapu*, an Inca sign system, which was still in use in his lifetime. A painting commissioned in the seventeenth century also displays this same vivid attention to the details of the *tocapu* symbols which adorn the dress of an Incaic noble woman, Beatriz Clara Coya (Hemming 1970: 470). The numerous rectangles, filled with geometric dots and ciphers, allude to a symbolic system which is only imperfectly understood by researchers today (Figure 9). Thomas Barthel (1971) and Victoria de la Jara (1974) have attempted to decipher the figures as an alternative system of writing. Although no clear one-to-one correspondence is demonstrated conclusively, it is safe to assume that the symbols portray a hierarchical reference to the elites in Inca society.

The indigenous chronicler, Guaman Poma, also illustrated the headpieces and the shields of authority as well as the 150 designs of circles, triangles, dots, and zs embroidered on the garments of the nobility (Kauffmann Doig 1978: 302–303). The persistence of the *tocapu* sign in portraits of Incan nobles for two hundred years after the Spanish invasion attests to its cultural importance as the predominant "script" of the empire (Rowe 1967: 265).

While no researcher has yet deciphered the meaning of these symbols, we must assume that they possessed more than mere decorative value within Incaic culture. The manipulation and organization of symbols was, in the domain of the empire, both a restricted activity and one of easy access. Santacruz Pachacuti Yamqui himself explains that each town was referred to by a sign system well recognized in the Andes, the *pacarina*. Manco Capac is credited with originating this custom whereby each province and each town chose an object to symbolize its origin. Some groups chose lakes, waterfalls, hills, even gorges to differentiate themselves from others; another alleged purpose was to clearly and easily identify the diverse groups:

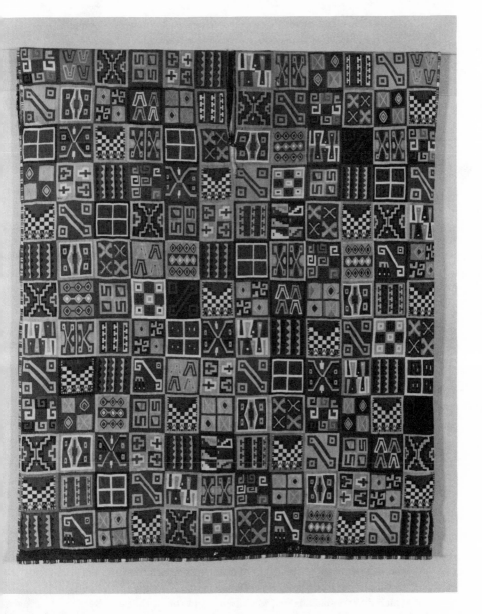

*Figure 9. Tocapu* designs on an Andean poncho. By permission of Dumbarton Oaks Research Library and Collections, Washington, D.C.

Y assi mando que los vestidos y traxes de cada pueblo fuessen diferentes, como en hablar, para conoçer, porque en este tiempo, no echauan de ver y conoscer a los yndios que nación o qué pueblo eran; y por ser más conocidos, los mandó que cada prouincia y cada pueblo se escogiesen o heziessen de donde descendieron, o de donde venieron. . . . ([1613] 1927: 145)

And thus [Mancocapac] commanded that the dress and the garments in each town [should be] different, just as their speech is different, to identify [them], because in this time period, they didn't observe and identify which nation or what town the Indians were from, and to be better known [identifiable] he commanded [them] to choose or to create where they were descendants of or where they came from. . . .

Knowledge, then, was conveyed through visual signs, and this cultural mapping was so complete that one could identify at a glance the participants at a ceremonial gathering. One such scheme is identified in the *Relación* where all the chieftains (*curacas*) are seen in their places (*lugares*) and seats (*asientos*) representing each province and gathered together at a ceremonial plaza (ibid.: 166). This sign system is further explained by the Inca Garcilaso, who writes of the intricate system of assigning housing sites in Cuzco to peoples of recently conquered territories according to a pattern that depicted the entire empire:

. . . cada uno de [los curacas guardó] el sitio de su provincia; que si estaba a mano derecha de su vecina, labraba sus casas a su mano derecha; . . . por tal orden y concierto, que bien mirados aquellos barrios y las casas de tantas y tan diversas naciones como en ellas vivían, se veía y comprendía todo el imperio junto, como en el espejo o en una pintura de cosmografía. ([1609] 1963: pt. 1, bk. 7, chap. 9, 258)

. . . each one [of the chieftains] maintained a site according to his province; if it was on the right-hand side of his neighbor, he built his houses on the right side; . . . all ordered and in harmony, those neighborhoods and all the houses of so many and such diverse nations just as they lived in them, that just by looking at them one understood the [layout of] the empire, like in a mirror or in a painting of the cosmos.

Natural phenomena also entered into this semiotic system: divinations with coca leaves or the entrails of animals and the interpretation of cosmic events served as prognostic devices.

Santacruz Pachacuti Yamqui's assimilation of the Spanish symbols of the new cultural order sometimes is less than complete. His statement of belief in one God the Creator of the World is accompanied by a phrase which ostensibly proves his Christianity, yet it also proves the "pagan" origins of his system:

> Como digo, creo en Dios trino y vno, el cual es poderoso Dios que crió al cielo y tierra y á todas las cosas en ellas questan, como el sol y luna, estrellas, luzeros, rrayos, rrelampagos y truenos, y á todos los elementos; &. . . . ([1613] 1927: 130)

> As I have said, I believe in God three and one, the same one who is the powerful God who created the heaven and earth and everything that is in it, like the sun and the moon, stars, morning and evening stars, lightning, the flash of lightning and the thunder, and all the elements; etc. . . .

This statement, with its repetition of stars, morning and evening stars, lightning, flash of lightning and thunder, is not an account of the Creation according to Genesis. The celestial enumeration reveals a structure peculiar to the Andean system of classification, not one derived from Christian teachings.

Menéndez Pidal (1958: 64–65) notes that the juxtaposition of synonyms is the most salient stylistic feature in Spanish literature of the sixteenth century; we see this device in Santacruz Pachacuti Yamqui's list that we just read. Yet, here this purposeful writing of *estrellas* and *luzeros* creates a contrast of these celestial bodies (*estrellas*) with those of the morning and evening stars (termed *luzero*) in the Amerindian cosmological map drawn in the manuscript. Research by Abdón Yaranga Valderrama (1979: 710) helps to explain the repetitive emphasis of the elements *rrayos, rrelampagos,* and *truenos* (lightning, flash of lightning, and thunder): These divisions refer to a tripartite deity (Illapa) still worshipped in southern Peru as a flash of lightning (*rayo*), thunder (*trueno*), and lightning itself (*relámpago*). Thus, his version of God's creative spirit enunciates some of the most powerful images in the Andean belief system while leaving other entities enveloped with the nonspecific "á todos los elementos" (everything). Santacruz Pachacuti Yamqui's termination of the enumeration with an ampersand—a frequent conjunctive device in manuscripts—may well indicate, on the other hand, our author's knowledge of Christian principles and the rules of Hispanic discourse. This European sign, often signifying "et cetera," usually indicates that something has been elided. It also signifies a rule of

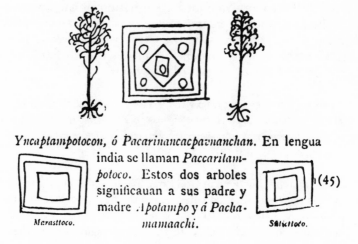

*Yncaptampotocon, ó Pacarinancacpavnanchan.* En lengua india se llaman *Paccaritam-potoco.* Estos dos arboles significauan a sus padre y madre *Apotampo* y *á Pacha-mamaachi.*

*Marasttoco.*     *Salixtloco.* (45)

*Figure 10.* An ideogram in Santacruz Pachacuti Yamqui's text. From Santacruz Pachacuti Yamqui [1613] 1927:144.

interpretation, according to Tyler (1978: 344): "When someone uses an et cetera marker, he assumes that his addressees can supply the missing information either from rote memory or because they know a rule which will generate what has been left out." Here, our author may be hiding behind an ampersand to avoid the scrutiny of the Spanish priests, who, as we have, may detect the remnants of Andean beliefs.

As a cultural interpreter, Santacruz Pachacuti Yamqui often conveys information through synonyms, as in his description of the rainbow "aquel arco del cielo, llamado *cuychi turumanya yayacarui*" (that rainbow, called *cuychi turumanya yayacarui*) ([1613] 1927: 141). Here, starting with the Spanish, he intentionally offers three more examples from the languages in which he is more fluent, Quechua and Aymara. When he translates from the other direction, from Quechua, he is sometimes at a loss for an exact wording in Spanish, especially when he is also working from a drawing of the same information (ibid: [1613] 1927: 44). His explanation of the ideogram (Figure 10) goes beyond what is literally conveyed in the *tocapu*s and the Quechua phrases:

Los hizo que colgase en los dos arboles frutas o pipitas de oro, de manera que llamasen *corichaochoc collquechaochoc tampo y uacan;* que quiere

dezir que los dos arboles significasen a sus padres, y que los yngas que
procedieron, que eran y fueron como frutas, y que los dos arboles se
habian de ser tronco y rayz de los yngas. . . . (Ibid.: 144)

He made them hang fruits and seeds of gold on the two fruit
trees, because of this they were called *corichaochoc collque-
chaochoc tampo y uacan;* which means that the two trees
stand for his parents and for the Incas from which they pro-
ceeded, who used to be and were like those fruits, and the two
trees must be the trunk and the roots of the Incas. . . .

His translation of the Quechua phrase "corichaochoc collquechao-
choc tampo y uacan" is not a literal one, which would be rendered
"el santuario donde se hallan los jardines de oro y plata" (the sacred
space of the gold and silver gardens). After drawing the figures and
naming them, he does not restrict himself to a literal translation;
instead, he explains the symbolic meaning. The tree figures repre-
sent the mother and father of Mancocapac and the fruit of the trees
will be the future generations of the Incas. Santacruz Pachacuti
Yamqui would have a reader understand a meaning for the word
"tree" which is related to the sacred mummies of the ancestors, defi-
nitions not found in the Quechua dictionaries of González Holguín
and Santo Tomás, written in this time period. In this passage, he,
Santacruz Pachacuti Yamqui, alludes to the symbolic meaning of the
Quechua word *mallqui*, "which stands for the dried bodies, the rit-
ual mummies of the ancestors" (Duviols 1977a: 186). Since this tree
figure is highly reminiscent of the *tocapu* designs and is also one of
his cosmological symbols in the map of the universe, the Andean au-
thor translates an entire cultural system, not a simple word image.

Here, Santacruz Pachacuti Yamqui wrestles with the problematics
of signs, where a sign represents a similar object (the tree) and also
serves a function as a symbol of his own parents and all the fore-
fathers. Yet other signs in the semiotic system of the Quechua-
speaking peoples were ascribed a fixed value. We have seen that
signs of hierarchy (the ruling scepters) and the signs of origin (cloth-
ing and hats) lend themselves to one acknowledged interpretation.
There is mention of less problematical signs, particularly in divina-
tion, which reflect one determined meaning. In contemporary usage,
a potato plant often is used to predict a good or bad harvest: ". . . a
perfect potato plant is uprooted and the potatoes counted off in two's
to divine the outcome of the crop. An *even* number signifies an *abun-
dant* harvest, while an *odd* number presages a *poor* crop" (Tschopik,
cited by Barthel 1971: 75).

In the mention of more complex symbols, as in our discussion of *huaca* and *supay*, the attribution is more arbitrary and context dependent. For instance, in Santacruz Pachacuti Yamqui's text the rainbow is perceived to be a good omen by Manco Capac. It also is interpreted in this manner in the *Miscelánea antártica:* ". . . buena señal es aquesta ya no se acabara el mundo por agua" (. . . this is a good sign that the world would not be ended with a flood) (Cabello Balboa [1586] 1951: 262). However, the parallels with Christianity disappear in evidence cited by the chronicler Polo de Ondegardo, who states that a rainbow signifies approaching death or calamity, although it is also greeted with reverence ([1561–1571] 1917: 198).

**An Andean Ideogram: Translating a Visual Code**

This rainbow icon and other symbols appear in an elaborate line drawing of Incan cosmology which Santacruz Pachacuti Yamqui crowds in at the bottom of a page in his handwritten manuscript. This Inca cosmogram is a representation of the most complex of the Incan semiotic systems; it is a copy of the images found on the wall of the sacred Coricancha, the Sun Temple in Cuzco. Here, the Andean chronicler chooses to reveal this belief system by means of drawings. No sentence explicates the religious hierarchy of symbols; an ampersand inserted in the text again leads us into a visual code which is only partially understood by the written labels attached to each figure.

In Figure 11, each symbol is labeled in Quechua and Spanish and occasionally in Aymara. Scholars have noted a difference in the handwriting found in this drawing and other places in the text; the emendations and commentary are believed to belong to the priest Francisco de Avila, according to R. Lehmann-Nitsche (1928). While Quechua wording does predominate in the marginal notes and drawing, there is sublabeling in Spanish and also four examples of Aymara in the sections on the stars (*"Achachi Ururi, Apachi Ururi, Coso, and Vvchhu"*). Four times the pen of Avila is alleged to cross the page; he adds, "este es el luzero de la mañana" (this is the morning star), "este es de la tarde" (this is the evening star), "niebla" (fog), and the Quechua word *sucsu* (ibid.: 114, 130, 125).

The central human figures, male and female, are the only symbols to be designated solely in Spanish, yet, oddly, in the visual code they wear typical Incaic garments. This arbitrary coding again is seen in the Hispanic assimilation in Santacruz Pachacuti Yamqui's drawing of a lightning bolt. According to several Hispanic chroniclers, large statues of the god of lightning depicted as a person, not a zigzag, did

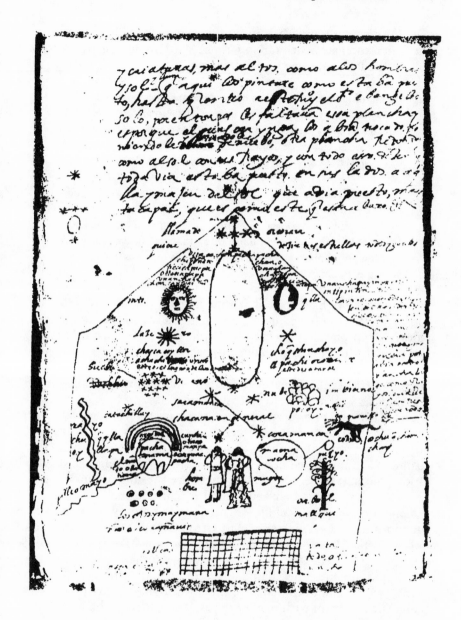

*Figure 11.* Santacruz Pachacuti Yamqui's cosmological ideogram. From Urton 1981:203 (Fig. 69).

exist in the main temple and in smaller sanctuaries (ibid.: 144–145) but Santacruz Pachacuti Yamqui chose the Hispanic abbreviations seen in the left-hand side of the drawing:

> [Santacruz Pachacuti Yamqui] no dibujó un personaje como dios de la tormenta, sino una linea en zic zac, es decir, el ideograma *europeo* del rayo, puede concluirse que se habrá olvidado de esta peculiaridad tan importante de testero de Coricancha, y que puso en su lugar el signo del rayo como estaba acostumbrado verlo en España. (Ibid.: 143)

[Santacruz Pachacuti Yamqui] did not draw a person as the god of the storm, but instead [he drew] a zigzag line, that is to say, a *European* ideogram of the lightning. One can conclude that he forgot this aspect so particularly important in Coricancha and he drew in its place the sign of lightning as one was used to seeing it in Spain.

Many scholars have looked at this diagram (Figure 12) drawn by Santacruz Pachacuti Yamqui as a visual code of Incaic ritual, agricultural, and political categories. Urton (1981), Lehmann-Nitsche (1928), and Müller (1972) analyze the astronomical designations of the celestial bodies; Isbell (1978), Earls and Silverblatt (1976), and Sharon (1978) explain the symbolic references to male-female relationships as well as Andean spiritual categories.

The celestial figures drawn in the chart have been studied by Gary Urton (1981). The meaning of the celestial figures is standardized by Urton, who "translates" them to our system of representation of the cosmos. The unlabeled stars at the top refer to Betelgeuse, Rigel, Orion, and part of Scorpio; below them are the sun and moon. *Lucero* refers to various first and second magnitude stars, as does the designation *choquechinchay*. These were commonly referred to as the morning and evening stars, but Urton does not claim they refer only to Venus. The *chacana en general* (bridge, stair) is commonly seen as Orion's belt. *Catachillay*, according to other chroniclers, is a constellation called the "llama silvestre hembra" (the wild female llama), while *choquechinchay* of the lower right designates a fierce puma constellation with brilliant eyes. The *collca* at the bottom is recognized as the Pleiades, the tail of Scorpio, and the Hyades in contemporary usage. In view of the agrarian patterns of the Incaic civilization, which is corroborated by contemporary observations, these stars provide a basis for weather predictions and indicate the moment for planting. Certainly, atmospheric conditions are also implicit in the words summer, winter, clouds, fog, hail, and lightning,

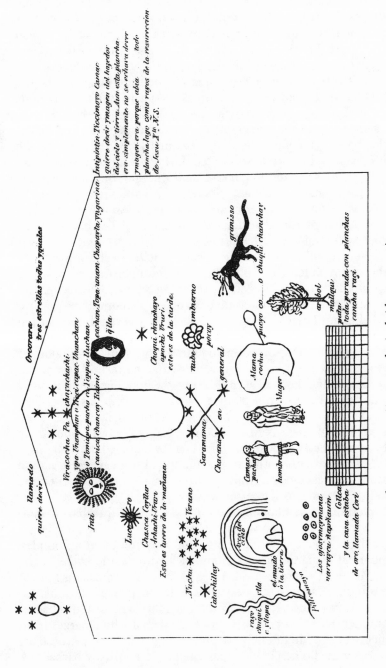

Figure 12. Santacruz Pachacuti Yamqui's cosmological ideogram, simplified. From Means [1613] 1928:n.p., by permission of the Connecticut Academy of Arts and Sciences.

which increases the inclusiveness of the drawing as a key to Incaic charting of the heavens for agricultural and ritual purposes.

The agricultural patterning predominates when the chart is read mindful of the planting of corn in the dry season (July–August) and the planting of potatoes in the wet season (January–February). The Pleiades, it turns out, may be sighted for the time maize is planted until its harvest; clouds may obscure the skies for the rainy periods of potato planting, as the drawing reveals. In addition, the sun is almost always sighted for the planting of maize using a horizon calendar (ibid.: 76–77). Potatoes are most frequently associated with the moon's phases; they are best planted during a waning moon (ibid.: 85). Corn is, we see, pictured in its cooking pot on the left side of the chart in the domain of the sun. Therefore, a symbolic dichotomy is revealed based on the two principal crops in the Andean fields.

A discussion of the genealogical references of the chart begins with perception of the male (left) and female (right) divisions. This designation coordinates with the accepted belief in the sun as male and the moon as female. The Aymara wording on the cosmogram further alludes to this distinction; luzero in Aymara means "grandfather star," and the afternoon star designates "grandmother" specifically (Lehmann-Nitsche 1928: 115). Read in a vertical manner (on the male line), the chart indicates a celestial, androgynous progenitor (Viracocha), a male great-grandfather (the sun), a grandfather (Luzero), and a male human figure. The same pattern is designated for the female line. Looked at in this way, the drawing parallels other descendant charts, called a panaca, which Zuidema has described, where male and female lines are distinguished (Isbell 1978: 210). The sexual symbolism is further complemented by a camac pacha (male earth) directly opposite a mama cocha (female lake). The tree, or mallqui, represents both tender saplings of future generations and ancestors or preserved mummy figures, as we read in Santacruz Pachacuti Yamqui's explanation.

The plethora of symbols in the middle range of the chart is concerned with the cycles of water: lightning, rainbows, rivers, lakes, springs, hail, clouds, and fog. This band may represent a complex metaphorical explanation of the annual hydrographic cycle in the Andes. Much of the explication of this cycle resides in what is known of the amaru, a large snake associated with the tropical regions. Although it is not pictured here in the diagram, Santacruz Pachacuti Yamqui mentions this powerful cultural symbol who emerges from the underworld: "Muy fiera bestia, media legua de largo y grueso, de dos braças y medio de ancho, y con orejas y colmillos y barbas" (A very fierce beast, half a league in length and fat, two and a half arm's length around, with ears and fangs and beards) ([1613] 1927: 184). A study by Earls and Silverblatt (1976) indicates that the *amaru* may serve as a mediator between sky and earth; it also is depicted in a number of transformations such as lightning, rainbow, and a feline figure. So, according to their study, an extended metaphor is erected whereby the cluster of symbols conveys a system of thought. Sharon synthesizes the conclusions in Earls and Silverblatt's article as follows:

> Today it is believed that during the rainy season the *ccoa* cat emerges from the highland springs (*puqyos*) in the form of clouds. Near the end of the dry season the *amaru* serpent gushes forth from the springs and into the irrigation canals in the form of a flow of water, mud, and stones. It also manifests as the lightning that announces the arrival of the first downpours of the rainy season. (1978: 98)

Thus, we now better understand the variance in meaning of this symbol, which also surfaced in the interpretation of the sign of the rainbow. A full description of its meaning necessarily involves comprehension of the processes of transformation, the seasonal and stellar cycles of nature, and the interaction of human beings and the agricultural systems on earth.

The inclusion of sketches in Santacruz Pachacuti Yamqui's *Relación* allows us to see the power of the pictorial sign to convey a message of Andean categories of thought. His written text often is much less clearly articulated, perhaps due to the imposition of Spanish syntax to describe the history of the conquests and ruling elites in the Andean region. To deliver his message, Santacruz Pachacuti Yamqui creates a hybrid work, a grafting of verbal and pictorial signs.

### The Code of Verbal Discourse

We have discussed at some length the visual coding (the *tocapu*, the *quipu*) operant among the Incas; now we must spell out the rules for verbal discourse in this same society. The Incas, who developed a highly coded oral tradition based on a mnemonic device, the *quipu*, also codified formal and precise manners of verbal expression in the discourse of society. The many entries in the seventeenth-century dictionary by González Holguín ([1608] 1952) record interest in speech and verbal modes of expression:

*simi cazcachik:* el que la pronuncia, y sabe propria, y galana-
mente (he who pronounces it and knows it well and with flair)
(328)

*mattucta rimani rimaytam matuchani:* hablar no claro, o no
pronunciar bien (to not speak clearly or to not pronounce well)
(233)

*arui aruictam rimani:* hablar confuso ó escuro (to speak con-
fusedly or obliquely) (538)

*ccuru kallu:* el que no sabe bien hablar y habla despacio y atiento
(he who does not know how to speak well or who speaks
slowly or hesitantly) (132)

*mircca simicta rimak:* el que habla lengua mezclada de otras
agenas (he who speaks with a hodgepodge of other languages)
(242)

*aclluchacuni:* pronunciarlo todo muy mal sin quedar nada (pro-
nounce everything badly without making sense) (16)

To better understand the role of language in contrast to the pri-
macy of the visual in Incaic society, we must turn to González
Holguín's seventeenth-century dictionary to contrast the functions
of two verbs utilized for the act of speaking, *ñini* and *rimani*. *Ñini* is
used in the reportive sense of "dezir algo" (to say something) but
also carries the sense of "strong" speech of commanding and passing
judgment on others ("dezir, y pedir, y mandar, y sentenciar") (to say,
and to ask a favor, and command, and to sentence) (ibid.: 261). Here
the dictionary calls our attention to the delocative action of this
verb; it can enclose a quote and it can embed a new speech context.
*Rimani* is defined only as *hablar* (to speak), but we have an addi-
tional sense of its meaning in a form which includes the augmen-
tative *ycu*. *Rimaycuni* means "Murmurar hablar de otro mal" (to
whisper, to speak badly of another), which contrasts with *ñiycuni*,
"dar aviso, avisar, hazer saber" (to notify, to advise, to make known)
(ibid.: 317, 261). The negative qualities attached to the gossiping
function of the verb *rimani* are highlighted later, when we analyze
the nature of Quechua speakers' knowledge of events.

*Ñini* exclusively is used to indicate quotative and citative clauses,
and there is a formal structure set aside for that purpose. When a
speaker wishes to include reference to someone else's speech, the
appropriate message is cited and marked with *ñispa*, a nominal-
ized form of *ñini*. The quoted material retains its own syntactic
forms, which correspond to it; the *ñispa* lets us know that direct
speech—the actual speech of another person—is being quoted, as
in the following passage: "'¡Haliyáw, hawanta payay, wiraqocha!'
*ñispa* . . . Y gritan '¡Oh, señor granizo, pasa por alto!' diciendo" (And

they shouted, "Oh, Lord of Hail, pass far overhead!") (Cusihuamán 1976: 281).

Quechua shares with other languages the need to distinguish various types of speech acts (gossip, talk, commands) and to impart information as to whether talk is reported directly (I say) or indirectly (he/she said). Yet Quechua speakers go beyond these basic grammatical functions to select factors which are "socially vital" in their particular society, as V. N. Voloshinov suggests for the structure of every language: "It is the function of society to select and make grammatical (adapt to the grammatical structure of its language) just those factors in the active and evaluative reception of messages that are socially vital and constant and, hence, that are grounded in the economic being of the particular community of speakers" (1971: 151).

A look at the rules for reporting the testimony of a person indicates the societal values privileged in Quechua discourse. Quechua, in addition to the reported form of *ñispa*, also has a more varied manner of demonstrating the source of the information related. The reportive enclitic *-si* is used to relay messages from another person or from any other source. If the speaker wishes to acknowledge what another person has said or written, *-si* is the preferred form and is usually translated as "they say" or "once upon a time" (Cusihuamán 1976: 242). In addition, there is a reportative past tense (*sqa*) which is used to narrate an event where there is no direct participation by the speaker, such as mythic discourse, dreams, or situations where the speaker is unconscious (ibid.: 170).

Santacruz Pachacuti Yamqui's frequent inclusion of speech by others lets us see how these speech rules are played out. When a monologue is presented embedded within his authorial context we detect how the speaker's speech is received, its possible manipulations, and the process of orientation in the social interrelations among speakers. The process is subtle but profound, for it tells us more than just which words were said by whom.

Santacruz Pachacuti Yamqui's assimilation of the Quechua rules for reporting discourse may have influenced his selection of Spanish verbs and background material which frequently appear in his manuscript. He has a keen interest in the speech act; his use of these Spanish verbs goes beyond mere denotation, and he provides us with acoustic, visual, and kinetic dramatizations of the mode of speech. He subtly teaches us in his text that loud speech is positively associated with a strong and enthusiastic leader: "Les da gran voz, exclamandole, diziendo anssi" (He spoke in a strong voice, exclaiming, saying [it] like [that]) ([1613] 1927: 177). He employs various synonyms for the "act of saying" which help interpret the situational contexts of the direct quotes in the text: "hacenle burlas" (they teased him), "los haze afrenta, deciendo" (they offend him, saying), "les porfiaua al ynga, diziendo" (he persisted with the Inca, saying), "reprende . . . con gran yra" (he scolded . . . with a lot of anger).

The technique of narrating reported speech within a mythic/historical discourse is seen in a passage from the *Relación* where the young Inca, Capacyupangui, enters to speak face to face with a feared *huaca* (sacred spirit), the object of much veneration:

> . . . acabó de llamar al ñiablo, dizen que el diablo entró con vn rruydo de viento que todos se sudaron frio y temor, y entonces el moço ó nuevo ynga dizen que dixo: "abran esa puerta y las ventanas, yo los quiero conocer que figura ó que talle trae este á quien con tanta veneración y aparato lo habeis esperado." Y como acabó de abrir la puerta, dizen que [el *huaca*] se escondió el rostro quaçi medio pasmado y no los supo responder; y dizen que el atrevido ynga *Capacyupangui*, dixo: "dime, como os llamaes?" Y entonces dizen que dixo con gran verguença que se llamaba *Cañacguay Yauirca.*" (Ibid.: 163)

> . . . he had just finished calling the devil and they say that the devil came in with a great noisy wind and everybody got in a cold sweat and full of fear, and then they say the young man or the new Inca said: "open that door and the windows, I want to meet that figure or [see] what size this person [is] who you have waited for with such veneration and preparation." And just when he finished opening the door, they say, the *huaca* spirit hid his face, a little afraid and didn't know how to answer; and they say that the bold Inca *Capacyupangui,* said: "tell me, what's your name?" And then they say that he said, very ashamed, that he was called *Cañacguay Yauirca.*

Santacruz Pachacuti Yamqui sets the stage artfully; all discourse surges forth to heighten the young Inca's verbal strength ("*el atrevido ynga*" [the bold Inca]) and to silence the utterance from this *huaca* whose mere appearance caused spectators to break out in a cold sweat. His *dixo* (he said) shows us the very words that the young Inca uttered; his care to write "dizen que dixo" (they say that he said) shows his respectfulness of the oral tradition. Even while writing in Spanish, Santacruz Pachacuti Yamqui honors the Quechua rules for clearly defining sources of knowledge.

Although Santacruz Pachacuti Yamqui was a Quechua speaker and chose to include many Quechua proper nouns in his text and in his cosmological sketch, he rarely quotes discourse in Quechua. There is one person, Ttonapa, said to be a prefiguration of Saint Thomas, whom he does not quote (or quasi-quote) at all. He characterizes him as a "splendid orator" who speaks "loving words," but he does not cite them. In other instances (as seen above with *Capacyupangui*), he cites in Spanish. In the rare cases in which he includes Quechua phrases, his discourse springs forth as ritual language: *curacas* (chieftains) use Quechua phrases to banish evil, an Inca rids himself of afflictions, and formulaic phrases are recited at the *apachitas* (shrines made of rocks) (ibid.: 141, 147, 167).

We can explain this sudden code switching from one language to another on selective occasions; Santacruz Pachacuti Yamqui resorts to usage of the aboriginal language in the midst of his Spanish text because he describes a situation for which only those words would be appropriate. Ritual language usually differs from ordinary discourse in that the system of the ritual often depends on specific verbal forms quoted in a particular sequence. So tightly woven are actions and words that the mere mention of the words serves to connote the symbolic importance of the entire ritual: "Ritual as one observes it in primitive communities is a complex of words and actions . . . it is not the case that words are one thing and the rite another. The uttering of the words itself is a ritual" (Tambiah 1968: 175). So awesome are the ritualistic expressions in Quechua that when Santacruz Pachacuti Yamqui notes the demons' names in Quechua, he quickly adds a marginal note "Dios me libre" (God protect me) (ibid.: 181) and draws the sign of the cross to exorcise their influence on him. Lengthy Quechua lyric texts transcribed by Santacruz Pachacuti Yamqui again represent a ritual context and are utterances to celebrate a state occasion: the birth of a son, the prayers of chosen priests, a prayer to Viracocha, a statement to exorcise demons, and a ritualized curse.

Before beginning a close study of one of these lengthy Quechua texts, I would turn first to a discussion of Quechua poetics based principally on Quechua texts preserved by Cristóbal de Molina, el Cuzqueño. In one poem there is a vivid poetic example to illustrate that the act of creating is equivalent to the act of speaking, at least when Viracocha utters the words:

| | |
|---|---|
| "qhari kachun | "Let there be man, |
| warmi kachun" | let there be woman," |
| ñispa, llut'aq, ruraq | saying, molder, maker. |
| | (Rowe 1953: 86, my translation) |

Emphasis is placed on this creative principle through repetition and insistence on verbal forms; the communicative *decir* (*ñiy*) is first present in the act of creation in the gerund form (*ñispa*), which marks a direct quote. *Ñiy* is also coupled with verbs "to mold" (*llut'ay*) and "to do, to make" (*ruray*) in a nominalized form, linking the verb "to say" with the agent of actions (*llut'aq, ruraq* = he who molds, makes). In another ritual discourse, the second verb of "making" or "doing" is omitted and merely understood by the insertion of the nominalized form of *ñiy, ñeq:*

| | |
|---|---|
| Wiraqochaya, | Lord, |
| "p'unchaw kachun, | "let there be day, |
| tuta kachun" | let there be night," |
| ñispa ñeq | saying, he who says, |
| "Paqarichun, | "Let there be dawn, |
| illarichun" | let there be light," |
| ñispa ñeq | saying, he who says. |
| | (Ibid.: 90, my translation) |

Even closer associations are invoked in pairing the two concepts of creation and verbal locution within one verse form:

| | |
|---|---|
| "wak'a willka kachun" | "Let the sacred *huacas* exist," |
| ñispa, kamaq | saying, he who infused life. |
| | (Ibid.: 94, my translation) |

In this verse and in one other, then, Viracocha's act of pronouncing the various vowel and consonant phonemes not only creates the things which will populate the world but also represents a more significant act, *camay*—animating or breathing a spirit into an object.

Previously, Quechua scholars have translated this verb as "to create" or "to order." Gerald Taylor, in an article titled "*Camay, camac, et camasca* dans le manuscrit quechua de Huarochirí" (1974–1976), proves that the meaning is more complex. He quotes el Inca Garcilaso de la Vega's explanation of *camay:*

> ". . . *cama*, que es animar; el cual verbo se deduce del nombre *cama*, que es ánima: Pachacamac quiere decir el que da ánima al mundo universo, y en todo su propia y entera significación, quiere decir el que hace con el universo lo que el ánima con el cuerpo" (Cited in Taylor 1974–1976: 233)

("cama, which is to give energy; the verb is arrived at from the
noun *cama*, which is spirit: Pachacamac means he /
she who gives spirit to the entire universe, and in its true and
whole meaning, it means he /she who does with the universe
like what the spirit does with the body")

The verbs *ruray* and *churay* do not encompass the sense of spiri-
tually animating or sustaining the world. *Camay*, in a hierarchy of
power, is superior to the other verbal actions, as Taylor notes:

Garcilaso nous explique que ces termes se réfèrent au domaine
matériel et sont propres aux hommes et non à Dieu; le *yachachic*
est celui qui enseigne les arts et les offices, le *rurac* celui qui
les pratique, tandis que *camac* fournit "ser, vida, aumento y
sustento, etc." (Ibid.: 233)

Garcilaso explains to us that these terms refer to a material
domain appropriate to humans and not to God; the *yachachic*
is the person who teaches arts and skills, the *rurac* is he who
actually does them, whereas *camac* gives "being, life, increase
and maintenance, etc."

Thus, when reading *ñispa, churaq, camaq* in other pre-Hispanic
verses, we understand that the creative principle differs from men-
tion of the "word" in the biblical Genesis:

| | |
|---|---|
| "Qozqo Tampu kachun; | "Let Cuzcos and Tampus exist; |
| 'atikoq llasakoq kachun" | let there be conquerors and despoilers," |
| ñispa, churaq, kamaq | saying, he who placed, he who infused life. |
| | (Rowe 1953: 93, my translation) |

In contrast to the Christian God saying simply, "Let there be light"
and light appearing, the Quechua-speaking creator has the process,
the actual steps to creation, defined and emphasized. *Ruray, churay,*
and *camay* reflect differing aspects of power; "saying" alone is not
enough in the Andean genesis. *Ñispa* serves in a grammatical func-
tion to indicate speech which has been uttered, and the other two
verbs describe the processes of creation. *Churay* represents the act
of "criar poner en su ser" (to create, to place in existence) (González

Holguín [1608] 1952: 122) and *camay* the act of infusing life spirit. Throughout the ritual poems there are references to the verbs of creation and the spoken word. The choice of these lexical items reflects a hierarchy of values which govern Inca processes of conceptualization and categorization.

Ritual texts found in Santacruz Pachacuti Yamqui's manuscript are similar in their insistent reference to speaking, ordering, and existence within a cosmological system. However, instead of a description of the Creator ordering and making, we see frequent reference to the nature of the speech act between Creator and created human being. We hear the human cry out to the Creator, yet in the ritual texts the message is unidirectional; the supreme deity, as we saw in the case of Ttonapa, never answers back and never gives a verbal sign of existence. Sometimes the human poet demands to know the actual location of the Creator, in addition to pleading for a verbal reply:

| | |
|---|---|
| maycanmicanque | Who are you? |
| ymactan ñinque | What do you say? |
| rimayñi | Speak then. |
| | ([1613] 1927: 164, my translation) |

## Ways of Knowing and Understanding: Rikuptiy, Yachaptiy, Unanchaptiy, Hamuttaptiy

The human desire to know, to be informed, the demand that the Creator make his/her presence known clearly is the enunciated message of the previous verse. We have seen how "saying" is equivalent to ordering the universe and thus we appreciate this human demand made to a deity. While this verse ends in ominous silence, one other passage in Santacruz Pachacuti Yamqui's text offers hope that knowledge will be attained and the world will be explained. In this long ritual poem, the acquisition of this specialized knowledge is outlined through the usage of four verbs which progress toward attainment of this goal:

| | |
|---|---|
| ricuptyi | When I see, |
| jachaptiy | when I know, |
| vnanchaptiy | when I make signs, |
| hamuttaptiy | when I discern the future, |
| ricucanquim | you (will) see me, |
| yachavanquim | you (will) know me. |
| | ([1613] 1927: 148, my translation) |

At first, the simplicity of the verbs and their concepts (seeing, knowing, making signs) hides more profound conceptualization which can emerge with a detailed analysis similar to the contrasts found among the verbs for speech and creation. The mere ranking of these verbs is significant; elaboration of a chain of verbs is an important construct, for the "temporal order of speech" mirrors the order of narrated events in time or rank (Jakobson 1971b: 350). This progression is significant again because of the deictic markers (*pty*) which indicate a shift from human action to actions of a supreme being. The *pty* (*pti*) subordinate signifies that the subject of the main clause (you will) is not the same as that of the subordinate clause (when I . . .). It also expresses a relationship in time: "action which begins, and perhaps ends, previous to the action denoted by the main verb . . ." (Parker 1969: 50). Thus the brief Quechua phrases indicate an interaction of persons (human and deity), the steps of attainment of knowledge (verb forms), and a temporal reference which explains that only after a mastery of each stage will the divinity acknowledge human presence.

The first verb in the series is related to knowledge through the perception of sight (*rikuy*, to see). The usage of this verb in this capacity (as a means to understanding) extends to the present day. In the contemporary lyrics I have collected in Ecuador, visual images dominate the poetic expression, and references to the verb of "seeing" as "experiencing" abound in the transcribed texts. "Seeing" is a primary means by which information is stored and then later retrieved for expression in song.

The remaining verbs in the passage all refer to cognitive processes, modes of understanding which indicate a particular type of knowledge not readily evident at first glance in the translations. *Yachay* has a frequently cited denotation of *saber* (to know) and is distinguished from the verb *riksiy* (to be acquainted with a person). Yet, as we saw in Taylor's quote from the Inca Garcilaso, the verb is often restricted to a person who knows and teaches arts and skills, a manual and practical knowledge. In Ecuador, this verb root also refers to a person who has attained knowledge of the supernatural (*yachak*) and uses these powers to harm or to cure others.

*Unanchay* appears at intervals in Santacruz Pachacuti Yamqui's text in addition to its inclusion in this Quechua verse. In its most concrete manifestations (as a substantive), *unancha* is glossed as "estandarte, ynsignia, escudo de armas" (a standard, an insignia, a coat-of-arms) and "hierro del ganado" (a cattle brand) (González Holguín [1608] 1952: 355). In this capacity, its usage is indexical, but at other times it acquires iconic properties. In the *Relación* ([1613]

1927: 209, 158), this word figures prominently in the description of the banners of various leaders "*unanchas* enarboladas" (signs with trees) but also in a more figurative sense as when referring to the images of the deity in the drawings of the Coricancha: "Viracocha Pachayachachiypa unanchan o Ticci capac Unanchan."[4]

The meaning of *unanchani*, the verb form, is closely related to its usage as a sign: "hazer señales entender considerar traçar" (to make signs; to understand, consider, track down) (González Holguín [1608] 1952: 355) and a more contemporary definition of "designar, prefijar, pronosticar, anunciar proféticamente" (to designate, to foresee, to foretell the future, to announce prophetically) (Lira 1944: 1042). This knowledge indicated comprehension of a distinctive sign (a brand, a heraldic seal) as well as a more complex referential sign of the image of the supreme being. Comprehension here involves a level of representation where a sign substitutes for a more concrete conceptualization.

The third category of understanding is indicated by the verb *hamuttani*, which receives considerable attention from González Holguín ([1608] 1952: 147–148): "advertir y entender y notar las vidas agenas para murmurar de ellas," "traçar y dar orden por la esperiencia en negocios," "traçar, o considerar cómo saldrá bien algo, ordenarlo y endereçarlo bien," "conjecturar sacar por discurso lo que será bueno y sucederá bien y lo que no" (to notice, understand, and observe the lives of others in order to gossip about them, to follow up and command because of experience in trading, to follow up or consider if something will turn out well, to arrange it, to straighten it out well, to conjecture, to get out of conversation what will be good and turn out well and what will not). This verb would seem to indicate a more complex level of understanding in that there are allusions to perception, observation, and ordering of thoughts and actions on the basis of this comprehension. Also included is an element of predictive knowledge (*conjecturar*) and the intimation that this information is conveyed through spoken discourse.

These two categories of comprehension (*unanchay, hamuttay*) are not mutually exclusive in all instances; both *hamutapu* and *unanchapu* mean "consejero diestro" (a wise counselor) (ibid.: 148). However, other glosses distinguish between the sign function of the former and the more complex symbolic attributes of the latter. *Hamu* is defined as "genero especie de cualquier cosa" (a species kind of whatever thing) (Santo Tomás [1560] 1951: 291) and "clase, especie" (a class of, a species) (Lira 1944: 212). According to González Holguín ([1608] 1952: 147), the person who attains this superior level of understanding is called a *hamu hamu soncoyoc:* "el que es universal versado y entendido en todo que lo penetra y da razón de todo" (he who is broadly skilled and comprehends all, [he] enters into it and can give a clear explanation).

The passage then provides a model which defines the various stages that govern human attainment of knowledge, according to the Incas. Each ascending hierarchical category must be purposefully mastered in order to begin to communicate with a supreme deity. Only then can a possible act of communication and recognition be attempted. The repetition of the initial set of verbs (*rikuy, yachay*) in the last two lines is meaningful, for the human referent is no longer active and it is the deity who now manipulates the domains of knowledge. The return to *rikuy* and *yachay* in the last lines indicates that the intercommunication between god and man begins on this level, but the situation is altered: The verbal referent is to a richer, fuller category since it points to reciprocal interaction with the deity. Although the other two verbs of higher understanding are not included, they are implied through the example of the human processes of change. There is no doubt that the god(s) possess superior powers, as many varied titles and descriptions are explicit in this regard: "fundamental Viracocha, Viracocha unique in the world, creator of this world, molder, former of man, skillful worker." A more lengthy analysis of three complex attributes (*pachayachachic, tecsi, usapu*) is undertaken by Pierre Duviols (1977), in which he emphasizes the all-inclusive powers of this creator god (gods). Obviously, the successive stages of human and divine communication are impregnated with profound significance when Viracocha recognizes the person he/she created in speaking to him/her.

This abstract model for attainment of knowledge closely parallels recent research in cognitive psychology, where similar patterns have emerged. Michael I. Posner (1973: 18) alludes to a basic iconic code (existing in memory processes) which "preserves certain relationships present in the physical stimulus." The capacity for storing information is enhanced by this facility for visual reproduction of complex hierarchical systems of knowledge. Human subjects, when questioned, often report that they can "construct a visual representation which includes more information than they can verbalize" (ibid.).

However, this level of processing is restricted to short-term memory unless it is combined into a system of symbolic codes which "suggest something else rather than by reason of resemblance" (ibid.: 26). This stage corresponds to the category *unanchay*, which functions both as an index and an icon in its quality of representation. Finally, there emerges a system for clustering information where material is recalled through construction of "easily identified categories" (ibid.: 31). The memory image at this level bears little resemblance to a first-order complete, vivid perception and consists of second and higher order assemblies. This schema most closely approximates the functions of *hamuttay*, where knowledge of a species or genre or a pattern of existent phenomena is suggested.

Ultimately, the model presented in the text can be utilized to go beyond mere patterns of cognition and memory; the schema also serves to illuminate a comprehensive belief system present in the Andes. We have referred often to the indexical functions of *unanchay* in its simplest form, in the knowledge of the signs of office (*suntorpaucar*), the banners of kings, and the dress of the people from various provinces. This category allows for directly correlated knowledge, as when Manco Capac wished to identify his subjects as to provenience. *Unanchay* also takes on more iconic properties, as seen in the discussion of the image in the Coricancha diagram which was labeled *unanchan* (Figure 13). Here the referent is one step removed from a causal relationship and depends on a meaning derived from cultural conventions. This image is still dependent on visual perception to convey representation of conceptualization. Such is the case in another drawing (Figure 14), which Santacruz Pachacuti Yamqui ([1613] 1927: 160) describes as a "plancha de oro fino que dizen que fue ymagen del Hazedor del verdadero sol" (a thin sheet of refined gold that they say was the symbol of the creator of the sun itself). In this same manner, we understand the sketch of a young tree (*mallqui*) to be an image of the ancestors who, like the tree, must be cared for and nourished.

By far the deepest level of understanding is denoted by the verb *hamuttay*, which alludes to comprehension of the essence and functions of matter. Knowledge at this level is total and universal in that one recognizes and processes information from many different levels beyond that of knowledge derived from signs. Few individuals possess this capability, but apparently Maytacapacynga was one who attempted a global understanding. When he is quoted in the *Relación*, Maytacapacynga refers to a special type of knowledge of the supreme creative force which was not based on signs or rational explanations of discourse:

> conocer solo con el entendimiento por poderosso Señor y dominador y
> por Hazedor, menospreciando á todas las cosas, elementos y criaturas
> mas altos como a los hombres y sol y luna. ([1613] 1927: 160)

*Figure 13. Unanchan*, as drawn by Santacruz Pachacuti Yamqui. From Santacruz Pachacuti Yamqui [1613] 1927: n.p.

*Figure 14.* The images of the creator, the sun, and the moon. From Santacruz Pachacuti Yamqui [1613] 1927:160.

to understand merely with his mental capacity because he was a powerful lord and a conqueror and creator, contemptuous of all things, elements and higher beings like humans and the sun and the moon.

He refers to absolute comprehension, which encompasses all visual and representative cues, yet disdains specific signs, to see and understand a cosmological design. When humankind indeed reaches this level of understanding, the nature of existence at all levels is known and humans comprehend fully the order imposed on the world. Posner (1973: 60) points out that Plato has an apt manner for stating this concept: "The lowest form of thinking is the bare recognition of the object. The highest, the comprehensive intuition of the man who sees all things at once."

The care with which Santacruz Pachacuti Yamqui wrote his chronicle has enabled us to understand his text from many perspectives. In addition to narrating the history of the Incas, he offers us a corpus of ritualized Quechua texts which give evidence about the modes of discourse prevalent in his society as well as some notions of the dimensions of Andean cognition. His inclusion of the cosmological drawing is significant; the sketch surpasses his verbal powers of ex-

pression and provides us with a heuristic tool worthy of construct-
ing a comprehensive explication of Andean ideology. His text allows
us to glimpse the extent to which he has assimilated Hispanic cul-
ture through his references to Christian theology and the European
literary tradition. More importantly, his manuscript also reveals
to us the extent to which he preserved the essence of his indige-
nous heritage in the sketches which often convey more than his
written words.

# 4. *Cultural Translation of the Andean Oral Tradition*

THE DIFFERENCES between the Spanish language and Quechua are well described in a story told by Indian peoples of the Ayacucho region of Peru. Three Quechua speakers, they say, agree to go to Lima to buy some Spanish words to curtail the ambitions of a landowner who is taking advantage of the community. Each Quechua man could only buy one word of Spanish because "a lot of words would be too expensive." Which words should they buy? The equivalents of *ñoqayku*, and *munaspayku*, and *chaytam munaspaykum*. They travel by train to Lima, arrive at the house of a member of their community, and tell him that they want to buy some Spanish words. He agrees to sell them these three words at 50 *soles* each word. When they reply that the cost is too great and that he should give a break to people from his hometown, he tricks them and says, "Hey, for you, it's 60 *soles*."

They do not realize they have been tricked and they each happily take their word home with them. However, the trip is marked with calamity when, on their way back, they walk by a bloody corpse. The rural police arrest the three Quechua word buyers and begin to question them in Spanish. The three Indians quickly decide to use their newly acquired Spanish words to defend themselves: "Who killed this man?" said the policeman. The first Quechua speaker said, "Nosotros" (*ñoqayku*, we did). "Why did you kill him?" said the policeman. The second word purchase was used by the other villager in his answer, "Porque queremos" (*munaspayku*, because we wanted to). His reply was followed by the policeman's statement, "OK, you're all arrested." "Eso es lo que queremos" (*chaytam munaspaykum*, that is what we want), said the third man from the village, using the last word they bought in Lima.

Brought before the judge in the rural court, the three Indian men attempt to use their Spanish one more time, as all the legal proceedings are conducted in this language. The magistrate's questions are answered using the same Spanish phrases, of course, which again seals the fate of the three Quechua speakers. The judge sentences the Indians to twenty-five years in jail on the basis of their Spanish defense of "We did," "Because we wanted to," and "That is what we want" (Ortiz Rescaniere 1973: 176–183).

This story from the contemporary oral tradition of Peru makes us smile sadly, yet it also serves a more serious purpose. Within this Quechua narration we see the extent to which Quechua speakers regard Spanish as the dominant language in Peruvian courts and in legal battles over landownership. Their strategy to defend their communal land is to buy some Spanish, using community funds. We also see the duplicity of the men's own ethnic "brother" who moved to Lima as he tricks them in the sale of words. He charges them 60 *soles*, not the first-mentioned 50, when they beg him to lower the prices for men from his own hometown. They lose the court battle for their freedom, even though they are confident of a strong defense because of their ownership of the precious Spanish words. The pessimistic vision of the story is only dissipated by the solidarity inherent in the message of the original Quechua phrases. *Ñoqayku* and *munaspayku* reflect the unity of an entire village to protect their land through marshaling village resources to have things turn out in a manner beneficial to their own people. This solidarity, translated into Spanish or English, is not easily conveyed in words other than the original, for Quechua embraces a syntactical feature which marks inclusivity and exclusivity. Thus, a Quechua speaker may say a *we* which denotes that the listener is included in the group or say a *we* which particularly states that the listener is excluded. The Quechua story is replete with references to exclusivity, clearly demarcating this group of Quechua speakers and excluding others with the usage of the nominal and possessive ending *yku*.[1]

### A Gloss for "Huaca": Is Translation Possible?

A precedent for this solidarity by means of language emerges in the prose of the Inca Garcilaso de la Vega, a mestizo whose father was Spanish and whose mother was an Inca; although he was born in Peru he nevertheless lived much of his life in Spain. Paralleling the ideology of Antonio de Nebrija and the classical tradition, the Inca Garcilaso reiterates the conception of language as the necessary "companion" in the unification and spread of empire. As he writes the history of his own native people, he insists on the beauty and subtlety of Quechua and he reaffirms, in a nostalgic yet historical gesture, his ties with his land of birth, Peru.

As Alberto Escobar has noted (1972: 154–155), the Inca Garcilaso's writing celebrates the "sense of community" to be found by means of language, coupled with a cultural tradition which is shared by speakers of Quechua. He excludes from this "language community" even those Spaniards who have mastered the native language. At times his tone is critical of the Iberian attempts to interpret the deep meanings of Quechua phrases and concepts. He states, in one passage, that he can best serve as interpreter, providing glosses and commentary, because as foreigners "they [the Spanish] interpreted beyond the innate meaning of the language" (cited in ibid.: 253–254, my translation).

Exemplary of his instructive "glosses" is his analysis of the word *huaca*, which is prefaced with his critical commentary:

> En lo que se ha dicho, se ve largamente cuánto ignoran los españoles los secretos de aquella lengua; . . . por do vienen a escribir muchos versos, interpretándola mal, como decir que los Incas y sus vasallos adoraban por dioses todas aquellas cosas que llaman *huaca*, no sabiendo las diversas significaciones que tiene (Garcilaso de la Vega [1609] 1963: pt. 1, bk. 2, chap. 5, 49)

> As for what has been said, one sees very plainly how much the Spanish are ignorant as far as the keys to the language; . . . for this reason they write with a great deal of error, interpreting badly, such as saying that the Incas and their followers worship as gods all those things that are called *huaca*, not being aware of all the meanings that [word] has.

His own "interpretation" is a full one that encompasses two pages and embraces a full range of positive and negative values (much as we saw for *supay* in chapter 2). His lengthy definition of *huaca* alludes to its abstract qualities as well as its more concrete manifestations:

> Quiere decir cosa sagrada, como eran todas aquellas en que el demonio les hablaba: esto es, los ídolos, las peñas, piedras grandes o árboles en que el enemigo entraba para hacerles creer que era Dios. Asimismo llaman *huaca* a las cosas que habían ofrecido al Sol, como figuras de hombres, aves y animales hechas de oro, o de plata, o de palo, y cualesquiera otras ofrendas, las cuales tenían por sagradas; porque las había recibido el Sol en ofrenda, y eran suyas, y porque lo eran las tenían en gran veneración. También llaman *huaca* a cualquier templo grande o chico, a los sepulcros que tenían en los campos, y a los rincones de las casas, de donde el

demonio hablaba a los sacerdotes y a otros particulares que trataban
con él familiarmente, los cuales rincones tenían por lugares santos, y así
los respetaban como a un oratorio o santuario. También dan el mismo
nombre a todas aquellas cosas que en hermosura o excelencia se aventa-
jan de las otras de su especie, como una rosa, manzana o camuesa, o
cualquiera otra fruta que sea mayor y más hermosa que todas las de su
árbol; y a los árboles que hacen la misma ventaja a los de su especie le
dan el mismo nombre. Por el contrario, llaman *huaca* a las cosas muy feas
y monstruosas que causan horror y asombro; y así daban este nombre a
las culebras grandes de los *antis*, que son de a veinticinco y de treinta
pies de largo. También llaman *huaca* a las cosas que salen de su curso
natural, como a la mujer que pare dos de un vientre, a la madre y a los
mellizos daban este nombre por la extrañeza del parto y nacimiento; . . .
otras naciones lo tomaban en contario, que lloraban, teniendo por mal
agüero los tales partos . . . Y por el semejante llaman *huaca* al huevo de
dos yemas, y el mismo nombre dan a los niños que nacen de pies, o
doblados, o con seis dedos en pies o manos, o nace encorcovado, o con
cualquier defecto mayor a menor en el cuerpo o en el rostro, como
sacar partido alguno de los labios. que de éstos había muchos, o bisojo,
que llaman señalado de naturaleza. Asimismo dan este nombre a las
fuentes muy caudalosas que salen hechas ríos, porque se aventajan de las
comunes, y a las piedrecitas y guijarros que hallan en los ríos o arroyos,
con estrañas labores o de diversos colores, que se diferencian de las
ordinarias.

Llamaron *huaca* a la gran cordillera de la Sierra Nevada que corre por
todo el Perú, a la larga, hasta el estrecho de Magallanes, por su largura y
eminencia, que cierto es admirabilísima a quien la mira con atención. Dan
el mismo nombre a los cerros muy altos, que se aventajan de los otros
cerros, como las torres altas de las casas comunes, y a las cuestas grandes
que se hallan por los caminos, que las hay de tres, cuatro, cinco y seis
leguas de alto . . . (Garcilaso de la Vega [1609] 1963: pt. I, bk. 2, chap.
4, 47–48)

It means something sacred, like all those [places] where the
devil spoke to them: that is to say, the idols, the cliffs, large
stones or trees that the enemy entered in order to make them
believe that he was God. Likewise they call a *huaca* all the
things that they had offered up to the Sun, such as images of
humans, birds, and animals made of gold, silver, or wood, and
whatever other offerings, those they felt were sacred; because
the Sun had received them and they were his, and because they
were, they esteemed them. Also they call any large or small
temple a *huaca*, and those graves that they have in the

countryside, and in the corners of their houses, from which the
devil spoke to the priests and the other persons who had deal-
ings with him, those corners [of the house] they regarded as
sacred, and thus they respected them like a holy spot. Also
they give the same name to all those things which in beauty or
excellence excel above all the others of their type, like a rose, a
fruit or *camuesa*, or any kind of fruit which is bigger or more
beautiful than all the rest in the tree; and for those trees which
also excel among those of their species they give the same
name. On the other hand, they call *huaca* all the ugly and
monstrous things that cause terror and surprise; and so they
gave this name to the large snakes found in the *antis* [terri-
tory], which are twenty-five, thirty feet long. Thus also they
name anything which strays from its natural path a *huaca*,
like a woman who gives birth to two [children] from one womb,
they call the mother and the twins this because of the oddness
of the birthing process and the birth; . . . other peoples [nations]
look at it in a different manner, crying because those births are
seen as a bad omen . . . And for similar reasons they call a
*huaca* an egg with two yokes, and the same name they give to
children who are born feet first, or doubled over, or with six
fingers or toes, or who are born hunchback, or with whatever
small or large imperfection on one's body or one's face, such as
having a divided lip. There were a lot of these, or cross-eyed,
which they regard as marked by nature. This same name they
give to very gushing springs that emerge as rivers, because they
are better than the regular ones, and to the little rocks and the
back teeth that are found in rivers or streams, with strange
markings or multicolored ones, which are different from the
others.

They call a *huaca* the large mountain chain, the Sierra Ne-
vada, that runs the whole of Peru to the Magellan Strait, be-
cause of its length and its size, which really is admirable for
anyone who looks at it well. They give the same name to the
large hills that stand out from the other hills, like the high
towers above the average houses, and for the steep grades that
you find on the roads that are three, four, five and six leagues
high . . .

It is apparent, given the extirpation of idolatry in Peru, that some
meanings of *huaca* were understood by the Spanish priests: desig-
nated sites where devils appeared and spoke, temples, small altars in
the household, golden objects, multicolored stones from the rivers,

and snow-capped mountain peaks. What is added in this version is the mention of alternate categories: the most beautiful of the species and the ugliest, the most fearsome monster, twins, a double-yoked egg, a child with a harelip or six fingers. His definition is infinitely more complex and not easily reduced to binary categories of good and bad; in fact, the numerous examples almost defy categorization using European concepts.

In such a long explanation, the Inca Garcilaso demonstrates his superior cultural knowledge and reinforces a personal identity bound up in his first language. This passage also demonstrates the impossibility of assuming a one-to-one correspondence between words in the act of translation. As the discussion of *huaca* demonstrates, the difficulty resides in translating an entire message of cultural beliefs. Interpretation involves a shift in codes:

> Translation from one language into another substitutes messages in one language not for separate code-units but for entire messages in some other language. Such a translation is reported speech: the translator recodes and transmits a message received from another source. Thus translation involves two equivalent messages in two different codes. (Jakobson 1971a: 261–262)

Even more useful, as Jakobson points out, would be a bilingual reference which "define[s] what unifies and what differentiates the two languages" (ibid.: 262). The Inca Garcilaso serves as a cultural translator (he would say interpreter) in only one direction. His comments narrate a specific Quechua cultural system to be read principally by Spanish-speaking readers. He leaves implicit the Iberian message codes which inform the Spanish speakers; perhaps if he had delineated the Iberian categories of thought he might have succeeded more fully in his task as translator.

If there is no Spanish concept which serves to translate *huaca* from the source language (Quechua) to the target language (Spanish), how is translation to come about? Circumlocutions may bridge the cultural gap and create an equivalency which is adequate for expressiveness. Some translations may be fulfilled by acknowledgment of their form (sea = flat water) or functions (anchors = those things that make the boat stay) or both form and function (mainsail = the cloth that takes the wind so that the boat enters the trail) (Larson 1984: 167–168). In other circumstances, cultural substitutions will not wholly suffice. The biblical fig leaf may not be replaced in translation by an avocado without a loss in meaning.

As we have seen, in conceptual issues more cultural divergence may surface. Ezra Pound's distinction between "what a man sez" and "wot a man means" accurately captures the dilemma (cited in Kelly 1979: 60). Jakobson, in an illustrative passage, has us remember the importance of disposing of the words *sunrise* and *sunset* in post-Revolutionary Russia; the use of the outdated Ptolemaic imagery in a modern age of Copernican doctrine was offensive to some Soviet visionaries. However, Jakobson reminds us further of basic translation techniques of everyday life; we easily manage to translate the original Ptolemaic sunrise/sunset into a "sign in which it appears to us more fully developed and precise" (Jakobson 1971a: 262).

The Inca Garcilaso, in his discussion of *huaca*, attempts a verbal description—what Jakobson (1971a) calls an "intralingual" translation—which is partially successful in correcting Spanish presumptions regarding the cultural system of the Quechua speakers. For Guaman Poma and Santacruz Pachacuti Yamqui, two indigenous chroniclers also writing at the same time as the Inca Garcilaso, linguistic (intralingual) translation of cultural signs may not have been possible. Enmeshed in the political realities of the Peruvian colony, in close proximity with the clergy, they both profess their Christian faith as they attempt to explicate an Andean world vision. Both resort to black and white illustrations to bridge the gap between lexical representations and basic cultural assumptions. These two writers, for different reasons, sometimes choose an intersemiotic translation; in Jakobson's terms, "an interpretation of verbal signs by means of signs of nonverbal sign systems" (1971a: 261). In the book by Guaman Poma, many of the Quechua texts he inserted are not translated; the illustrations, similarly, may be viewed as an alternative text for the vast majority of illiterate indigenous readers (Adorno 1974: 28–29). His illustrations of the "discovery" and Conquest help to give shape to the lengthy narrative, and his commentary on the corrupt clergy is accompanied by drawings of "virtuous moral behavior" (ibid.: 28).

Santacruz Pachacuti Yamqui's verbal text leaves off at an ampersand, and the complex line drawing barely fits into the remaining space on the manuscript page. The illustration immediately follows a discussion of the image of the True God and Creator, flanked by the images of the sun and the moon. The visual, not the verbal, discourse reveals much more than his Spanish text about the conceptualization of Andean knowledge. His recourse to images parallels the preliterate stage in Andean culture where the *quipus* served as memory devices and the *tocapu* designs on the wooden cups and textiles conveyed specific meaning. In a lengthy and convoluted written text, this cultural recoding (translation) by means of illustration does justice to the highly ordered world of the Andean tradition.

## Manco Capac's Poem: A Model for Cultural Translation

Unfortunately, neither Guaman Poma nor Santacruz Pachacuti Yamqui chose to illustrate literally the long ritual poems which are embedded in their texts. Translation of these fragments of the Quechua oral tradition is difficult because of inadequate phonetic transcription in the originals and imperfect Spanish glosses which assume cultural understanding. These few texts written down by Amerindian chroniclers and a few Spanish observers are all that is left of a rich oral tradition which flourished before the Spanish invasion. Analysis of the origins of this oral tradition facilitates our comprehension and appreciation of the pervasive tradition of riddles, songs, myths, and narratives which persists in Quechua-speaking communities of the contemporary period.

Mindful of the pitfalls inherent in the process of translation, we turn to an exemplary ritual Quechua poem found in Santacruz Pachacuti Yamqui's manuscript. The verses are found scattered about in the text, enmeshed in a history of Incan rulers. Thus we read about the aging first ruler, Manco Capac, who, on his knees, implores that prosperity be granted to his son, Sinchi Roca, the next designated ruler, before we see the text of the poem.[2]

Before we enter the linguistic and cultural labyrinth of the poem in great detail, let us read the Quechua text written by Arguedas and a simplified translation I created from Arguedas's and Bendezú's transcription of Quechua. In the original manuscript this poem is written in a solid, dense paragraph; the construction of verses in the poem is the work of modern scholars and each contemporary version represents a form not found in the colonial text. In printing the long paragraph broken up into these shorter lines, we in fact are assimilating the passage to our Western system even if, in the end, we "legitimize" this text by having it approximate our own poetic tradition.

| | |
|---|---|
| ah, wiraqocha tiksi qapaq | O life force, source of all things, ultimate power, |
| kay qari kachun | you say, let man come into existence, |
| kay warmi kachun | you say, let woman come into existence. |

Wilka ulka apu

hinantin achikcha

kamaq

Maypin kanki?

manachu rikuykiman

hananpichum

urinpichum

kinrayñinpichum

qapaq usñuyki?

hay ñillaway

hanan qocha mantaraya

urin qocha tiyankayqa

pachakamaq

runa wallpaq

apuy yanaykikuna

qanman

allqa ñawywan

rikuytan munayki

rikuptiy

yachaptiy

unanchaptiy

hamut'aptiy

rikuwankim

yachawankim

intiqa killaqa

punchaoqa tutaqa

poqoyqa chirawqa

manan yanqachu

kamachisqam purin

unanchasqaman

tupusqamanmi

chayanmi

mayqanmi

topa yawrita

apachawarqanki?

hay nillaway

uyarillaway

manaraqpas

saykuptiy

wañuptiy

Deity of the sacred . . .

5 just like one who foretells all,

you create [by giving life's breath].

Where are you?    /

May I not see you?

Above?

10 Below?

Or to one side?

[Where is] your royal seat?

Ay! speak to me.

From the upper lake, spreading
out

15 to where the lower lake exists, [is]

ruler of the world,

maker of humans,

Supreme One [commander of]
your creatures.

Toward you,

20 with my imperfect eyes,

I desire to see you.

When I see,

when I really know,

when I make signs,

25 when I discern the future,

you will see me,

you will know me.

The sun, the moon,

day, night,

30 wet season, dry season,

on their own

do not function, but regulated,

predicted by signs

and measured out,

35 they appear [before us].

To whom

your royal scepter

did you send?

Ay! speak to me,

40 listen to me

while I'm still
vigorous,

[while] I still go on living.

(My transliteration based on Arguedas 1955: 124–126; Bendezú 1977)

Translation of Quechua nouns and verbs in the form of questions, pleas, and statements gives us an English text which is only partially equivalent to the original. The brevity of each line allows us to glimpse the ordering of the Andean universe within the patterns acceptable to grammatical rules in English. To negate the prescribed European conceptual order we must look at some verses in more depth; we must examine the semantic field of several verbs and widely recognized descriptions of events in Incaic society.

When we look closely at segments of the text, we see that even the first line of appellation, "ah, wiraqocha tiksi qapaq," is difficult to translate because of the many suppositions regarding the meaning of the first word. *Wiraqocha*, literally translated, is composed of *wira* (fat, grease) and *qocha* (lake, or greasy lake). This word, which later is used to designate the Spanish conquerors and the modern upper-class "whites" in the Andes, is little understood without reference to the concept of *wira* as a substance of life and power. There are many tales and myths which describe the horrible supernatural beings that suck out the fat of living human beings and thus rob them of their life force (Urioste 1983: 123, n. 1). When the lexicographer González Holguín included the term in his seventeenth-century Quechua dictionary it was already a dead metaphor:

> Viracocha. Era epicteto, del sol honrroso nombre del Dios que adorauan los indios y de ay ygualandolos con su Dios llamauan a los españoles viracocha. ([1608] 1952: 353)

> Viracocha. It was an epithet of the honored sun, the name of God that the Indians worshiped and because of that they called the Spaniards Viracocha, referring to them in the same [term] as their god.

*Tiksi* is an honorific which alludes to the principal course, the foundation of life, the origin of force, and in this case the founder of the *ayllu* (Duviols 1977a: 59). *Qapaq*—a reiteration of he/she who animates with the essential life spirit, orders, and structures—complements the notion of the embodiment of power, not unleashed and free, but ordered and conveying life force. We have noted previously the care with which the honorifics are ranked (maker, molder, imposing order, infusing the human spirit); there is overlap in the powers of creation, yet there is also a means of differentiating each act.

Following Santacruz Pachacuti Yamqui's diagram, Viracocha must be addressed as androgynous, and the translation attempts to convey this aspect of a male/female deity. The confusion in the interpretation of the Supreme Being partially arises from the early priests' desire to prove that the Incas were close to discovering the one true Christian God (the European conception). Much Spanish discussion of the concept of Viracocha seems to depict this individual as a male and closely identified with an entity like God the Father. Close reading of the chronicles, however, attests to the plurality of deities within the empire. Indeed, we are told by Santacruz Pachacuti Yamqui that Manco Capac immediately recited a prayer to Ttonapa after he concluded this long prayer to Viracocha ([1613] 1927: 148–149). Yet, the many epithets of Viracocha alternately may reveal the differentiation of Andean sacred beings, not a belief in one god, and an implicit acknowledgment of their separate identities (Duviols: 1977a: 53–63). A translator with a particular masculine conception of the Godhead should be conscious to not allow the Christian image of one God, a male God, to shape the translation.

As the Quechua language does not require definite articles or gender agreement between noun and adjective, the sexual identity of Viracocha is not explicated. Yet the following two lines contrast this sacred androgyny with a concrete reference to a human male and female:

kay qari kachun                     you say, let man come into
                                    existence,
kay warmi kachun                    you say, let woman come into
                                    existence.
                                            (Lines 2–3)

The verbal ending *chun* indicates an imperative command spoken by the Primordial Force who in effect creates sexuality. In contrast to Christianity, both man and woman are created in the same moment and equal, although, granted, the male is mentioned first.

Viracocha, we learned from Santacruz Pachacuti Yamqui's illustration, is represented by an oval plaque in the Coricancha. Nevertheless, the narrator of the poem expresses a desire to see him/her in more substantial form: "Where are you? / May I not see you?": "maypin kanki? / manachu rikuykiman" (lines 7, 8).

The act of seeing requires special consideration; it parallels the earlier discussion of the dimensions of speaking and the powers of oratory (chapter 3). In an agriculturally based society, one must be ever vigilant to see the signs; the interpretation of these signs is a necessity for human survival. Many times sorcerers were consulted, entrails of sacrificed animals observed, fires lit to divine the will of the gods. The task of interpretation is to know the future, to see it

manifest. The plea to see Viracocha attests to the mysteries of his/
her being, which also indicates his/her absolute sacredness. The
Inca Garcilaso mentions Inca belief in an invisible God, Pachacamac,
one who did not allow itself to be seen by its subjects. Other gods, he
claims, were seen by their worshipers; the Sun God was one of them
(Garcilaso de la Vega [1609] 1963: pt. 1, bk. 4, chap. 4, 46). The plea
"May I not see you?" also indicates rules of privilege; Quechua sub-
jects were not allowed to glimpse the Inca, who sat behind a screen
when giving a royal audience (Rowe 1946: 259). The desire to see the
god surfaces again later in the poem:

| | |
|---|---|
| qanman | Toward you, |
| allqa ñawywan | with my imperfect eyes, |
| rikuytan munayki | I desire to see you. |
| | (Lines 19–21) |

The phrase "allqa ñawywan" is problematic to most translators;
Bendezú prefers to transcribe the phrase as "a ti con mis ojos en
blanco" (toward you, with my unseeing eyes) (1977: 22), while Lafone
Quevedo and Father Mossi gloss it as "con mis ojos que desfallecen"
(with my eyes that are failing [me]) (in Lafone Quevedo 1950: 307).
González Holguín, among his other descriptions, states that *allca* is
"unfinished," "no acabado" ([1608] 1952: 19). Another more likely
interpretation would be "full of spots of color, or changing colors"
(Lira 1944: 36) and the equivalent of *tiqlla* a two-colored llama
(Flores Ochoa 1978: 1013). Given the model of knowledge which im-
mediately follows this phrase, with its ever-increasing hierarchies of
learning and knowing, an attempt to attain the all-encompassing
knowledge of the deity, a gloss of *imperfect* may well fit the context.

The central section of the poem, as we have seen in chapter 3, in-
volves an elaborate model for knowledge and cognition in the An-
dean world:

| | |
|---|---|
| rikuptiy | When I see, |
| yachaptiy | when I really know, |
| unanchaptiy | when I make signs, |
| hamut'aptiy | when I discern the future, |
| rikuwankim | you will see me, |
| yachawankim | you will know me. |
| | (Lines 22–27) |

The conceptual verbs for *knowing* (to see, to know, to discern signs,
and to know completely enough to prognosticate) follow a hierarchi-

cal patterning which leads to ever-higher levels of cognitive abstraction. These are the attributes of a wise man, a *sinchi* leader, and the reiterative yet differentiated nature of the verbs reveals their importance in the society. Only after Manco Capac attains knowledge of total understanding will Viracocha then acknowledge Manco Capac's existence (through sight, through understanding).

| | |
|---|---|
| hananpichum | Above? |
| urinpichum | Below? |
| kinrayñinpichum | Or to one side? |
| qapaq usñuyki? | [Where is] your royal seat? |
| | (Lines 9–12) |

The interrogative communication of "above, below, or to one side, [where is] your royal seat?" reinforces an elaborate sign system which accords great importance to the royal seat of authority, the *usñu*. A throne, a carved wooden stool, was erected on a platform in each provincial capital to be used when the Inca was called upon to adjudicate (Rowe 1946: 258). Moreover, Zuidema has made us aware of the usage of the *usñu* in plotting the movements of the constellations and stars (Zuidema 1979). The interpretation of the directionals, "above, below, to one side," is rich in resonance and must be evaluated in terms of astronomy and the significance of *hanan* and *urin*, the two main divisions of the organization of Cuzco. Manco Capac himself was credited with originating such a custom of divisions, which was duplicated in all areas of the empire (Garcilaso de la Vega [1609] 1963: pt. 1, bk. 1, chap. 16, 28). No differences in superiority were intended while dividing Cuzco's population in this manner. However, those of upper Cuzco were the close relatives of the Inca and those in lower Cuzco were the relatives of Mama Ocllo (ibid.). Thus, it is speculated that "upper" references designate the primary kin of the emperor and the subsidiary sons and distant relatives in "lower" Cuzco. According to this interpretation, Manco Capac as the originator represents both divisions; Sinchi Roca and four other rulers are from Hanan Cuzco, while five of the other rulers came from Urin Cuzco (Zuidema 1978a: 8).

Although traditional dynastic lists of rulers in chronicles written after the Conquest make succession look well planned, when an emperor died there was not always a clear choice of successor. One of the functions of the custom of incestuous royal marriage common among the Incas was to "limit the number of potential claimants to the throne and to minimize conflicts over the succession" (Conrad and Demarest 1984: 134). Indeed, Guaman Poma states that the

king's sons (brothers of two different mothers and one father) would
go into seclusion to choose a new king. When one was chosen, and
all had equal opportunity, descendance was traced from the position
of the new king (Zuidema n.d.a.: 27). Conrad and Demarest cite an
example of warring factions contending for the crown, Pachakuti
and Inca Urcon, where the latter originally was his father's choice
for succession (1984: 112). In light of this analysis and other accounts
of vigorous infighting to choose a successor, the prayer may reveal
Manco Capac's desire to know who will succeed him and where the
*usñu* should be placed. A later question, addressed to Viracocha,
poses this very thought:

| | |
|---|---|
| mayqanmi | To whom |
| topa yawrita | your royal scepter |
| apachawarqanki? | did you send? |
| | (Lines 36–38) |

The royal scepter has been specifically given to Manco Capac as an-
other visible symbol of authority, as revealed in Santacruz Pachacuti
Yamqui's text (Millones 1978: 14). Here, the interrogative nature of
the phrasing conveys doubt as to who would be the successor to the
aging ruler.

Another tightly ordered passage in the long poem is based on op-
positions of sun/moon, day/night, wet season/dry season:

| | |
|---|---|
| intiqa killaqa | The sun, the moon, |
| punchaoqa tutaqa | day, night, |
| poqoyqa chirawqa | wet season, dry season, |
| manan yanqachu | on their own |
| kamachisqam purin | do not function, but regulated . . . |
| | (Lines 28–32) |

We have seen this complementarity expressed before in the drawing
of the Coricancha temple. Manco Capac's usage of these symbols in
the ritual discourse reinforces our interpretation of them as ex-
amples of agricultural and ritual patterning. A basic distinction is
manifest in the celestial symbols, which have much to do with agri-
cultural practices. Potatoes are planted in the *poqoy quilla* (De-
cember–January), in the domain of the moon (Urton 1981: 24, 85),
and corn is planted in the dry season (*chirau*) of July, August, and
September when the sun is shining (ibid.: 120–121). These seasons,
days, and celestial bodies do not function on their own (*yanqa*) but

come and go because they have long ago been ordered by an outside force (*kamachisqan*).

The conclusion to this discourse on the celestial signs further iterates their assigned functions; they are measured and bounded and appear on cue:

| | |
|---|---|
| unanchasqaman | predicted by signs |
| tupusqamanmi | and measured out, |
| chayanmi | they appear [before us]. |
| | (Lines 33–35) |

Thus, the movements of the skies have been predicted by signs (*unanchasqaman*), and this phrase is complemented by another, *tupusqamanmi*, which restates the ideology of prediction. We know from the previous chapter that *unancha* figured prominently in the cultural configurations of the Incas. Simply stated, *unancha* functioned to indicate a person's position in the society (the royal scepter) or his or her birthplace. At a more complex level it referred to a higher conceptual process where as a sign it represented an abstract concept, such as an oval signifying Viracocha. *Tupu* is a measurement of distance and, in a more metaphorical sense, an example (Santo Tomás [1560] 1951: 365, *ejemplar*, example). In this passage, then, paired with *chayan* (to arrive or to reach a high point), it indicates a moment when things come to fruition, where one entity reaches a tenuous balance with another, *chayani*: "allegar al lugar alla, o alçancar a o que esta en alto" (to arrive at a distant place, or to catch up with or that which is high above) (González Holguín [1608] 1952: 100). In both verbs, *unanchasqa* and *tupusqa*, the past tense *sqa* is used to report a specific temporal sequence in Quechua—the time of myths, legends, and events where the speaker is not directly participating (Cusihuamán 1976: 170).[3] The present tense of the verb *chayan* indicates this present-day meeting up with the previously ordered past (*sqa*) in the heavens.

The entire poem reflects a concept of fluidity, of movement, as opposed to stasis. Things are in flux—the days to nights, the passing of the seasons—yet in their changing they are ordered in a patterning which needs to be read and understood by means of interpretation. The necessity of "seeing well" is paramount—to interpret the celestial signs, to perceive lordly pleasure and displeasure, to forecast planting, and to ward off illness in the empire. Similarly, the whereabouts of the sovereign throne must be known to appoint the next ruler and to apportion justice, to issue decrees which concern the governance and well-being of the Incan territory. In a world of plural deities and contextual interpretation of signs, Manco Capac pleads for a complete understanding of the nature of existence so that he can "read" the written text of the heavens.

Manco Capac also would welcome a verbal sign, not solely a visual clue to the workings of heaven and earth. He initiates a dialogue: *hay nillaway* (Ay! speak to me) is repeated twice in the text, as is *uyarillaway* (listen to me). Communication with the deity is restricted; direct intercession with a deity was a privilege only accorded to the Inca (Demarest 1981: 17). Other subjects of the Inca could use a confessor to intervene (the Aymara were considered the best in this), but only the emperor was allowed to confess directly to the deity (Rowe 1946: 305). We also know that many shrines and oracles had priestly interpreters to transmit the meaning of the divine world, verbally, to the awaiting listeners. Santacruz Pachacuti Yamqui mentions in his text that both Atahualpa and Huascar consult the shrine at Pachacamac for a clear message as to the winner of the battle between the two of them. When the oracle tells both Atahualpa and Huascar that each will win, Huascar consults with Pachacamac a second time, asking for a "definitive answer," and is told, for certain, that he will win the war (Millones 1978: 41; Santacruz Pachacuti Yamqui [1613] 1927: 223).

The final lines of the poem reveal the Inca's knowledge of his limited human, earthly powers. Manco Capac, for all his diviners and priests, alludes to his lack of perfect knowledge of the "order of things"; he also admits the possibility of his own death, likewise inevitable, but not necessarily foreseen or yet interpreted:

| | |
|---|---|
| uyarillaway | listen to me |
| manaraqpas | while I'm still |
| saykuptiy | vigorous, |
| wañuptiy | [while] I still go on living. |
| | (Lines 40–43) |

*Manaraqpas* conveys within it, with the extender *raq*, a sense of time still remaining but also a circumscribed, limited sense of life span. Therefore, facing a diminishing of his life force, Manco Capac's questions attain a poignant urgency for the divine will to be made present, to be known.

Although we have observed that in Incan lore certain days and events are marked and fixed in a cyclical pattern, other occasions and circumstances depend more on a "contextual kind of divination" through omens. "Every event the least bit out of the ordinary,

departing from the established order, will be interpreted as the her-
ald of another event, generally an unlucky one, still to come (which
implies that nothing in this world occurs randomly)" (Todorov [1982]
1987: 64).[4] And with the absence of writing, these events can fall vic-
tim to even more change as history is rephrased ("rewritten") ac-
cording to the dominant *ayllu*, or god, of the triumphant army.

Although the exact interpretation of this poem is hampered by the
lack of a linguistically accurate version, we have glimpsed the work-
ings of the act of translation within the oral tradition. In this poem,
one of the oldest versions extant, the act of translation calls for an
understanding of Andean metaphysics and the underpinnings of the
society. In an oscillation between entries in colonial dictionaries and
contemporary ethnographies, a rendering of the earliest recorded
text extends itself into the present century. Now the text, in its
barest form here, may be read with a memory of its explicated se-
mantic depth, which we have garnered from the previous discussion.

## The Mythic Origins of a Contemporary Quichua Song

Our conception of the oral tradition implies acknowledgment of an
ongoing dialogue within a group of speakers who share the same lan-
guage, Quechua. Through word choice and articulation of valued
metaphors, cultural identity is promoted. A society's philosophical
and ideological orientation may be revealed with a detailed analysis
of texts, semantic fields, and conversation. These principles of or-
ganization, systemic categorizations, are passed down from one gen-
eration to another: We often find the preservation of two verbal
endings to indicate the past tense, one stating that the speaker actu-
ally witnessed the event and the other indicating that the facts are
second-hand. This human interest in clarifying the "truth" of an
event is evident in an emphasis on a semiotic (sign) system of *tocapu*
designs, which ordered the potential chaos of the universe, as well
as the ability to "read" coca leaves, which form patterns, blown by
the wind.

The translation of Manco Capac's ritual poem uncovered some
of the beliefs which were shared by Quechua speakers at the time
Santacruz Pachacuti Yamqui wrote down the words in the seven-
teenth century. The persistence of the oral tradition, from the time
of the Spanish invasion to the present day, becomes visible in a
translation of a modern Quichua song. Its basic structure, we shall
see, is drawn from the spoken tradition of several centuries ago.

The efforts of the anonymous writer(s) of the Quechua manuscript
of Huarochirí, dated to the beginnings of the seventeenth century,

enable us to trace basic mythic patterns recorded in that century to their survival in a Quichua song taped in Ecuador in the latter half of the twentieth century.[5] Our awareness of the Andean structure and themes common to the two examples of Quechua oral tradition allows for a fuller appreciation of the significance of the song. As in the "reading" of the previous text, cultural references will be explored through semantic analysis and ethnographic details.

The manuscript *Runa yndio ñiscap machoncuna*, found in volume 3169 of the National Library in Madrid, is a loosely organized collection of myths from the coastal valleys of Peru (Lurín, Rimac, and Chilca). Its pages represent an attempt to record Quechua oral lore with a writing system appropriated from the Spanish. As in the case of Santacruz Pachacuti Yamqui's *Relación*, there are many additional comments inscribed in the manuscript which may belong to the Spanish priest, Francisco de Avila.

The passage of interest, which I will summarize, occurs in the early sections of the manuscript and concerns the life of the deity Quni Raya (Urioste 1983: 8–13). Quni Raya, a powerful Viracocha, took the form of a poverty-stricken beggar who walked the earth. He impregnated a beautiful *huaca*, Qawi Llaqa, when she ate a *lúcuma* seed which he had covered with his semen and placed near her purposefully. She gave birth; not knowing who the father of the child was, she called all the *huacas* together. She then commanded her one-year-old child to crawl to his legitimate father. When the child sat in Quni Raya's lap, Qawi Llaqa could not accept the patched and shabbily dressed beggar as the father. She ran away and she didn't look back or she would have seen him change into his sparkling, brilliant, shining clothing.

Quni Raya followed after her and met up with a number of animals, all of whom he questioned as to his lover's whereabouts. The condor assured him that he would find her, that she was near, and Quni Raya praised the bird, saying, "You will live a long time and you alone will eat all the animals that live in the *puna* when they die." The skunk, on the other hand, he did not praise because it said that he wouldn't find Qawi Llaqa. Quni Raya then stated that henceforth the skunk would walk about at night, stinking, and all people would look down on him / her.

The puma said that Qawi Llaqa had passed right near and Quni Raya blessed the feline, saying, "You will be loved by all. You will eat llamas . . . and your skin will be used in the major ritual celebrations." The fox did not fare well when he said Qawi Llaqa was far away; the fox would be cursed by men and its pelt would rot. The falcon, answering affirmatively, was blessed as Quni Raya gave it the right to eat hummingbirds and the other birds. In the festivals, a falcon headdress would be placed on the heads of the dancers. The parrots were chastised for their warnings that he would not meet up with Qawi Llaqa; people would avoid them, their food would be scarce then, the Viracocha said. Indeed, the negative prognostications turn out to be true, for the male god does not come into his lover's presence again until the close of the episode.

The theme of unrequited love which runs through the myth often is enough to sustain our interest in this episode. However, to better understand the myth of Quni Raya, we must turn again to the Andean concept of *tinkuy*, which, in general terms, is described as a designated place where a meeting of opposites takes place (see chapter 2 for additional description). Quechua speakers frequently call attention to such locations, as the meeting of two rivers or where the hairs on a dog's neck join together and form a ridge. Quni Raya and Qawi Llaqa gather for a *tinkuy* in Anchicocha, a geographic spot located significantly between the snow-capped mountain range and the sea, which mirrors the contrast between Andean highlands and coast (Ortiz Rescaniere 1980: 25).

The emphatic mention of *tinkuy* in daily conversation attests to its value as one of the primary categories for Andean society. It is a domain where two contrary or opposing forces or concepts co-exist and intermingle. This idea is apparent in González Holguín's gloss of "la junta de dos cosas" (the coming together of two things) ([1608] 1952: 342). However, this co-existence, this meeting up of the two forces, is not without a sense of competition, too. The seventeenth-century dictionary gives one variant of the word as "to be opposites, to compete," with an underlying sense that this competition takes place between equals: "a pair of equal things such as gloves" (ibid.). In rereading the myth we can measure the oppositions and the complementarity of Quni Raya and Qawi Llaqa in terms of maleness and femaleness, ugly and beautiful, fertilizing agent and fertilized, and the brilliant shining sun as opposed to the land.

The characteristics ascribed to the animals further connote a relationship to the distinction between highlands and lowlands and the ruling divinities in each sector. Quni Raya only praises those animals associated with the highland environments: the condor, the puma, and the falcon. For Hermann Trimborn, there is further categorization within the domains of light versus darkness. These three daytime animals are linked with Quni Raya, a disguised beggar who is a shining bright god, whereas the others are all nocturnal animals and would be his opposite (Trimborn 1953: 140). The ritual importance of the puma and the falcon is highlighted in Quni Raya's dis-

*Figure 15.* Woman singer of Saraguro, Ecuador, wearing the distinctive dress of her community.

course; he specifically states that each, animal and bird, shall be worn in festive celebrations draped over the dancers' heads. The fox, a coastal symbol, is not so similarly elevated by Quni Raya. Both Albornoz and Calancha, Andean chroniclers, mention the mummy or golden figure of a fox which hung in the temple of the lowland coastal deity, Pachacamac (Rostworowski 1983: 45).

The persistence of the oral tradition is evident in a contemporary version of this same myth taped by Alejandro Ortiz Rescaniere in 1975 in a town near Huarochirí. The modern version specifies more clearly the geographical domains of the two gods; Quni Raya lived in a high-altitude zone near the Mala River, while Qawi Llaqa lived in the zone between coasts and mountains in Anchicocha (Ortiz Rescaniere 1980: 22). In this version Quni Raya only meets up with three animals and he curses or praises each one. The fox is told that he/she is a "bad omen"; the condor is called a "master of the animals" and the "chief" of birds; the lion (puma, we should say) is also called a "master of the animals on the earth" (ibid.: 23–24). Thus, four hundred years later, the same basic oppositions remain the same; the fox, a lowland figure, is cursed for his reply to Quni Raya.

A Quichua song I taped in the southern Andes of Ecuador is structured on the same basic pattern where animals (and one plant) are questioned as to the whereabouts of a *wawa* (baby) who has disappeared.[6] The cursing or blessing of the fauna (and, in this case, flora) is not present; instead, the principal speaker describes the significant attributes of the animal or plant he/she meets up with on the road in the lyrics of the song:

| | | |
|---|---|---|
| Ushkitulla | | Little ole turkey buzzard, |
| puka washalla | | red back, |
| sañi *cristal*la | | dark-colored breast, |
| sañi chakilla | | dark-colored feet, |
| ichapashlla kan*situ* | 5 | by any chance did you |
| ñu wawita rikurkangi? | | see my baby? |
| Mana mana *amiguita* | | No, no, my friend. |
| mana rikushkanichu | | No, I haven't seen |
| kambak wawitata. | | your baby. |
| *Gavilan*situta tapuy | 10 | Ask the sparrow hawk; |
| ichapashlla paysitu rikurka. | | perhaps he saw the child. |
| *Gavilan*situlla | | Little ole sparrow hawk, |
| *kuchillu piku*lla | | knifelike beak, |
| yurak washalla | | white back, |
| sañi chaquilla | 15 | dark-colored feet, |
| Ichapashlla kan*situ* | | by any chance, did you |

| | |
|---|---|
| ñu wawitata rikurkangi? | see my baby? |
| Mana, mana *amiguita* | No, no, my friend, |
| mana rikushkanichu | no, I haven't seen |
| kambak wawitata. | 20 your baby. |
| Achupallata tapuy | Ask the *achupalla* plant; |
| ichapashalla pay*situ* rikurka. | perhaps he saw your child. |
| Achupallitalla | Little ole pineapple, |
| kasha aychalla | [meat] fruit thorn-covered, |
| uchupa sikilla | 25 ash-colored stalk, |
| ichapashalla kansitu | by any chance, did you |
| ñu wawita rikurkangi? | see my baby? |
| Mana, mana *amiguita* | No, no, my friend. |
| Mana rikushkanichu | No, I haven't seen |
| kambak wawitata. | 30 your child. |
| Tarugitata tapuy | Ask the deer, |
| ichapashlla pay*situ* rikurka. | perhaps he saw your child. |
| Tarugitalla | Little ole deer, |
| llilla *gachulla* | with spinning around horns, |
| *jurnu* singalla | 35 with hot-oven-like nostrils, |
| pallka shillulla | with divided hooves, |
| pallka rurulla | with divided balls, |
| ichapashlla kan*situ* | by any chance, did you |
| ñu wawitata rikurkangi? | see my baby? |
| Mana, mana *amiguita*. | 40 No, no, my friend. |
| Mana rikushkanichu | No, I haven't seen |
| kambak wawitata. | your child. |
| *Sapituta* tapuy, | Ask the toad; |
| ichapashlla pay*situ* rikurka. | perhaps he saw your child. |
| *Sapitulla* | 45 Little ole toad, |
| *verde* wiksalla | green belly, |
| lliki shimilla | broken up mouth, |
| *saltak* ñawilla | bulging eyes, |
| ichapashlla kan*situ* | by any chance, did you |
| ñu wawitata rikurkangi? | 50 see my baby? |
| Ari, ari *amiguita*. | Yes, yes, my friend. |
| Ñuka *alba* shulla *sirinota* fallakukpi | When I was gathering up the early morning dew, |
| shiri shirillatagmi jichush rirka. | your baby left, leaving behind the cold, cold earth [fields]. |
| Ñuka wawita | My child, |
| ñuka *vidita* | 55 my life, |
| ñuka *alas de pluma* | my feathery wings, |
| *Criashka* wawita | tenderly brought-up baby, |

| | | |
|---|---|---|
| ña kunankamanka | | now, right now, |
| maypishi tiyakupak *uras?* | | where in the world could my child |
| Ñami *amiguita* | | [be] up till now? |
| kunankamanka | 60 | Well, my friend, |
| *tíu pullu cruz*pimi tiyangá. | | now your child is |
| Ñuka wawita | | in the old buzzard's stomach. |
| ñuka *vidita* | | My baby, |
| ñuka *faldapi cria*shka wawita | | my life, |
| Maypicha kunanka tiyakun? | 65 | my child, brought up in my lap, |
| | | where in the world is he/she now? |

Although a similar basic structure lies under both the song and the myth, the song version does not embody the highland/lowland dichotomy so pronounced in the myths. The animals, and the plant, are all found in the high-altitude Andean ecological environment. The turkey buzzard, *ushku* (*Cathartos burroviana cass;* Howard-Malverde 1981: 53, n. 26), often is seen flying above the *páramo,* high grasslands, at 3,500 meters above sea level (Howard 1980: 240). The *taruga,* Andean deer (*Odocoileus virginianus gray;* Cordero [1892] 1967; 95), the *gavilán* (*wamán*), and the *achupalla* plant (*Pourretia piramidata;* ibid.: 3) are also found in higher elevations. Although the *sapu* (terrestrial toad; called *jambatu* in Quichua) may be found at varied altitudes (from 1,000 to 5,000 meters; Urton 1981: 180), it is a frequent symbol found in Andean highland tales.

In a reading of many variants of turkey buzzard tales from the Andean area, the bird functions as a male lover of an unaccompanied young woman, who for various reasons has delayed marriage; she often is forcibly carried off by the bird (Howard 1980: 240). The *wamán* often has the same function in the harvest songs from the Ecuadoran Andes (Chimborazo). For example, he is called a "night traveler," an abductor (Jara 1982: 248; my translation), wandering around and taking his pleasure everywhere:

huamancitu, huamancitu                  My dear turkey buzzard, little old
                                        turkey buzzard,
tuta tuta puridur                       [you] wander far and wide at
                                        night . . .

The small Andean deer partakes of the same erotic symbolism in numerous Andean songs of Ecuador where the animal represents an "illicit lover or a foreign lover" from "outside" the village who comes for sexual pleasure (ibid.):

| urita ric taruquita | Deer who's been to the lowlands, |
| janacta ric taruquita | deer who's been to the high-lands . . . |

The symbolism of the *achupalla* is less well known. It is listed in the earliest dictionaries as a plant with leaves like a pineapple, a fruit also native to the Indies. The song, however, focuses on the thorns, not the fruit. There may be a reference to a use in fashioning love potions, for thorns (*waqanki*) were used by the Incas in this manner (Rowe 1946: 314). However, in the Saraguro region of Ecuador, *achupalla* is more well known as food for guinea pigs.

The toad has long been associated with bad luck, is seen as a bad omen, and is said to have been created by the devil (Cayón Armelia 1971: 156). At the same time, it is an animal often used in ritual processes; it is often released at the juncture of two roads to effect a cure of a disease (ibid.), and sorcerers were known to sew up the eyes and mouth of a toad and bury it where a victim was likely to sit down (Rowe 1946: 314). The toad is used as a verbal insult for people who have "lively eyes" (*ojos saltones*); this may be an extension of the belief that the twitching of an eyelid means that a "person was likely to hear something good or bad" (ibid.: 304). It is likewise an insult to be hurled at those who like to talk a lot ("Hamp'atu hinan rimaysapa" [Like a frog, you're a real talker]) (Cayón Armelia 1971: 156).

In analyzing the narrative of the verses, the sexually charged symbolism of the animals is foremost. The turkey buzzard, hawk, and deer are synonymous with lovers who abduct and ravish young females. Other aspects of the poem also are laden with the sexual undercurrents. Although it is omitted in this version, another singer describes the hawk as having a *lomo rijito* (Spanish for lusty), a backside amenable to fornication. The deer possesses *jurnus singalla* (nose, hot like a furnace), which the singer said indicated that the nostrils flared open, as when people are murmuring and gossiping. The toad is linked very commonly with the forces of evil, and we have mentioned its use in curing. It may also be a standard item in bewitching, and it is fitting in this regard that this animal is the last person to see the child.

The communicative role of the toad in Quechua symbolism, its dancing eyes and garrulous mouth, leads us to expect a well-articulated message at the conclusion of the song. However, the answer given by the toad is full of ambiguity. If we are looking for a message it unravels out of some elaborate code switching in Quechua and Spanish and a plurality of interpretations of these phrases:

51   Ari, ari *amiguita*
     Yes, yes, my friend.
52   Ñuka *alba* shulla *sirinota* fallakukpi
     When I was gathering up the early morning dew,
53   shiri shirillatagmi jichush rirka
     your baby left, leaving behind the cold, cold earth [fields].

The interpretation of the events as a misadventure of an amorous
sort is embedded in the choice of the verb *jichush* (abandoned, or left
by a mate for another). This is more explicit in another song variant
of the phrase "shiri shiri sarush jichurca," where *sarush* conveys the
idea of "stepped upon, beaten," she was abandoned. The exact equiva-
lent of *shiri shiri* is not found in any dictionary, but the singer glossed
the words as *gritando* (crying out). If the transcription were altered
to become *chiri chiri*, the adjective means *molestoso* (bothersome),
as a spoiled child who cries a lot (Lira 1944: 179). In this spelling the
words also indicate a person with "unkempt hair," wildly disordered,
which is a veiled allusion to sexual encounters (see chapter 5, p. 00).
The latent meaning of a sexual encounter is substantiated in pas-
sages of the turkey buzzard tales analyzed by Howard-Malverde; the
young female protagonist is devoured by the turkey buzzards when,
after intercourse, she is taken to meet his relatives, far from her par-
ents' home (1981: 134–147).
   A closer look at this passage also reveals a line heavily laden with
both Quichua and Spanish nouns in "ñuka alba shulla sirinota fa-
llakukpi." *Alba* and *sirinota* are terms widely understood in Spanish,
denoting dawn and the morning dew. *Shulla* merely states the idea of
dew, this time in Quichua. The code switching, where Spanish word-
ing alternates with Quichua, is a reflection of the bilingual nature of
the population. Sixty percent of the inhabitants of Saraguro are flu-
ently bilingual in Spanish and Quichua and 95 percent commonly
speak a "rather corrupted Spanish" (Schmitz 1977: 70). The poem is
laden with many assimilated Spanish lexical items. Sometimes the
Spanish vocabulary replaces a common Quichua word, as in the use
of *gavilán* (line 12) for the Quichua *anga* or *wamán; gachu* (line 34)
for *cara; sapu* (line 45) for *jambatu; piku* (line 13) for *shimi;* and
*alba* (line 52) for *pakarina*. At other times, a Spanish word has been
chosen to replace a word which formerly existed in Quichua, such as
*cuchillu* (line 13), *saltak* (line 48), *cresta* (line 3), and *uras* (line 59);
equivalent Quechua words are readily found in González Holguín.
The latter part of the song is heavily laden with Spanish phrasing;
stock phrases as "vidita," "alas de plumas," and "faldapi criashka"

may convey the emotion appropriate for a child's wake as well as provide the boundaries of closure for the song. "Tíu pullu cruzpimi" (literally, in uncle chicken's cross; line 62) allows a playful semantic ambiguity highlighted in Quechua riddles. *Tíu pullu* is parsed by the singer as *gavilán* (buzzard) and *cruz* as (stomach). The last line literally communicates a clear message of death for the wayward child: "Right up to this minute [your child] is sitting in the old bird's [stomach]." As in other parts of the poem, this line enjoys a resonance which alludes to the myths of the turkey buzzard. In one of the mythic variants, the parents find their deceased child, a victim of the buzzards, and erect a cross there (Howard 1980: 242, variant 4). This would partially explain the symbol of *cruz* in the statement. Aside from this literal interpretation, the phrase *tíu pullu* is one found in the Andean myths of Ecuador. It marks an uninhabited area of the high *páramo* lands in Ecuador; one narrator of the myth specifies the exact location as near the modern city of Latacunga.[7] In the myth of *tíu pullu*, the husband and wife team who live in the deserted *páramo* eat the flesh of recently deceased human beings. A human postman, who wishes to spend the night in their house, barely escapes with his life (Chuquín 1977: n.p.). Latent here we might find a sense of redemption from death by the erection of a Christian cross or an escape from this feared area which threatens human existence.

The syntactic structure of the song conveys an additional message which may aid in understanding the semantic referents of plants, animals, and a lost baby. The temporal markers in the song reveal great uncertainty in the mother's discourse as she searches for her child. The question which structures the song, "ichapashlla can*situ* ñu wawita rikurkangi?" (by any chance, did you see my baby?), illustrates a heightened sense of unknowing and uncertainty as the dubitative *icha* is combined with *pash*. The figurative meaning, "by any chance," is slightly distant from the literal adverb "perhaps" and "also." When we finally get to the toad's answer, we are relieved that he answers in very concrete and solid terms and that he focuses on the exact moment of the event. He specifies "at that very moment" by his use of *llatak* (line 53) and further indicates a clear temporal past where he was a witness, *rirka* (line 53). The mother, however, does not quite accept his explanation and forms another question, replacing *ichapashlla* with *maypishi*. The vague first question is transformed into an interrogative of location, as *may* means "where." However, as Ross notes (1963: 92), the use of *maypishi* enables the speaker to frame an indirect question which "shows a desire to know but does not frame a direct question."

The toad's answer again is ostensibly concrete ("in the old buzzard's stomach") but also allusive to complex Andean images of the buzzard. The mother seems to grasp the significance of the toad's utterance, however, for her last question, *maypicha*, indicates a change from the previous *maypishi*. In the conscious selection of *cha* the mother still supposes but admits "mistaken opinions, fears, and hopes" (ibid.: 95) which contrast with the excessive doubts implied by *shi*. In her shift from *shi* to *cha*, the mother indicates less doubt about the loss of her child. She seems to exhibit more understanding of the forces which have carried off her baby, even though for us, as readers, the message is still mysterious.

This poem exhibits many layers of interpretation which reach beyond the literal narrative glossed in the words of the singer. Syntactically, the singer's version revealed a line-for-line rendition of its message and, indeed, was especially helpful in the explication of the "old bird's stomach." Yet, to understand the full range of meaning, the animal symbolism is analyzed, the mythical components are traced to more contemporary turkey buzzard tales, and the text is viewed in light of an ancient pattern of oppositions present in the myths from Huarochirí.

A reading of the song in a less literal manner may yield a translation which makes it meaningful for our highly literate culture. The toad's words may offer subtle explications of illness and death so that the mother understands the loss of her child; this song primarily is sung at the wake of a child in Saraguro, Ecuador. This interpretation hinges on an understanding of the semantic depth of the word *sereno* (dew) and synonyms in Quechua related to it. We have discussed the etymological definition of *sirino/sereno* as "humidity that falls during the night" (Corominas 1954: vol. 4, 201). The *Diccionario de autoridades*'s entry of 1732 also provides the usual definition of a "substance [humor] which descends over the earth after the setting of the sun" (Real Academia Española [1732] 1964: vol. 5, 6, 96). However, in this listing is an exemplary phrase which conceptualizes some malefic force in the *sereno*: "Temo que me coja la noche antes de llegar a mi posada, y que me haga mal el Sereno" (I am afraid that night will fall before I arrive at my inn and that the *Sereno* [dew] will make me ill) (ibid.).

Although Spanish dictionaries provide no further references, a glance at the Quechua definitions provide the necessary link between dew and illness. *Sirino* in Quechua is described as *chiri ppucuycuk* (literally, he/she blown on by the cold [wind]) (González Holguín [1608] 1952: 113); another variant of this Quechua phrase is even more explicit: "Que le ha hecho mal el sereno" (He/she has been

*Figure 16.* Woman and infant, Saraguro, Ecuador.

made ill by the *sereno*) (ibid.). The illness is described in terms of one of the qualities of the *sereno, chiri* (coldness), and is specifically named as palsy (*chirayay uncuy*) or as paralysis in general. If the toad were gathering the morning dew when he last saw the baby, then the cause of death could be traced. Wind and cold are blamed for many Andean illnesses, as research by C. Muñoz-Bernard has documented for southern Ecuador.

> El viento y el frío, que constituyen el aire malo, son responsables de la mayoría de las enfermedades. . . . Estas [cuestiones de frío] corresponden en regla general a lo que la sobiduría [sic] popular llama pulmonías (con el síntoma correspondiente de la parálisis or "paralizo"). Los campesinos creen que el frío ataja la sangre impidiendo que el agua mala que se encuentra en el cuerpo salga. (Muñoz-Bernard 1976: 58)

> The wind and the cold, which make up the "bad air," are responsible for the majority of the illnesses. . . . These matters of "coldness" generally are part of what the folk wisdom calls pleurisy (with a corresponding symptom of paralysis or "*paralizo*"). The *campesinos* believe that the cold partitions off the blood, trapping the "bad water" in the body.

Thus we see how the Quechua-speaking peoples may preserve and pass on to succeeding generations a belief commonly held in the seventeenth century.

A conclusion which explicates the ravages of death provides a neat closure to the Quechua song. Investigation of the properties ascribed to the *sereno*, the symbolism of the toad, and the syntactical acceptance of death by the mother protagonist all support this interpretation. The ancient pattern of questioning the animals, as found in the myth of Huarochirí, still structures the discourse of the song. However, the content of that message has been altered considerably. No longer do we witness the tumultuous warfare and oppositions of competing Andean gods set in a period of empire building. The song reflects a world centered on community and offers consolation to a grieving parent who seeks the whereabouts of his/her child. In part, death is robbed of its final sting, for the song provides the music and the imagery to which the community happily dances, relieved that one more person escapes the misery of this earthly passage (Figure 16).[8]

# 5. Translating Supay: Women's Place and Women's Strength in Contemporary Quichua Songs

TRANSLATING QUECHUA women's songs means shaping discourse to convey precisely an Amerindian view of what the term *woman* represents in Andean society. This calls for active reader participation, for these translations often challenge a predominant ideology of male and female in European thought. Before looking at the Quichua songs, we must pursue a definition of femaleness in industrialized societies by tracing some of the philosophical dimensions of this concept.

An all-pervasive dichotomy is unfortunately embedded in a European tradition which devalues the functions of women in society. Simone de Beauvoir's title, *The Second Sex*, sets forth this dominant ideology, and, underpinning much of this structural analysis, are Lévi-Strauss's words in his influential book *The Raw and the Cooked* (1969: 276): ". . . human society . . . is primarily a masculine society . . ." Although Lévi-Strauss's theoretical constructs of nature / culture have done much to elucidate cultural categories, in matters of sex roles they have had the effect of limiting woman's importance in society. Women are often described as the unformed natural components of society, while men are praised for their capacity to carry out the more abstract projects of society. It appears that "biology is destiny," according to Sherry B. Ortner (1974), who bases her conclusions on writings of de Beauvoir and Lévi-Strauss. Women are seen as closer to nature because of their generative powers; women by virtue of their bodily functions (menstruation, breast feeding) are relegated to the domestic family context, caretaking children in the process of socialization. There is no question that the domestic role is an important one and should be valued; it is the mother who molds the child to society's "civilized" goals. In this way, though, women's full participation in society is limited, for they are the primary agents in only the early stages of the socialization process. In Western societies, women are characterized as "more practical, pragmatic, and this-worldly than men," and societal institutions persist in associating women with the "lower levels" of the cultural process (ibid.: 81).

Eleanor Leacock and June Nash, in tackling the problem of women / nature versus men/culture, retrace the Western origins of the dichotomy in "Ideologies of Sex: Archetypes and Stereotypes" (1977). They assert that many studies are marred due to enthnocentric approaches to the role of women, especially in regard to the nature/culture controversy. Although they acknowledge de Beauvoir's contribution, they also ferret out her acceptance of Hegel's formulation "that man is the active principle, in consequence of his differentiation, while woman is the passive principle, because in her unity she remains undeveloped" (ibid.: 619). De Beauvoir likewise employs Hegel's terminology of woman as "immanent" and man as "transcendent," and she often sums the situation up in terms which acknowledge a debt to Lévi-Strauss:

> In spite of the fecund powers that pervade her, man remains woman's master as he is the master of the fertile earth; she is fated to be subjected, owned, exploited like the Nature whose magical fertility she embodies. . . . Her role was only nourishing, never creative. In no domain whatever did she create; she maintained the life of the tribe by giving it children and bread, nothing more. (De Beauvoir, cited by ibid.: 620)

For Leacock and Nash, this vision of women is based on patterns of European cognitive systems where Nature is seen as a feminine entity which exists to be "mastered."

Carol P. MacCormack takes up the women/nature metaphor in her essay, "Nature, Culture and Gender: A Critique" (1980). She also focuses on the message of Genesis for Western culture which promises human dominion over nature and, with women seen as part of nature, men have dominion over them. However, as she points out, the eighteenth-century classification of women is more ambiguous, for they were defined both as "natural (superior) [and] instruments of a society of men (subordinate)" (ibid.: 7). She calls our attention to the polysemic nature of words such as *nature, wildness,* and even *women;* not all societies view these categories in the same manner as Europeans conceive of them. According to MacCormack, Lévi-Strauss errs and "mis-trusts the people's own assessment [of categories] as a possible screen hiding deep structure" (ibid.: 18), whereas other researchers are more vigilant in avoiding the structuring of universal categories according to our own dominant codes. Olivia

Harris's research, for example, on Andean symbolic categories in Bolivia (1980) finds that in a series of identifications, the Laymi do not identify the "wild" with "female":

> human : wild :: day : night
> day : night :: sun : moon
> sun : moon :: male : female
>
> On the other hand, while syllogistic thought might proceed to deduce that the wild is therefore identified as female, I found no indication that Laymis themselves made this step. To apply "logical" procedures in this case is to forget that what are being compared are complex concepts, and that in each identification it is different and specific characteristics of these phenomena that are selected for comparison. (Ibid.: 85)

Before turning to ideas of maleness and femaleness in songs gathered from Quichua-speaking communities of Ecuador, we first turn to a brief analysis of this theme in the dominant Spanish-speaking classes of Andean society. In everyday speech, Spanish has an expressive word to designate masculine mastery of females in Latin America: *macho*. This word increasingly fills an English-speaking need to express this same power relationship, so we see *macho* loaned and then incorporated into the English language. Originally, *macho* was a Mexican-Spanish word used to describe a nonhuman male thing, a male plant or a male animal. In the twentieth century, however, it now represents excessive masculine virility, a "tough guy." *Macho* is first mentioned in the *Nation* (1928), but it is not until the fifties and sixties, notably in the writings of Norman Mailer and Saul Bellow, that *macho* is fully accepted in English usage (*Oxford English Dictionary, a Supplement* 1976: 777–778). Some claim *machismo* is a degeneration of sixteenth- and seventeenth-century attitudes toward honor and shame as tied to manliness. Often labeled a lower-class phenomenon of the professional *bravo*, the bullying braggart, the dandified tough, its manifestations are clearly seen in every social class in Latin America. The acceptance of the *macho* as the predominant cultural image of Latin America is reinforced by the United States's exposure to *machismo* by virtue of the large influx of Hispanic populations to urban areas. Women's roles, understandably, parallel this image; women are seen as either "saint" or "sinner" to fulfill masculine expectations.

   *Marianismo*, or the idealization of women and their role, is likewise a tradition in Latin America: "[*Marianismo*] is the cult of feminine spiritual superiority, which teaches that women are semi-divine, morally superior to and spiritually stronger than men" (Stevens 1973: 91). In behavior patterns, this means that women are expected to be submissive to the demands of men, make personal sacrifices in regard to the family's needs, exhibit infinite patience, and often not seek personal satisfaction through a career (ibid.: 94–95).

Reference to the labels of *machismo* and *feminismo* are pervasive in the discourse of Latin America. The statements of a Quechua-speaking Bolivian woman, wife of a miner, who instructs women to take a more active role in the politics of their country, contain both concepts as contrastive terminology:

> . . . al luchar entre hombre y mujer, le estamos dando gusto a esos capi-talistas que han sido los que han creado el machismo, que quiere decir que el hombre no acepta la participación de la mujer y de esta forma nos están dividiéndo para que no podamos luchar juntos, unidos. Por eso también los capitalistas han creado el feminismo, es decir, que las mujeres peleen contra los varones. ([Barrios de] Chungara 1980: 25)

> . . . with infighting between men and women, we are doing just what those capitalists want who have created this *machismo,* [a word] which means that men do not accept the participation of women, and in this way they are dividing us up so that we cannot fight side by side, unified. For this reason, the capitalists also have created feminism, [a word] which means that women fight against men.

In her speech, *machismo* and *feminismo* are introduced as alien concepts, labels invented by "capitalists" to cause a rift in the normal cooperation of males and females in Amerindian societies. Domitila Barrios de Chungara's comments emphasize an alternative to the "universal subjugation of woman" construct built from a European model. When we examine the chronicles and the codices of the New World, we find other evidence where women are valued and equal in the societies of the Andes.

## Andean Women in Pre-Conquest Society

In works written after the Conquest, in the chronicles of the Andes, some evidence survives to convince us of the high social and religious status ascribed to women in the Incaic Empire. Irene Silverblatt gives a thorough analysis of women's lot in pre-Conquest society in "Andean Women in the Inca Empire" (1978). While she acknowledges the cultural bias inherent in the chronicler's perspective (that of male dominance in the religious and political spheres), there are gleanings from the data to offer another interpretation. Within the political structure, overtly male dominated, women are mentioned in the *curaca* elite which governed throughout the empire. The queens, called *coyas*, controlled some land for their personal use and were cited in the mythical lore as superb agronomists who supervised experimental fields of cultigens (ibid.: 40–45). Ideologically, *woman* was synonymous to *conquered group* in Quechua semantics, and it is true that women were redistributed throughout the empire by means of the institution of the *aclla* (ibid.: 48). These virgins were controlled by the Inca elites, chosen from regional areas, and were dedicated to the service of Andean deities or became secondary wives of the Inca. Noblewomen, including *aclla* women, performed essential sacred tasks highly valued by their society. They excelled in the spinning and weaving of royal cloth and the making of ritual beverages. The *coya* (queen) presided over the cult of the moon (seen as female); she directed a number of female attendants and she organized the tending of agricultural plots (ibid.: 54–55).

While rereading the chronicles provides glimpses of women's power distributed in the political and religious spheres, the center of power appears to be a masculine preserve. Men may not always have been located in the center of things. Rostworowski finds, in the ancient myths of Huarochirí, a female deity who breathes life into all of humankind (women and men); this reference to shared power may later be superseded by dominant masculine religious symbols (1983: 85). Nevertheless, another institution, the system of parallel descent through which genealogies are traced, provides an alternative model to female subordination. In this system, Santacruz Pachacuti Yamqui's drawing of the temple of Coricancha again is important, for it reveals the Incan genealogical system. Although the first figure is one of an androgynous god, the remainder of the drawing stresses a strict division into male and female domains (see Figures 11 and 12).

The configurations in the drawing adequately map the structure of kin relations: "The principle of parallel lines of descent, in which men conceived of themselves descending from a line of men, and women from a line of women, was one of the key rules ordering pre-Columbian Andean kinship, . . . The parallel descent structure of the kin group marked out lines through which classes of material goods (as well as ritual objects and obligations) were transmitted" (Silverblatt 1980: 152). When a *curaca* died, leaving his wife a widow, she returned to her own *ayllu* with her daughters, leaving her male children in their father's *ayllu* (Rostworowski 1983: 94).

Both parents were asked for their consent to a marriage of their offspring, and brides often received a portion of their inheritance at marriage (Silverblatt 1980: 153). Andean inheritance patterns differed from those of Europe: "By Andean custom (which is still practiced today), a woman maintains independent rights over all goods, including lands, that she might inherit. The concept of joint or common property did not (and does not) exist" (ibid.: 163).

This system of sharing, which balanced the relations between men and women, was modified under the Spanish. The conquerors utilized Inca men more frequently in appointing positions of *kuraka*; Incan women ascended in status through marriage within the Spanish hierarchy of power. But the contraction of marriage to a Spaniard often brought to the fore the contradiction in ideologies, where the Spanish woman was considered a minor entrusted to her husband's authority. Silverblatt, in examining colonial documents, highlights cases where indigenous women protested the legality of Spanish laws of inheritance. Notable is the case of Clara Payco, who stated in her will, "Even though I have no kinsmen, my husband has no right whatsoever over my lands" (ibid.: 163).

### The Contemporary Quechua Woman

The contemporary departure from the role of symmetrical relationships is discerned further in the image of the Andean couple described in Hildebrando Castro Pozo's *Nuestra comunidad indígena* (Our indigenous community):

> El hecho, muy común en la sierra que, a simple vista, valoriza plenamente la estimación que . . . los maridos [tienen] por sus mujeres, es el que se observa cuando bajan de las punas a las ferias: los hombres marchando a pie o cabalgando en asnos, sin más bagaje que sus ponchos y petaca-carteras o *chuspas* de lana a medio llenar de coca; mientras que las mujeres, cargadas como bestias, llevan en el *quipe* [sic] todos los productos que van a vender, a más el fiambre y de *yapa* la *huahua*. No he podido constatar un sólo caso en que un burro o un varón bajen cargados y la amable compañera tan sólo con el fruto del cariño *quipichado*. ([1927] 1979: 83)

There is one item, very common in the Sierra [Andes], which, in one glance, gives an idea of how husbands value their wives,

and it is what you see when they come down from the high
grasslands to the markets: the men walk on foot or are
mounted on asses, not carrying anything other than their
ponchos and their wallets or their small woolen bags half filled
with coca leaves; while the women, burdened down like
beasts, bear in their carrying cloths all the products that they
are going to sell, in addition to a snack and even the baby. I
have not ever seen one instance of a burro or a man heavily
laden and the woman companion sweetly carrying only the
fruit of their love in the carrying cloth [on her back].

This image that Castro Pozo offers us is a common misconception
about indigenous gender relations which is commonly held in the
Andean countries. His indignation upon viewing this scene may
convince us because it coincides with our European constructs of
etiquette and courtesy accorded females. However, instead of con-
centrating on the issue of whether the man or the woman is riding
on the burro, it may be more profitable to look deeper into the *quepe*
that the Andean woman carries on her back. A glance at its contents
reveals another perspective on the special relationship between men
and women in the Andes. Most likely, inside the folds of the carry-
ing cloth are a number of products to be sold in the market—agricul-
tural products that this woman has decided are not needed to feed
her family.

Olivia Harris, in a study of indigenous women in Bolivia, expli-
cates the extent of women's decision-making powers within the
framework of the married couple:

> Though Laymis [a Bolivian ethnic group] see all major deci-
> sions in the household economy as being taken jointly by all
> adult members, they also recognise that the woman is in a bet-
> ter position to make certain decisions: she can calculate how
> much of each of the staples will be needed for subsistence in
> the coming year, how much can be sold, and how much must
> be kept for seed. Again with their daily herding activity women
> are in a good position to make the vital decisions about the
> livestock of the household: which animals should be slaugh-
> tered, which shorn, which are good breeders, and which should
> be sold. (1978: 31)

These observations are reiterated by Sarah Lund Skar, an anthropolo-
gist who studied in Matapuquio, Peru: "In the household unit, the
means of production are held individually by both husband and wife

and the division of labor, where it exists, is complementary and not exclusive. The basic attitude to individual ownership coupled with economic inter-dependence, marks the relationship between the sexes as one of mutual respect and competition" (Skar 1979: 449). She gives us a more concrete example of this "mutual respect and competition": "The competition between spouses arises from the fact that each keeps a careful eye on the productive capacities of individually owned resources. There is a constant measuring-up between the two adult household members to see that the other half is providing a fair share. . . . The portion of the harvest which can be used for barter is decided upon by the woman of the household, though the man may arrange the actual transaction" (ibid.: 454).

Another study from Peru by Daisy Irene Nuñez del Prado Béjar tells us what happens with a harvest of corn in Huaro, Peru. Although corn is considered to be a product of the efforts of husband and wife, once it is harvested the corn falls under the domain of the wife. If the husband of the couple wishes to see a part of the harvest, he must ask his wife first; however, she has full powers to exchange it for goods or to make it up into *chicha* (fermented drink) to earn some money, all without consulting her husband:

> Aún en el caso de que se haya realizado una venta en total de la cosecha, la plata de la misma deberá ser entregada a la mujer quien dispondrá de ella a su antojo, porque "ella sabe de eso el hombre que va a a saber pues." (1972: 37)

> Even if the husband has carried out the entire sale of the harvest, the money from that transaction should be handed over to his wife, who will dispose of it as she wants because "she knows about all this stuff; men, what do they know."

## Gender Definitions in Quichua Songs

A number of songs I recorded among indigenous women in Ecuador contain personal commentary on the theoretical positions discussed above. Within the Quichua songs, women's roles are defined specifically as one of symmetrical relationships. The following songs were sung by a woman in the central Ecuadoran province of Chimborazo in the community of Colta-Monjas. The region is well populated and the land, which borders the lake, has been "redistributed" to favor the Indians. Before the official period of agrarian reform in the 1960s, the Indians purchased their land in the breakup of an old hacienda. The community is made up of small landholdings (three *hec-*

*tareas*, or seven acres, on the average per family) (Revilla and Revilla 1965: 111); thus, 70 percent of the male adult population go to the coast to work or become traveling salesmen of household goods (Forman 1972: 61). In an ideal situation, the woman participates equally in the activities of planting, weeding, and harvesting; women also carry their share of heavy loads, burdening themselves with up to seventy kilos of *totora* reeds en route to the central market. In the making of cloth a division of labor is marked; only women spin the cloth, while it is the man's job to weave it (ibid.: 48).

"Ishki purishun, ishki kawsashun," one of the songs I recorded from a forty-one-year-old Quichua-speaking woman in Ecuador, illustrates a willingness to accomplish domestic tasks (Figure 17). This is the most favorable attribute a man looks for in choosing a wife, stemming from the value placed on work in an indigenous community. Accordingly, the song begins with a long list of the woman's domestic duties which she is willing to carry out: child care, leading the animals to pasture, and washing, cooking, spinning, loving:

| | | |
|---|---|---|
| ay ñuka kusalla | | My dear husband, |
| ay ñuka runalla | | my dear man, |
| kantami kuyasha | | I'll really love you, |
| kantami *servisha* | | I'll really wait on you. |
| tuta jatarishpa | 5 | Getting out of bed while it's still night, |
| | | |
| kanmu *servishami* | | I'll wait on you. |
| amsa jatarishpa | | Getting out of bed in the dark, |
| kanta kuyashami | | I'll take care of you. |
| alli taksashami | | I'll really wash the clothes well, |
| alli pushkashami | 10 | I'll really spin well, |
| alli yanushami | | I'll really cook well, |
| alli *servishami* | | I'll really take care [of things]. |
| ari kusa wawa | | Yes, my husband, babe, |
| ari runa wawa | | yes, my man, babe, |
| mana llakinichu | 15 | I won't cry, |
| mana manzhanichu | | I'm not afraid. |
| kan may rikpipish | | Wherever you go |
| wasi kwidashallami | | I'll take care of the house. |
| kan mayta rikpipish | | Wherever you go |
| shuk *granota kwidas*hami | 20 | I'll take care of the crops. |
| wasi *kwidas*hami | | I'll take care of the house, |
| wangu pushkashami | | I'll spin with the distaff, |
| millma tisashami | | I'll comb out the wool, |

*Figure 17.* Woman singer winnowing grain from the recent harvest in Colta-Monjas, Ecuador.

| | |
|---|---|
| *poncho* awachisha | I'll have them make you a poncho, |
| *bayeta* awachisha | 25 I'll have them make me some cloth. |
| kanman churachisha | I'll give you that to put on. |
| ñukapish churasha | I'll put mine on too. |
| wawa *kwidashami* | I'll really take care of the kids, |
| *grano kwidashami* | I'll really take care of the crops, |
| allpapipish tsagmakushami kusaku | 30 I'll also be hoeing the fields, husband. |
| allpapipish *trabajashami* kusaku | I'll also really work in fields, husband. |
| *papas* jamashami | I'll really weed the potatoes, |
| *habas* jamashami | I'll really weed the broad beans, |
| *grano*ta pukuchishpa | I'll make a brew of the crops. |
| chipish katusha | 35 I'll also sell it right here. |
| kulki japishami | I'll take the money, |
| wawaman karasha | I'll feed the kids, |
| wawata *kwidasha* | I'll take care of the kids. |

This long list makes it look as if all the domestic tasks are delegated to the woman. However, as she mentions later in the song, her hard work is for a period of time while her husband, for economic reasons, is not living at home. Many men take jobs as peddlers, to obtain cash so that their families may enter the monied economy. Here Rosa María sings of her expectations, of his return home with his earnings. However, she apparently does not plan to pry into his moneybags; thus we observe firsthand the "respectfulness and competition" mentioned by Skar (1979):

| | |
|---|---|
| maymantapish shamuy | Wherever you go, come back. |
| maymantapish tigray | 40 Wherever you go, return. |
| kan shamunapuka | Even before you come back, |
| shuyakushamari | I'll be waiting for you, for sure. |
| kan tigranapuka | Even before you return, |
| chapakushamari | I'll be waiting on you, for sure. |
| tukuy imatapi | 45 Everything, whatever, |
| rurakushamari | I'll surely be doing. |
| kuchi *kwidashami* | I'll take care of the pig, |
| *wagra kwidashami* | I'll take care of the cow. |
| kan kuk liwanllalla | Not even your precious money, |
| shamukpipish kusa | 50 when you come back, husband, |
| kan *comercia*shpalla | not even your business deals, |
| shamukpipish kusa | when you come back, husband. |

| | |
|---|---|
| mana ñuka kari | Never, my man, |
| chayta chapashachu | will I spy on that. |
| mana ñukakalla | 55 Never will I |
| chayta shuyashachu | wait around like that. |

Yet implicit in this song is a "marriage contract" of sorts. Both members of the couple must work, together and separately, to maintain the family and provide a good standard of living for the children:

| | |
|---|---|
| kanpish *trabaja*ngi | Both [of us], you work |
| ñukapish *trabajo* | and I work. |
| kawsashunmi kusa | We'll get by, husband. |
| kawsashunmi runa | 60 We'll get by, my man. |
| ishki *trabaja*shpa | Both [of us] working, |
| alli kawsashunmi | we'll live well, for sure. |
| ishki *trabaja*shpa | Both [of us] working, |
| alli tiyashunmi | we'll be fine together, for sure. |
| wawakunamunpish | 65 The kids, too, |
| karashunmi kusa | we'll feed, husband. |
| wawakunamunpish | The kids, too, |
| churachishun kusa | we'll dress up, husband. |
| kanpish churachikpa | You dress up |
| ñukapish churaypish | 70 and I'll be dressed up, too. |
| alli kulkiwanlla | With well-earned money |
| kawsashunmi kusa | we'll get by, husband. |
| alli wagratalla | What fine cows |
| charishunmi kusa | we'll have, husband. |
| alli kuchitami | 75 What fine pigs |
| charishunmi kusa | we'll have, husband. |
| kanka kusa wawa | You, my little husband, |
| shukti *trabaja*way | work with me, in one task. |
| ñukapish kusaku | Me, too, my husband. |
| shukti *trabaja*sha | 80 Indeed, in another task, I'll work. |
| ishki *trabaja*shpa | When the two of us work, |
| kushi kawsashunmi | We'll live happy. |
| ishki *trabaja*shapa | When the two of us work, |
| kushi purishunmi | we'll get along fine. |

The song optimistically mentions the results of so much hard work, in one job, in another job, as long as the two of them are working. As we see in lines 73–76, they will invest the earnings in livestock, specifically pigs and cattle. As little money is accumulated from agricultural products in their household subsistence economy,

María Rosa apparently is counting on the cash brought back in from her husband's efforts as a peddler. Livestock is bought as an investment in indigenous communities, and it is sold to pay for major expenses of religious celebrations, to send a child away to high school, and to pay for medical care of critical illnesses. However, for all the energy expended at hard work, one notes that money is not easily accumulated. In 1965, 77 percent of the families owned three pigs each, while only 39 percent were owners of even one head of cattle (Revilla and Revilla 1965: 114, 116).

Along with the insistence on sharing the work, another note predominates in other lyrics. Although the singer doesn't lay claim to a cent of her husband's merchandise, she strictly controls some household products, such as eggs and guinea pigs. Women often manage to store up a few items like these, along with onions, that are left over after providing for the needs of their families. Money or bartered exchange is earmarked for special projects, planned by the wife with an eye toward her own or her family's needs (Forman, personal communication). In the following lyrics, in a traditional song found in the central Andes, María Rosa personalizes the narration to include her purchase of a new skirt and some cloth to replenish her own wardrobe:

| | | |
|---|---|---|
| Jala Rosa María | | Come on, Rosa María, |
| Jala Pancho Francisco | | come on, Pancho Francisco. |
| kambak pushkak *comercio* | | Your spun merchandise |
| mana *perdi*chishachu | | I'll not cause you to lose. |
| kambak millmak *comercio* | 5 | Your wool merchandise |
| mana *perdi*chishachu | | I'll not cause you to lose. |
| alli kuy charini | | I've got some fine guinea pigs, |
| alli lulun charini | | I've got some fine eggs, |
| alli kuy charini | | I've got some fine guinea pigs, |
| alli lulun charini | 10 | I've got some fine eggs. |
| alli lulun katusha | | I'll sell some fine eggs, |
| alli kuy katusha | | I'll sell some fine guinea pigs, |
| alli lulun katusha | | I'll sell some fine eggs, |
| alli kuy katusha | | I'll sell some fine guinea pigs. |
| chita katushpaka | 15 | When I sell those, |
| chita *vendi*kushpaka | | while I am selling those, |
| kulki japikushami | | I'll really grab hold of the money. |
| *medio* japikushami | | I'll really grab hold of the coins, |
| | | for sure. |
| anaku randishami | | I'll certainly buy a skirt, |

bayeta randishami                          20   I'll certainly buy some cloth,
chayta churajushami                             I'll certainly put them on me.

## Physical Abuse: Indigenous Women Speak Up

In a study of the ideology of women's songs, another topic apparent
in the contours of male/female relationships is wife beating. Turn-
ing again to Castro Pozo's impressions, we are led to see the absurd
motivations for the commonplace violence. One indigenous man
"pegó la tunda del siglo a su cara mitad por haberse levantado con
los zapatos con que se casó" (battered his better half because she got
out of bed in the shoes that she was married in) and another "quería
desollar a la 'Señorita' porque no había aprendido a 'pelar' un car-
nero" (wanted to seriously injure his wife because she hadn't learned
how to skin a sheep) (Castro Pozo 1979: 104). In another comment,
Castro Pozo does not stress the reasons for a beating, saying instead
that certain husbands are "pegalon[es] y celoso[s] hasta con los pe-
rros" (abusive and jealous even with their dogs) (ibid.). The ideology
which evolves in the Andes as a result of this treatment is summed
up in a statement from the Sierra: "Porque te quiero te aporrio [*sic*]"
(Because I love you I beat you up) (ibid.: 94).

The theme of wife beating is nothing particular to the Andes;
there are references to this abuse in Europe for the fifteenth century,
along with societal mechanisms drawn up to control the actions of a
violent husband. One such mechanism is "charivari," also called
"katzenmusik" and "rough music." The latter amounted to "a spe-
cialized form of ridicule for the wife beater":

> The offending husband might be subjected to a chorus of ca-
> cophony of men, women, and children beating bells, kettles, fry-
> ing pans, and other assorted instruments. Proceeding through
> the community to his doorstep, they would raucously recite
> rhymes or songs such as:
>
> Ran, tan, tan; ran, tan, tan
> To the sound of this pan;
> This is to give notice that Tom Trotter
> Has beaten his good wo-man;
> For what, and for why
> 'Cause she ate when she was hungry,
> And drank when she was dry.
> Ran, tan, tan; ran, tan, tan;

Hurrah-Hurrah! for this good wo-man!
He beat her, he beat her, he beat her indeed,
For spending a penny when she had need.
(Dobash and Dobash 1981: 568–569)

If we pursue the answer to the question "for what, and for why?" we confront a list of motives drawn from studies of cultures all over the world: jealousy, alcoholism, economic uncertainties, job dissatisfaction, a breakdown in communication between the couple and others (Prescott and Letko 1977: 72–96). To understand the complex situation of domestic violence in the Andes, Ralph and Charlene Bolton's *Conflictos en la familia andina* (Conflicts in the Andean family) (1975) is rich in examples drawn from a number of indigenous households near Cuzco. The table of contents provides a rich survey of the variety of themes:

La paternidad negada (Paternity which was denied)
El esposo violento (The violent husband)
El balde confundido con un amante (The bucket that was
    thought to be a lover)
La suegra entrometida (The meddling mother-in-law)
El hijo protector de su madre (The son who protected his
    mother)

The titles exude a Cervantine richness of imagination and lead us to easily visualize the vicissitudes of plot. Beyond their literary value, the texts are important as testimony from the indigenous people as they reveal the details of their lives to the judges, the mayor, and the anthropologists who are drawn into the conflict. This unfolding oral history allows us to learn of the dynamics of society and the treatment of women within it.

Women often say that beatings begin after the birth of their children. Often during trial marriage, *sirvinakuy*, there is no hint of violence that is to come after the formal marriage:

Entonces, después que comencé a vivir con Bartolomé, después de un año, tuve un hijo y después otro. Cuando tuvimos dos hijos llevamos a cabo nuestro matrimonio. Después de esto comenzó a tratarme peor y peor. Me pegaba más y más cada vez que estaba borracho. Seguramente que no pegaba antes, cuando vivíamos en *sirvinakuy*, porque no había niños y no estábamos completamente casados. Yo podía dejarlo no más. Pero ahora tenemos hijos y no puedo dejarlo. (Bolton and Bolton 1975: 54)

Then, after I began living with Bartolomé, a year after that, I had one child and then another. When we had two children our marriage took place. After this [ceremony] he began to treat me worse and worse. He hit me more and more each time that he got drunk. He didn't ever beat me before, when we were living together in *sirvinakuy*, because we didn't have any children and we weren't really married. I could walk right out on him. But now we have children and I cannot leave him.

Another cause for conflict is jealousy: "La gente siempre está recordando a sus enamoradas o enamorados, incluso después de que han casado. Por lo que irán donde sus amantes" (People are always thinking about their lovers, even after they're married. So, they go to where their lovers are) (ibid.: 44). There is also the case of a lazy wife who provokes reversals of traditional family roles:

> Es por eso que yo le digo "hombrecito." No hace nada ni presta atención a su esposo. Isidro cocina y le sirve la comida. No sabe hacer nada [ella]. Va a su casa y se sienta allí. (Ibid.: 61)

> That's why I call her "little man." She doesn't do anything, doesn't pay any attention to her husband. Isidro cooks and serves the meals. She doesn't know how to do anything. She goes to her house and she sits there.

Women often enlist the help of the families to prevent more abuse at the hands of their husbands. One woman, married to Bartolomé, called on her sister to come protect her. When her husband ignored her sister's pleas, her own mother appeared and said, "¡Qué lisura! Estás pegando a mi hija. ¡Te voy a demandar si la sigues pegando!" (What a way to be beating up my daughter! I'm going to have you brought to court if you keep on beating her!) (ibid.: 55). More frequently, the *padrinos* (comparable to best man and maid of honor at the wedding) are urged to act. In the case of the lazy wife and the husband in the kitchen, the *padrinos* beat both of them with a whip to convince both of them to change their ways (ibid.: 60).

One means by which physical abuse is introduced in the relationship of man and woman is the courtship pattern in the Andes. Sexual play often involves a "stealing" of items, pushing of each other, and even hitting:

> El indio aprovecha de la época de las cosechas, durante las cuales reina mucha alegría y a propósito para manifestaciones amorosas. Los varones

quitan a las mujeres ciertas prendas de vestir y a continuación, los
galanes empujan y golpean a su elegida. (Costales Samaniego 1968: 328)

The Indian benefits from the harvest season in which there is a
lot of festivity and an ambience for sexual overtones. The men
"steal" certain articles of dress away from the woman and even
push and hit the women they have selected.

These male overtures are either accepted with signs of laughter and
happiness on the part of the female or they are rejected with clear
signs of hostility (ibid.). No such overt physical aggression is re-
ported in the chronicles of pre-Hispanic customs; *sipas-tarina*, or
ways of looking for a wife, describe throwing a small stone down a
ravine to attract her attention (Farfán 1945: 139).

Although it was sung by a male *paki* (a soloist for harvest songs),
one long and well-known harvest song from the central Andes is
useful, for it describes a courtship pattern with two young lovers. In
the version I recorded in central Ecuador (1975), a young boy tries to
knock a spindle out of a young woman's hands and she, somewhat
hostile, warns him that her brother or her sister may go tell her par-
ents about this:

| | | |
|---|---|---|
| kasikangi *mozo loco* | | Be careful, crazy boy. |
| ñuka sigsig pakirimun | | My spindle stick is breaking off |
| | | on me. |
| kasikangi *mozo loco* | | Be careful, crazy boy. |
| ñuka turi chapakunmi | | My brother is spying for sure. |
| sigsig pakarikpikarin | 5 | If my spindle breaks, |
| ñuka mama ñuka tayta | | my mother, my father [will say], |
| imanishpa pakingilla | | why do you break it? [will say] |
| rimarikupangallami | | will chastise me for sure. |
| kasikangi *mozo loco* | | Be careful, crazy boy. |
| ñuka kaspi *piruru*ta [pirueta] | 10 | My stick is turning pirouettes. |
| kaspi *piruru*wantigmi | | My spinning stick |
| ñuka *baila*chikurkani | | I have made dance. |
| kaspi piruruwantigmi | | My spinning stick |
| ñuka buriachikurkani | | I have made hum. |
| kasikangui *mozo loco* | 15 | Be careful, crazy boy. |
| ñuka sigsig pakirikpi | | If my spindle breaks, |
| ñaña wambra willangami | | sister will tell. |
| turi wambra chapakunmi | | Brother is spying for sure. |
| *loco*tiklla *mozo* kangui | | You're a crazy boy, for sure. |

| | | |
|---|---|---|
| locotiklla wambra kangi | 20 | You're a crazy young guy, for sure. |
| ñuka mama yachashpaka | | When my mother finds out, |
| imatak chasna pugllangi | | why do you play like that? [she'll say.] |
| ima nishpa manallatik | | Why didn't you |
| wangu kaspiwan garuti | | with your distaff stick beat him |
| kantikchari pugllakukpi | 25 | when he played with you, |
| kantikchari *grasiya*rikpi | | when he courted you? |
| mama kashpapish manatik | | She's my mother, she doesn't |
| paypak *tiempo considera* | | remember what her time was like. |
| kasikangi *mozo loco* | | Be careful, crazy boy. |
| murumanga pakirimun | 30 | The speckled pot is breaking. |
| [unintelligible on tape] | | |
| ñaña wambra *parla*kunmi | | Sister is telling for sure. |
| kantatika manallatik | | I won't |
| *nombrashpa* willarkanichu | | tell on [you], naming you. |
| *de repente* kanwan ñuka | 35 | Maybe with you, you |
| *kumpaña*kpi chayllatik | | will accompany me over there. |
| ñuka pugllakukpikari | | When you play with me no doubt |
| chayta mamamun willasha | | that I'll tell Mother, |
| kutin *kumpaña*rikpika | | when I keep you company again. |
| kunan taytamun willagry nishpa nirkangi | 40 | [Now] go and tell your father, you said. |
| mamamunlla willagry nishpa rimapangimi | | Go and tell your mother, you told me. |
| kanllawantik *kumpaña*kpi | | When I am keeping you company, |
| kunanpish taytaman willayi | | right now tell [your] father. |
| chaymantami mana ñuka | | For that reason I don't |
| taytamunpish willapani | 45 | tell my father. |
| [unintelligible on tape] | | |
| *mozo loco* ñukawanka | | Crazy boy with me, |
| tupaywanchu pugllapangi | | scarcely meeting up with me, me, you [want to] play. |
| *mozo loco* kasikangi | | Be careful, crazy boy, |
| mana kanwan pugllashachu | 50 | I won't play with you. |
| *mozo loco* kasikangi | | Be careful, crazy boy, |
| ama ñukawan *grasiya*chu | | don't try to make me fall for you. |
| *bueno bueno mozo loco* | | OK, OK, crazy boy, |
| ña atingi ña *vinsingi* | | you win, you overpower me. |
| chayllatami *nombrash*kani | 55 | Now I've said your name. |
| *mozo loco* pugllandero | | Crazy boy flirt, |
| chayllatami *kwintash*kani | | I've told the whole story, |
| *mozo loco aterrido* | | cute little crazy boy. |

In another version taped in the central Andes, the violence accelerates as the girl's hair is loosened ("ñuca accha lluchurinman"); her spindle is going to break and her shepherd's crook will break (Jara 1982: 249).

Syntactically, the song is marked with a suffix, *takchari*, often found in situations of courtship and marriage. When the mother uses *tikchari*, she is specifically referring to the "playing around" (lines 25–26). In an explanation of this suffix in usage, a Quichua speaker states that it may be "used by a bashful girl when her parents ask her if she wants to marry a claimant for her hand, and the explanation given by the informant when quizzed about it is, 'No, she isn't sulky about it, but she's shy in front of her parents, so she uses *takchari*'" (Ross 1963: 97).

The sexually laden play reveals a clear element of feminine control in lines 11–14, where she states that she has the power to make her spinning stick whirl and hum; she alone makes it dance. It is she who announces the amorous conquest in terms that portray force: "ña atingi ña *vins*ingi" (you win, you overpower me). In the reiterated messages of being spied on and reporting the crazy boy's behavior, we see the slow erosion of *sirvinakuy*, where much sexual experimentation is expected of the youngsters.

In a close examination of the highly personal songs of Quichua-speaking Ecuador, the theme of physical abuse occurs with frequency. In the songs I taped in the Amazonian headwaters of Ecuador in 1974–1976, a predominant metaphor is composed using the verb *taksana* (to wash clothes). Its meaning was embedded in the lyrical texts; when I asked for an explanation I was told, "That's how he beats me, like you pound clothes on a rock, in the river":

> ñukaga mana pishisha shayangilla warmi mani (me, I'm a
> never-lacking, standing-tall kind of woman)
> > kasna warmirachu (that's the kind of woman [I am])
> > ñukara taksawangiri kusa (husband [who washes] me like
> clothes) . . .
> > kusashitu imasna taksakpis pasangalla warmimi (my dear
> little husband, no matter how often he "washes clothes" I'm
> a "pay no attention" kind of woman)

In the central Andes, one metaphor is composed using the loan word for grinding mill, *molino*, and the Spanish verb *fregar*, to actively scour or rub:

| | |
|---|---|
| ñuka aychataka | My flesh, |
| achkata *molingi* | you made pass through a grist mill. |
| ñuka *cuerpotaka* | My body, |
| achkata *fregangi* | you beat up on [it] a lot. |

Although the motive for this thrashing isn't stated, it does appear in the following verses that the woman did not provoke the violence:

| | | |
|---|---|---|
| kan piñakukpipish | | Even if you are getting angry, |
| imapina kusa | | what's it to me, husband? |
| kan piñakukpish | | Even if you are getting angry, |
| imapina runa | | what's it to me, my man? |
| imatak yuyangi | 5 | Whatever are you considering? |
| imata *pensangi* | | Whatever are you thinking about? |
| mana *servij* kusa | | Good-for-nothing husband, |
| ashkulayak kusa | | "dog" of a husband. |

Even though this woman understands few of the reasons for her husband's anger, she is very much aware of those people she can count on to stem his abuse. She can appeal to her women friends, but more importantly she will guarantee her personal protection through the members of her family. Syntactical semantics in the following verses help to appreciate her evaluation of those she can enlist in her cause. In referring to her women friends she uses a "looser" phrase of possession, *charini* (I have): "*amiga* charini" (I have a lot of women friends) and "*pamilya* charini" (I have a lot of family). The choice of possessor, *yuk* or *charina*, is important. The *yuk* morpheme is used with inalienable attributes and with possessions that are likely to be permanent; the contrastive usage of the verb *charina* indicates a neutrality with regard to permanence of possession (Cole 1982: 94–95). Her switch to the more permanent possessive *yuk* ("tawka *familya*yuk" and "tawka aylluyukmi"), which attaches to noun forms, allows her to say the same thing, that she is the possessor of a large kin group—one more way to stress a point.

| | | |
|---|---|---|
| ñukapish, ñukapish | | I also, I also |
| *amiga* charini | | have a lot of women friends. |
| ñukapish, ñukapish | | I also, I also |
| *pamilya* charini | | have a big family. |
| ashta rickungilla | 5 | You'll see lots of them, |
| ñukanchik karilla | | our he-men. |

| | | |
|---|---|---|
| tawka *familyayuk* | | Such a big family, mine, |
| tawka aylluyukmi | | such a big *ayllu*, mine. |
| kanchik kusa-wawa | | We are, my husband, babe. |
| ama piñachingi | 10 | Don't bother me. |

## Women's Values: *Supay* as a Metaphor of Self

If the situation doesn't change, in spite of the intervention of women friends and relatives, women may have no other choice than to leave their husbands for good. This choice is somewhat eased by the transition of matrilineal inheritance in the Andes, where women may separate from their husbands and take the material goods they brought into the marriage: "As does kinship, the pattern of inheritance reflects the essential parity of matri- and partrilines in the Indian society. The land and other major possessions that a woman or man brings to her or his conjugal household continues to belong to the individual and will be considered separately for purposes of inheritance" (Forman 1972: 36).

However, the decision to separate from a husband is not an easy matter; the decision may hinge on a woman's reliance on a strong *ayllu* network. Without networks of kin, planting and harvesting are difficult even if she owns a lot of land; in the Andes, agricultural tasks are organized around reciprocal labor (*mink'a*). Women, single or widowed, are disadvantaged under this system:

> . . . women depend on men in order to gain access to communal land where potatoes are grown and to arrange for male assistance in the fields and the transportation of crops. Even when widows or single mothers establish independent rights to communal lands, they are still dependent on men for crucial tasks in the agricultural cycle. Men can acquire such help through labor exchange or by hiring laborers. Women are disadvantaged because they do not have the same access to labor exchanges as men. (Bourque and Warren 1981: 128)

In the extreme circumstances where a woman decides on separation, the song becomes a communication event. Women describe singing the song over and over again, as they cook and work at household tasks, to attract their husband's attention. The message rings clear in the song; the women no longer accept this treatment:

| | |
|---|---|
| ñukapish ñuka | Even I, I |
| yuyaymi kusakumi | have my ideas, husband. |

| | |
|---|---|
| ñukapish ñuka | Even I, I |
| kulkiwan kawsashami | will live off my own money. |
| ñukapish ñuka    5 | I also, I |
| yuyaywan kawsashami | will live according to my idea. |
| kantapish manalla | From you never |
| rogashachu kusa | will I beg [for anything], husband. |
| cantapish manalla | From you never |
| rogaashachu runa    10 | will I beg, man. |

A similar strength and sense of self are found in the women's songs from the tropical lowlands of eastern Ecuador. Almost all the songs include the singer's name and a reference to her own *ayllu*. There is also an undercurrent of competition between the woman's family and the man's in the festivities, which include the consumption of fermented beverages. In this song Antonia (Figure 18) sings of drinking her husband under the table:

| | |
|---|---|
| manamari urmasha | Never ever falling down, |
| Antonialla supayga | Antonia spirit force, |
| Tangilalla warmiga | Tanguila woman. |
| Antonialla supayga | Antonia spirit force, |
| manamari urmasha    5 | never ever falling down. |
| Guiruwa runawna | The Grefa family, |
| urmashami sirinri | falling over they lie, |
| samballani runagami | strength-sapped family, |
| samballani runagami | strength-sapped family. |
| ñuka karishituga    10 | My dear husband, |
| manamari shinzhiri | for sure, not strong |
| kasnamari | like that for sure. |
| Arajuna runawna | People from Arajuno, |
| shitashkami sirinri | "wasted," they lie [there]. |

In this song, though, however outspoken she is in criticizing her husband's *ayllu* and their lack of staying power, she tempers her discourse with the addition of the independent suffix *ri* (line 11), which, in the lowland dialect of Ecuador, functions by adding some doubt to the situation; thus it ultimately blunts the force of the assertion (Orr and Wrisley 1965: 151). *Ri* is lacking, however, when she boasts of her own family and its strength, and only *mari*, the strong affirmative, marks her assertions (line 5).

The pervasiveness of the word *supay* (lines 2, 4) in these traditional songs learned from mothers and mothers-in-law argues for a semantic breadth which maintains intact the meaning of the word

*Figure 18.* Woman singer of the song "Antonia Spirit Force/Tanguila Woman."

as designating both good and bad spirit forces. As we saw in chapter 2, thirty-eight years after the Spanish Conquest the word has lost its fuller dimension and has acquired a restricted definition in the hands of the Spanish; *supay* is "devil." In fieldwork, I have found that *supay* also is used in this malevolent sense, such as *supay wawa* (devil's baby), which refers to a child born with a cleft lip or with hair covering its body. Such children are seen as a product of intercourse with a devil partner; they are often killed immediately after birth.

In most instances, however, *supay* carries positive connotations. *Supay* often appears in songs with themes of working in the *chakra* as well as in the aforementioned context of *fiesta* drinking patterns. When women use *supay* often their first name is attached to the phrase, or that of their *ayllu*, which designates a personal female strength handed down for generations. An outward manifestation of the passing on of this female strength is seen in the *paju* ceremonies. The woman who wishes to increase her yields in the *chakra* purchases the power from an acknowledged superior, a female agriculturalist. In this ritual, the woman with the "green thumb" extends her hands and allows the younger woman (or less successful gardener) to grasp one finger with her entire hand. She pulls on each finger, a motion similar to milking, and the power is transmitted. The entire process is not secretive or necessarily ritualistic; it is more practical and takes place with no real fanfare between the participants.

Laden within this conception of *supay* (power) is reference to the "chakra mama supayga" (mother of the *chakra*). As a mythical figure who is credited with teaching humans about cultivated plants, the women consciously appeal to her aid. Rituals of planting which are no longer practiced are still remembered by the older women. Songs are sung to make her "happy" and women paint their cheeks with dots of *achiote* (red vegetable dye). It is a mark of prestige to be called or call oneself "chakra mama" (mother of the fields) because one is worthy of the transmission of the force or strength. Once, when I made a particularly strong and fermented batch of *aswa* (manioc beverage), one of the men giggled and said to me "Allimi, aswa mama" (It's good, mother of [all] manioc beer).

When a woman boasts, through her songs, that she has the strength to keep standing up, that she will only lie down when she dies, the phrase is not mere poetic expression. Though "standing up" has profound levels of semantic meaning (which we will explore in chapter 6), in this context it may be taken at literal face value. Although men are responsible for the initial clearing of jungle land through

*Figure 19.* Woman cleaning dirt off the manioc roots to lighten her load back to the house.

slash-and-burn techniques, women and children scrape the under-brush down to the bare ground level of earth. This is very strenuous activity; a woman wields a machete, bent from the waist, always careful to maintain a lookout for snakes. After the manioc stems are planted, the women return to weed the *chakras*; the turned blade is used to level any weeds which sprout up in the five to six months before harvest (Whitten 1976: 74). The first weeding is often neces-sary shortly after planting, and thereafter the women go to weed again every three days. The growth of weeds seriously impairs the manioc yield; a well-weeded garden may last up to five years while one poorly maintained will be useful for half that time (Carneiro 1983: 87).

In the following song, one woman from the eastern slopes of the Andes sang about her physical strength in the fields, the powers transmitted to her by her family (Andi woman), and her sexual prow-ess as reflected in the context of *supay* (Figure 20):

| | |
|---|---|
| chagrama rikuk warmi | A woman who goes to the fields |
| supay pishisha | lacking strength, |
| imara pishisha | what strength will be lacking? |
| Andi warmi supayga | Andi women's strength. |
| kari warmi maniri | 5 I am, perhaps, man-woman. |
| imara tarabasha | I will do all kinds of work. |
| wañungalla sirisha | I'll only lie down to die. |
| kunanmari atarik | Now, for sure, I'm on my feet. |
| chakra warmi supayga | Spirit force in the *chakra*. |
| mana piwas pishinga | 10 [Nothing] will be lacking [in me]. |
| mana piwas paktanga | Nobody will equal [me]. |
| imara munakpiska | Whatever anybody wants, |
| ñuka munay shayasha | my desire is to keep on stand-ing up |
| ima tunu tarabasha | in every type of work. |
| shayangalla warmiga | 15 A woman [who] stands up, |
| mana valik warmiga | a worthless woman. |
| mana imaka pishishachu shayasha | No matter how diminished, I'll stand, |
| chawpi *parti* kariga | half man, |
| chawpi *parti* warmiga | half woman. |
| shinamari shayasha | 20 Like that for sure I'll stand up. |
| imara ñukaka pishiwanga | In what way will I be lacking? |
| kariska mana pishingamari | Men won't be lacking, for sure! |
| imara munakpiska | Whatever they desire sexually |
| ñuka munashkallami | I have sexually desired, for sure. |

*Figure 20.* Woman singer of the song "I'm Half Man, Half Woman."

| | | |
|---|---|---|
| ñukamari imara | 25 | Me, for sure, whatever |
| tarabana nikpiga | | work they want me to do, |
| ñukamari mani | | I'm [there for] that, for sure, |
| ima tunu tarabani | | all kinds of work. |
| manamari pishisha shayasha warmiga | | Never diminishing, standing up woman, |
| Andi warmi supayga | 30 | Andi woman spirit strength. |

In many of the songs from the tropical forest, *supay* of spiritual and physical strength is paired with the verb *pishina*, usually glossed as "to be lacking or to be drained of existence" (Herrero and Sánchez de Lozada 1983: 289):

| | |
|---|---|
| supay pishisha | lacking strength, |
| imara pishisha | what strength will be lacking? |

Although it may first appear to be a contradiction in terms (strength / force, lacking/diminishing), the following line contradicts this statement with a rhetorical question, "what strength will be lacking?" Through this song, the singer also "stands up to" the adverse commentary in the community from her husband or her husband's *ayllu* (lines 12, 27).

The singer also fashions another metaphor of self by her words "chawpi *parti* kariga, chawpi *parti* warmiga" (lines 18, 19). While occasionally "chawpi *parti* warmiga" is used in reference to a geographical location (a town halfway between two major settlements, generally a day's walk), in this song the usage is explained in the singer's own commentary. She possesses the attributes of woman and man, all in one person:

> Imara tarabanga nikpis ñuka mama, *señora*. Imara tarabanga. Maykan warmi kari aycha charini. Chawpi *parti* kari, chawpi *parti* warmi, kari-warmi, kari-warmi. Ima illapawas *animal*unawra wañuchinami illapasha. *Anzelo*was *anzelo*was mani. Ima tarpuras shitak mani, *señora*. Ima yuranawras ima muyunawras pitik mani. Maykan warmiuna mana ñuka *kwinta* shinanawngachu. Ñuka kasna upa upaynay. Warmisnalleira kasna putus putus rimashaylleira shinay. Shina tarabak ani.

> Do all kinds of work, my mother said, señora. I'll do all kinds of work. I have the body of women and men. I'm half male, half female, man-woman, man-woman. All kinds of animals I'll kill with a rifle. I'm good at catching fish: "with a fishhook, with a fishhook I am." Whatever [needs to be] planted, I'm a seed sower, señora. Whatever kind of tree, whatever kind of fruit, I cut [it] down. There are no other women like me. I'm quiet, quiet almost. Other women act [gossip] sort of angry, speaking angrily. I'm a good worker.

Also embedded within the song are references to other women, particularly the challenge "mana piwas paktanga" (nobody will equal

[me]; literally, catch up to me). The dubitative *ri* which begins the song "kari warmi maniri" (I am, perhaps, man-woman, line 5), is soon replaced with the affirmative marker *mari*. She is proud of her ability to work in her fields, yet she is also proud of her sexual prowess:

| | |
|---|---|
| imara ñukaka pishiwanga | In what way will I be lacking? |
| kariska mana pishinga*mari* | Men won't be lacking, for sure! |

Her pride in herself is tied to her superior strengths in hunting, fishing, cutting down trees, and planting. These attributes make her a desirable partner, and she cheerfully undertakes to do whatever task is necessary. Her choice of the verb *munana* (to want, to desire physically) aptly follows up her statement on her attractiveness to men:

| | |
|---|---|
| imara munakpiska | Whatever they desire sexually |
| ñuka munashkallami | I have sexually desired, for sure. |

The phrase has an ambiguous referent residing in whatever work they want done or whatever the desire in the way of sexual liaisons, she complements that desire. As we will see in chapter 6, women actively seek varied sexual liaisons in the tropical forest, and there are many songs purposely created to enhance a woman's sexual prowess.

## Man-Woman: Restoring the Balance

The rhetorical flourishes conveying the importance of womanhood and women's power in the Quechua songs may obfuscate the ideal male/female relationship in indigenous societies. As Tristan Platt records in Bolivia, there is a saying "Tukuy ima qhariwarmi" (Everything is man-woman) (1976: 21). Rock outcroppings, hills, pools of water fed from springs, dances, parts of the house structure are all made up of these two elements, unified in a concept of *yanantin* (unity, totality). We have already discovered a semantic field related to the concept of two separate mirror images becoming united in one basic unit and where the philosophical pursuit of equilibrium in Inca society was examined (chapter 2). In actual practice, within Quechua-speaking communities, a person "becomes an adult and full participant in communal affairs only after marriage" (Isbell 1978: 81).

However, when discussing women's place within Andean societies and not merely focusing upon the participation at home, the investigation of gender becomes more clouded. Although there may be complementarity between husband and wife in the matrimonial sphere, in the dynamics of the community—rituals, ceremonies, social gatherings—women are not featured prominently. At the family hearth or in the fields she is included in household decisions; in social gatherings it is often the men who govern the outcome of discussion (Harris 1978: 38). Thus, a basic contradiction arises which creates ambiguity when we define gender.

Modification of the concepts of complementarity in Quechua society may be expected in agricultural communities as money is introduced as a medium of exchange. Increasing dependence on developing markets for agricultural goods on the coast of Ecuador and Peru will affect the ideological evaluation of women. If we focus on subsistence activities, it is women "who call the shots" ("warmi kamachi") (ibid.: 39), but as more energy is directed toward producing surplus crops and purchasing commercial products, women lose their dominant status. Although Andean women are perfectly capable of performing transactions with coastal merchants, men handle the business contacts with the urban mestizo markets (Bourque and Warren 1981: 131). With successful "integration" into the national economy, women are increasingly judged from the perspective of the dominant Hispanic values often alluded to in the term *machismo*.

Consciousness raising, in the mode of Barrios de Chungara's rhetoric, will be the antidote to a devaluation of women's roles in the traditional exchanges of reciprocity and attention to equilibrium. As the society changes with the introduction of Hispanic or non-Amerindian values, societal contributions and worth are consistently measured in terms of the accumulation of the brightly colored national money. In the original Andean model for gender divisions, which are recorded in the songs and in the chronicles, another pattern is evident. To preserve that ancient model of balanced male/female relationships, to stem the erosion of Amerindian values, more opportunities must be extended to women in the areas of employment, education, and political representation. The feminism of which Barrios de Chungara speaks is not *femenismo gringa* (imported feminism), in which women "imitate all the vices that men have." She argues for a return to the classic Andean model where women are "intelligent beings, problem solvers" whose opinions are "respected both inside and outside the home" (1980: 9).

# 6. The Metaphysics of Sex: Quichua Songs from the Tropical Forest

THE QUECHUA-SPEAKING street vendor smiled when I spoke to her in her native language. She recognized that the dialect I spoke was different from Bolivian Quechua and, instead of selling her products, she began asking how I came to learn Quechua, what people were like in Ecuador, how they lived. As I spoke, I bought a few of her bright-colored yarns, some charms floating in used, cast-off hospital syringes, the soapstone carvings of animals and haciendas, and a dried llama fetus. Seeing my interest in these indigenous artifacts, she also pointed out her *warmi munachi*, small carvings of a man and woman locked in a tight, erotic embrace (Figure 21).[1]

When I bought eight of the figures, she surmised that I must be in dire straits sexually and offered to help out. She could make up a special charm to guarantee success in snaring a man and keeping him. She drew me closer, whispered in my ear, turning her head occasionally from side to side to see if other vendors were observing her: "Secretly, secretly you quietly place this in the bed or the room of the man you want. It's full of all sorts of powers; he will be your man." And she busily got to work, making a nest of green, orange, and reddish yarns, placing two spiral seeds (green and yellow) within the magic circle; next she added two *wuraruru* seeds (red and black) and one large natural-colored pod. Three bits of stone were also enclosed and then the entire charm was showered with miniature *milagros*, those metal symbols hung on Catholic altars to ward off evil and disease (Figure 22). Her last action, in the fading light of a sunset in La Paz, was to place the soapstone man/woman figure in the middle. "There you go," she said. "It's all yours."

My interest in the amulets was totally understandable from an indigenous perspective; the only surprise expressed by the vendor was my ability to address her in her own language. Love magic, as Dobkin de Ríos has documented (1978), is widely sought and bought throughout the coast, the Andes, and the tropical forests. Santacruz Pachacuti Yamqui, the seventeenth-century chronicler whose work we discussed in chapters 3 and 4, mentions much pre-Conquest interest in love potions. He mentions specifically a drug which causes aphrodisiacal effects, *uarnapo* (*Jatropha basiacantha*), and tells how one of the kings eagerly searched for *chotarpo uanarpo* to give away to others so they could use them to fornicate (Santacruz Pachacuti Yamqui [1613] 1927: 155). He also recounts a narrative of two lovers who, through the use of small stones (*china*), were so consumed by sex that they could hardly be separated (ibid.: 153–154). Luis Millones, Virgilio Galdo G., and Anne Marie Dussault (1981) also study the usage of these aphrodisiacs in the colonial chronicles. They suggest that the substances permitted the Incaic subjects to defy the authority and prohibitions of the state in the case of (nonroyal) incest and sexual relations between people of different classes. The mention of these events in the chapters of these early histories indicates a persistent theme of interest in sexual enhancement. The current sale of archaeological postcards and small ceramic pieces depicting copulation in many tourist shops is evidence that this interest is not limited to the indigenous population.

My success in obtaining the magical materials for bewitching a lover was easier in the environs of Lake Titicaca than in the confines of the tropical forests of Ecuador. My access to the lowland "love songs of enchantment" was more restricted. I was told that one reason women were reluctant to sing for me was that "I didn't understand their words well enough yet." Frequently, when a woman encountered me and my Quichua-speaking teacher, I'd hear the question, "Ña kawsanchu?" (Does she live yet?) as she nodded in my direction. This phrase ultimately translates to "Does she speak our language well enough yet?" The ability to converse, for power and for verbal play, is a dominant theme in nonliterate communities. Language skill is commensurate with the acquisition of logical analysis; children are said to be *sin razón* (without power to reason) until reaching the age of ten.

Acute embarrassment among the women prevented my taping songs for many more months. My inquiries were often brushed off with the reply, "Why don't you tape in that village over there? The women there *really* know how to sing." On a rainy day, six months after I first arrived in the Ecuadoran lowlands, one of "those" women walked up to my house and agreed to sing into my tape recorder. The singer insisted that we go off by ourselves to the porch of an empty schoolhouse, where she sang into a hand-held microphone. Although she showed little stage fright, she did voice a request, "Don't play

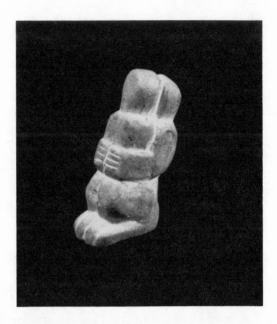

*Figure 21.* Close-up of the alabaster love charm, *warmi munachi.* Photo by Peter Scarpaci and Beth Carvette.

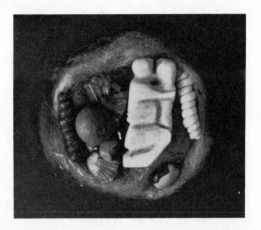

*Figure 22.* The *warmi munachi* love charm wrapped in colored woolen strands, from La Paz, Bolivia. Photo by Peter Scarpaci and Beth Carvette.

these songs when my husband is around." I honored that request, but it was many more months before I understood the significance of her utterance.

For the women in the tropical forest of Ecuador, singing these songs was a private function. Of course, a woman could sing in the company of her children and close female relatives, but more often the songs were enunciated in a setting conducive to contemplation, where clear images and thoughts were united in a domain of song. Norman Whitten's research yields information of women "think-singing" some songs, allowing for "integration with mythic time and enactment of mythic structure" (1976: 167). The women I recorded spoke only of gathering thoughts in a contemplative process; the singing was always a process of actual singing of the words and melody. The singer often went up to a high elevation, where the wind blew strong, so that her words would be carried far.

The songs are not categorized and labeled with any one term; however, the motive for singing was attributed to *llakichina*, usually glossed as "songs to make one sad." The older Quechua dictionaries insist on the communicative powers of this verb: "to cause sorrow or cause pain to another person" (González Holguín [1608] 1952: 211).[2] Its more restricted sense is not upheld in the lowlands of Ecuador, however, where it is also synonymous with "loving, to cause to love" (Leonardi 1966: 51). One preface to a song included a statement about the function of *llakina:* "ñuka kunan kantangarawni kanguna churiwna uyak maybi ñuka chingarikpi ñuka wañukpi kanguna llakisha rikusha charingichi churi" (I'm going to sing, you children [will be] listeners, when I become lost, when I die, you [children] saddened, seeing, will have [the song, my] son). The coupling of sorrow and love, pain and romance, refers to a heightened emotional state which is marked in the transmission of songs.

While some songs are readily understandable, with themes drawn from a singer's life or childhood, the taking of a husband, drinking songs, and planting songs, the songs of enchantment are the most private and least communicative to anyone beyond the singer and the person to whom she sings. Communication in these songs is distinct from everyday syntax and semantics. If the content of these songs were stated in everyday speech, even the men would understand the songs, but when they were sung, it was difficult to comprehend the message: "Kariwna rimawkpichu *intind*inawn, mana *kanta*shka mana *intind*inawn *kanta*shka *partim*andakmari" (If we said [the words] the men would understand, but not when we sing [them], they really don't understand [anything] from the [version in] song).

A stated theme is used to begin the song; the chosen image is frequently one seen in a tropical forest environment, such as a yellow-handed monkey, a newly blooming flower of the manioc plant, the toucan bird with its bright plumage, or the fearsome water boa. The thematic phrase is usually repeated two or three times, a type of entitlement procedure in a nonliterate society. Singers are aware of the demands of oral communication; the motive given for so much repetition in the "public" songs is so that "people can hear it well." Of course, repetition is also cause for mental pauses, a search to best continue the song within the demands of the form.

The more "private" songs pertain to a special memory of hallucinogenic visions which relate to life crises. Because of the seriousness of an event in the life of a singer, she often uses hallucinogens, usually datura. Highly symbolic, each song forms a nucleus of perception which is stored in memory. The image-producing capacity of datura is well documented in scientific studies which trace the effects of the plant hallucinogen. Sometimes a "screen full of visions" appears in much the same manner as a projection of a movie with tropical animals, rivers, and individuals engaging the drug taker's consciousness. Sometimes images, not continuous action, predominate (Dobkin de Ríos 1972: 117–118). The appearance of images, snakes in particular, is an expectation of users of *ayahuaska:* "A commonly reported vision is that a very large snake enters the circle around which a person is seated in the jungle or else enters the room where one is taking *ayahuaska*" (ibid.: 120). The person seeking a vision allows the giant snake to come into his/her presence; some patients report the snake entering their body, often through the patient's mouth (ibid.).

One experience of taking the drug often involves learning a song which both reinforces the descriptive images and is correlated intimately with major episodes in a woman's life. In narrating the vision in the process of song, each woman reenacts a central image which is useful in defining her personality. The images are culturally laden and bound to the environment which surrounds her, yet the associations with which she invests the images surge forth from many experiences in her lifetime. The image produced by hallucinogens may become a dominant organizing principle with which the singer integrates life episodes and an analytical tool with which she assesses the behavior of others. It focuses her attempts to understand significant aspects of her life which are troublesome, beyond her power to control, and laden with anxiety.

Many of the songs refer to difficulties in sexual and amorous relationships. Men in the tropical forest frequently leave home to embark on hunting expeditions, to purchase necessary household goods, and, more recently, to cut forest paths for oil company explorations. These trips away from home, although accepted by the wives, are seen as potentially disruptive because a man, through sexual liaisons, may be persuaded to abandon his children and wife. Sexual relationships with extramarital partners are not necessarily cast in negative moralistic censure, but the fear of abandonment by the spouse is significant. Even more threatening is the capture of a man's soul by a *sacha warmi*, a spirit woman, who serves as a man's knowledgeable assistant in the hunting of game but who also demands a close sexual union with the man she accompanies. A Quichua woman will tolerate the man's consorting with a *sacha warmi* for its promise of providing a protein source for the family, yet this relationship often carries her partner deep into the forest and far away on the rivers, away from his domestic obligations. Both human women and spirit women then pose a threat to the stability of the nuclear family. A mechanism of balancing the powers, of asserting domestic claims, is found in the song visions, which distill a methodology for winning back a spouse's heart and soul as well as his physical return.

### Discourse and Poetics: Sisa's Visionary Song

The integrating nature of the symbolism is outlined in a lengthy song taught to a lowland Quichua singer, whom I call Sisa, by a snake-woman (Figure 23). As a prelude to singing the song, Sisa told me of the event of taking *wanduk*, not for recreational purposes, but to resolve a crisis in her life. Her motivation to embark on a datura trip is to rid herself of a terrible pain in her lower spine, which hurt so much that she compared it to the pain of childbirth. She makes no mention of any other crisis in her telling of the event, yet in her hallucinogenic encounter with the snake-woman she participates in a deeper understanding of the nature of her life crisis: her children, reaching adulthood, will travel far and wide, virtually abandoning her in a pattern similar to that she experienced with her distant traveling husband.

Discourse with the snake-woman clarifies the problems Sisa will later experience. Her transcription of the encounter with the snake-woman in the vision demonstrates the nature of the clarification. When the snake-woman first questions Sisa as to why she has come to see her, she says that she's just walking around, ambling around the area for no specific reason. The snake-woman, however, pierces the veil of ambiguity and questions further: "Is there something that you don't know [or want to find out]?" The snake-woman encourages her to reflect on the cause of her sadness and her loving, yearning.

This encouragement of self-reflectiveness is particularly phrased "llakinamanda iyaringichi" (you-all think about the sadness, the loving). Specifically, the snake-woman addresses a plural *you* as the essence of the woman's identity in causing her to ponder an unper-

*Figure 23.* Woman singer of the "Ukumbi Snake-Woman" song.


ceived emotional state. The utterance of a plural future imperative (the command *iyaringichi*) is a definite shift from the singularity with which Sisa was addressed in the first question, "What are you [singular] doing here?" This switch from singular person to a plural form is in keeping with Lawrence Carpenter's insightful analysis of an individual's dual nature among the Quichua. This duality is marked morphologically and syntactically in Carpenter's study. Quichua speakers, in addition, specify the existence of two "hearts"—a physical organ (*kurasun*) and an "inside" heart (*shunku*), a spiritual center very important to an individual's well-being (1980: 7).

This depiction of two organs essential to an individual's existence attests to the fused relationship of the physical and spiritual. With two existences, both linked in a holistic manner, the means of fulfilling both natures becomes the basis of self-reflection and masterful interpretation. Often it is the shaman's lot to elicit the correct analysis of the symbolism; many times the interpretation resides in the participation of family members' commentary. In this song, the purpose is explicitly stated: In singing this song, the singer will avoid the pain of being alone and forgotten by her grown-up children.

The consolation obtained from the learning of the song is immediate. The snake-woman herself is reassuring; she has gone through a

*Figure 24.* Child in a canoe, tropical forest, Ecuador. Photo by Ted Macdonald.

similar period of worry about the loss of her children, as stated in the opening lines of the song she sings (Figure 24). Her assurance that the song is an effective remedy to loneliness is emphasized in the concluding statement: "Sing [the song] just like this. Don't abandon me [forget me], my children. Even far away, wherever [they've] gone, it [the song] will make [them] yours."

The explanatory discourse which precedes the song describes Sisa's reasons for taking datura (*wanduk*). So powerful is the boiled essence that she claims she "died" for several days with its strong effects:[3]

> Ungushkay ungushka wañungarawni shina nisha wañusha nisha. Pura nanaku *enteru* siki tulluka, wawa pagarina *uras kwinta*. . . . Wandukta upikani upiklleira ishqi punllara wañushka kaylla. Kimsa punlla tukunara tiyak kani. Chimanda purikani, anakma purikani. Chai *parti* sanka tiyashkay, huasi tiyashka. Wanduk warmi pichawaka, pichaka. Ukumbi warmi pungura paskaka, shamuk warmi shamusha.
>
> "Ima *milagro* kayma puringi?" nin.
>
> "Yanga puriunimi ñuka llaktamanda yanga puriusha," rimakani.
>
> Shina nikpi, "shuk *cosa* mana yachangi? Llakimanda iyaringichi," nin.
>
> "Shinalleira kambak kari mayta rikpis, churiuna ichusha riunawn iñachin,"

nin. "Atun tukun pay kasna tukungami," nin. "Karan llaktawna kay *Guaya-quil* lamarman—ima llakta tukuy llaktara riman—churiuna ichusha ichusha risha rinawkpica mamaga tiyarisha *kantawna*," nin.
  Chita nisha kamachina. Ñukaman kamachishka washa pay *kantanawn*.
  "Shina *kantay*," nin. "Churi wawawna ama ichusha tukungichi," nin.
  "Karu llaktara mayta rishashka kambaklleira ranga," nin.
  Kantak akas, chi *señora*. Kantaringarawni pay kantashkara.

I was sick, really sick, I'm going to die, I said [to myself], I will die, I said. One tremendous pain at the base of my spine, just like when I gave birth, just like that. . . . I did some datura, and I was "dead" right here two days after taking it. Three days later I was "here." After that I walked, upriver I walked, until I reached [a place] upriver. There where that cliff was, there was a house. A datura woman cured me, cleansed [me]. A blue-colored *ukumbi* snake-woman opened the door, she, coming over [to me], came over and said, "What in the world are you doing here?"

"I'm just wandering around for the hell of it, getting out of my village and I'm wandering around," I said.

Then she said, "Is there something you don't know? [something you want to find out?] You-all think about your sadness/loving, yearning," she said. "Just like your husband who travels all over the place, your children will leave you, abandoning you, they grow up," she said. "They get big, just like that, he [your son] will get [big]," she said. "To Guayaquil, to the ocean, to each and every town—all names of cities, she named every city—your children will go away, abandoning [you], forgetting [you], going away and when they go away, you, the mother, will be sitting there singing [your] songs."

With that [that's exactly how] she counseled me. After giving me [that advice] she sang.

"Sing just like this," she said. [Say] don't abandon me [forget me] children. Even far away, wherever [they've] gone, it [the song] will make [them] yours."

What a singer she was, that woman. Now I'm going to sing her song:

| | |
|---|---|
| ukumbi warmiga | *Ukumbi* snake-woman, |
| ukumbi warmiga | *ukumbi* snake-woman, |
| karan yakupichu | in every river, |
| puskuman armachisha | bathing in the foaming waters, |
| karanbi shayasha | 5    in each [river] standing |

| | |
|---|---|
| churi-wawa rikpiga | because your [my] son went away. |
| urayta risha | Going downriver, |
| uraymanda shamusha | coming back from downriver, |
| karan yaku chimbata | along each riverbank |
| puringa warmiga | 10 a traveling woman |
| killa simayukawachu armarisha purisha | with yellow love potion bathing, |
| | traveling. |
| ñuka purishkalla | I have traveled just like that, |
| ñuka churishitu | my dear little son. |
| ñuka chakillayta | On my feet |
| killu simayukahua | 15 yellow *simayuka* love potion |
| chapasha purikpi | waiting because he went away. |
| maykan llaktara rishaska | Wherever he went, |
| kaylla shamungi | come back here, right here, |
| ñuka churishituga | my dear little son, |
| | 20 from all the headwaters of the |
| tukuy yaku uma | rivers, |
| | from wherever you went, coming |
| tukuy rishkara shamusha | back, |
| karan lenusbichu | in each pool of water, |
| yaku puskullawa | with just the bubbly water, |
| armarisha shayasha | bathing, standing. |
| maykan llaktaras rishas | 25 Wherever you go, |
| ñuka maymanda shamungi | from wherever, come to me, |
| churishitunaska | my dear little son. |
| ima kusashitu | Just like a dear husband, |
| simayukawaga | with *simayuka* love potion, |
| armasha chapasha | 30 bathing, waiting, [I will wait] |
| mayta purishaska | to wherever you have gone. |
| atun yaku lenusbi | In the large pools of a big river, |
| rumipi tiyarisha | on a rock sitting, |
| puskuta armarisha | in the bubbles bathing, |
| payñarisha shayasha | 35 with combed hair, standing, |
| maybi puripiska | wherever you have gone, |
| mana kungariwangi | don't forget me, |
| mana kungariwangi | don't forget me, |
| karumanda warmi | woman from far away, |
| ñuka mamashitu | 40 my dear mother. |
| chapasha tiyawnimi | waiting, I am existing, |
| ima simayuka | whatever kind of *simayuka* |
| payñawa payñarik ashay | with a comb, I am combed, |
| | in each bubbly water place, |
| karan puskupi puskuta upyasha itarisha | bubbly water drinking, sitting, |

| | |
|---|---|
| yaku puskutami upyarisha tiyarisha | 45  drinking bubbly water, sitting |
| karan yaku umay | to each river's headwaters, |
| puringa warmiga | a traveling woman. |
| ñuka churi asha | My son is |
| maybi kusagasha | wherever my husband is. |
| simayukawa armashkay | 50  With *simayuka*, bathed, |
| ñuka wasi tiyani | I am in my house. |
| paktamungi churi | It will be time for you to come |
| | before me.[4] |

Although the narrative version of the encounter with the snake-woman is barren of images, the song version is colored with descriptions of the *ukumbi* snake-woman, the rivers, the foam on top of the water, and the snake's children. This kernel of expressive poetics appears in two shorter versions of songs which Sisa sang for me earlier.

| | |
|---|---|
| ukumbi warmi | *Ukumbi* snake-woman, |
| ukumbi warmi | *ukumbi* snake-woman, |
| uraymanda shamukanimi | from downriver I came for sure. |
| uraymanda shamukanimi | From downriver I came for sure. |
| puskuy puskuy armarisha | 5  Bathing in the bubbles, in the bubbles, |
| shayakshami | standing there |
| puspi | in the bubbles, |
| ñuka ayllumi armashami shayakuni | bathing with my family, I am standing, |
| simayuka warmiga | *simayuka* love potion woman. |

A second version, sung immediately after this short version, revealed more about the function of *simayuka* in the layering of the verses. *Simayuka* (love potion) is mentioned in the context of calling out to woo the return of the *ayllu* (members of the family) who no longer live in the house. The calling or singing is specifically accomplished with the strength of the wind that comes from downriver ("wayra shinachu uraymanda"):

| | |
|---|---|
| ukumbi warmigalla | *Ukumbi* snake-woman, |
| ukumbi warmigalla | *ukumbi* snake-woman, |
| ukumbi warmi shayashachu | *ukumbi* snake-woman, standing, |
| ñuka aylluguna | my family, |
| kayashami shayasha | 5  calling, standing |
| simayukawachu | with *simayuka* love potion, |
| purishka shinalleira | just as if [I had] walked, |

ñuka washallami shamungi

wayra shinachu uraymanda

ichayta shamusha

yana yana kuchapi

puskuy armarisha shayasha

ñuka churi wawanachu

puringa-a-a

later, come back to me.
Like the strong wind from
   downriver,
10  from upriver [your] arrival
in the black, black lake,
in the river bubbles, bathing,
   standing.
My little children,
you will all wander off.

This poetic discourse above, in comparison to the aforementioned longer version of the song, is more directly focused on the snake-woman herself. The singer's biography is not present here; this version, in abbreviated fashion, emphasizes the person in the hallucinogenic vision, the *ukumbi* snake-woman. The provocative image of the bathing and splashing in the foam of the river is later reiterated in the image of the human woman, Sisa, imitating the very same motions.

The mention of the snake, the rivers, the foam, and bathing in an area where water traverses rocks is rich in associations for Quichua-speaking people (Figure 25). These images are coded to reveal a woman's need to pick up strength and power (*urza*), generally acquired in these well-defined areas of the river. The theme of women's power has been examined in chapter 5, with a discussion of women's songs; women boast of their physical prowess, the transmission of the strength of a family from one woman to another (*supay*), and define their defiance of mistreatment at the hands of their spouses ("even though he beats me, I'll stand up to him").

The image of standing (*shayasha*) transforms the symbolic coding to an association of contemplativeness, where the singer's evocative forces of seeing and remembering are called forth, as well as providing a transition to the more erotically charged meaning. In the act of "standing" the son appears in the image, going downstream on his own, as his mother remembers him (lines 6–7): "churi wawa rikpiga/urayta risha." The next image pattern is his return from downriver significantly cast in a gerund form (*shamusha*, coming back), which illustrates a potential return as she produces the image.

The focus then shifts to the snake-woman again, the riverbanks, and her experiencing of existence articulated with the verb *purina* (to walk, to exist). This existence is explicitly linked to the powerful love potion (*killu simayuka*) with which, along with the foam in the river, she is bathing. The two substances, river foam and love potion, are conjoined in the domain of bathing in the river. Thus

*Figure 25.* Riverine settlement, tropical forest, Ecuador. Photo by Ted Macdonald.

conjoined, a meaning emerges which associates this snake-woman as powerfully reinforced by the strength of the river foam and the love potion. The prominence of these two concrete images serves to more graphically define existence (*purisha*), investing the woman with sexually explicit powers.

Focus on the sign itself, the *ukumbi* snake-woman, does not unravel the complexity of the associational imagery. In fact, the name *ukumbi warmi* does not reveal the kind of snake which appears in the vision and the song. According to the singer, the *ukumbi warmi* is not a harmless, nonpoisonous snake, which the name denotes, but is, in fact, the water boa, the boa wife of the water boa. She also has another form, for she can appear as a beautiful, white-skinned foreigner, with long black hair down to her hips. Without *wanduk* she would look like a snake, but with it one sees her in the human form, transposed. Because of the foam and the *simayuka*, the snake generates yet another image of itself which the singer is given to understand by means of the song and the snake's appearance. The image of the snake arises from memory, and it is with words that the singer attempts to infer the fullness of this existence. The succinct image of the snake is transformed to words which then undergo a second transformational level of associations.

A translation of the song must take into account the dual nature of the message it contains. The snake-woman who teaches Sisa the song is included in the song, and the singer also comments about her self. The repetitive usage of the gerund ending *sha* lends ambiguity, for it is identical to the first-person marker of the future tense *sha*. Thus, in line 5 "karanbi shayasha" could be translated "in each [river] stand*ing*," which refers to the snake-woman, or "in each [river] *I* will stand," which then refers to the singer. The shifting of lyrical voice is intentional, as singer and song-mistress are seen as one. Both women experience the same predicament with husbands who have taken up with many other women. The snake-woman tells Sisa that her husband will leave her: "'Kambak kari ichunga-rawn,' nin" ("Your husband will leave you," she says) and "when he does, you must sing this song" ("'ichukpi rawpika chita kant*a*ngi,' nin"). The snake-woman has a similar problem; her husband has been with a lot of women: "Pay shinalleira; paywa kari ashka war-miunara charin" (Her husband is just like this, too; her husband has [had] a lot of women). For this reason, the first eleven lines of the song refer to the snake-woman, and in line 12 the pronoun orients the listener to the singer's tale.

The song, for all its ambiguous personal references, is clear in the description of women splashing, standing in river currents, drinking the foam of the river, traveling in pursuit of men, or waiting quietly at home. Paralleling this description is one of men intertwined in the text; men, husbands and sons, leave home to venture off to distant places. It is to the men that the imperatives in the song are directed: "shamungi" (come home) (line 18); "mana cungariwangi" (don't forget me) (lines 37–38); and "paktamungi" (arrive back here) (line 52).

While the men are distantly wandering, the women are actively engaged in securing their return. Their technique for accomplishing this feat concerns the usage of *simayuka*, a type of love potion. This substance, which may be prepared from many types of materials, is chosen by the individual who wants to effect a charm. Often *sima-yuka* consists of an essence of the *tura tura* bird, the *yakumangu* bird, gratings from the *achiote* plant or from the wild potato plant. Women do not admit freely to cultivating *simayuka*, but each woman is able to allude to the types of *simayuka* that another woman has acquired. Although the word is frequently used in the tropical forests of Ecuador, the word is only listed in one dictionary of the many I have consulted (Leonardi 1966). There is a verb *yukuna* (to copulate) in the dictionary entries of Santo Tomás ([1560] 1951: 303); however, I cannot ascertain a possible derivation. Udo Oberem (1980: 286) acknowledges the magical power of *simayuka* to be-

*Figure 26.* Serving *aswa* (manioc beverage) in a ceramic bowl, tropical for-
est, Ecuador.

witch women in his reading of older sources, although he also does not cite lexical sources.

The sexual dimension of *simayuka* is understood, although it is mentioned devoid of overt sexual allusions in discussions of men's hunting magic. *Simayuka* figures prominently in the domain of men's power, as it is an essential ally to male activity. This essence is necessary to acquire the power to hunt successfully. For men, the symbolic power of the pulverized head of a boa is seen as the most powerful attractor. After killing a snake, the head is buried and allowed to decompose, and the man observes prohibition of sex, certain foods, and salt. Later, the head is dug up, pulverized, and stored away secretly.[5]

In questions of sexual alliance, the *simayuka* is usually imbibed or ingested and massaged into or rubbed onto another person. The Hispanic gesture of shaking hands is a perfect means of transferring the *simayuka* at a public gathering or fiesta. Another propitious moment, mentioned by women, is in the passing of the manioc beverage, which is served in shallow, wide-mouthed ceramic bowls (Figure 26). A woman intent upon establishing a liaison with a man will dip her *simayuka*-coated thumb into the liquid as she passes it on to her future desire. The *simayuka* causes the person to "go crazy" and "to loosen him/herself" (*lluspirin*).

### Semantic Domains: Verbal Metaphors

Three verbal concepts dominate this song and many others because they are useful in attracting male human lovers and spirit lovers. These verbs both define spatial categories and are synonymous with emotional states: *purina* (to walk, travel); *tiyana* (to be, to be located); and *shayana* (to stand, to stop). Their inclusion and prominence in the song allude to Quichua understanding of the nature of existence within their culture.

Analysis of Quechua verse uncovers a basic semantic coupling which often centers on the opposition of paired concepts. Bruce Mannheim, for instance, argues for a "relationship of semantic markedness, with one member of a pair characterized by a property that the other distinctly lacks" (1987a: 282). When he discusses *purina* and *tiyana*, Mannheim observes a "common element [of] a notion of kinetic or dynamic existence based in the cancellation of the boundedness property. . . . *Puriy* thus presupposes *tiyay* conceptually . . . *puriy* [is] the marked member, *tiyay* [is] the unmarked" (ibid.).

In an early gloss written by the priest González Holguín, *purina* is equated with "walking, liquid running" ([1608] 1952: 297), but this gloss is too restricted. *Purina* embodies notions of activity, motion, sexuality, and existence which go beyond this semantic restrictiveness. In the songs of the Ecuadoran lowlands, *purina* carries connotations as a verb which is a metaphor to define existence. Women, when asked to sing extemporaneous songs detailing their life (*kawsana*), often sang of the many towns and cities they had traveled to on foot, accompanying their husbands and lugging their young children on their backs. "Nuka purishkara" (my travels) often begins the songs filled with autobiographical details.

*Purina* is also used in a wide variety of expressions to describe the behavior of women. A "sumak purik warmi" (a woman who walks beautifully, correctly) is an ideal in Quichua culture. She walks along "seriously" ("*siriu* purina"), she walks in a "positive" manner ("alli purina"), and she doesn't wander "aimlessly" ("*mana yanga purina*"). In other words, she works long hours in her garden and resists the efforts of men to "bother her" ("mana piwas *molesta*shka"). As is conveyed in the last description, the verb also connotes adolescent, youthful sexual activity and passion. A similar connotation is noted among the Ilongots, where traveling is seen as youthful prowess, of potency and expansion, before one gets married and settles down (Rosaldo 1980: 149–150).

Lira's gloss of *purikukk* (1944: 772) as "one who does what he/she wants" comes close to the meaning of *purina* in the sexual connotation. Other phrases reinforce this interpretation, for "koskalla purik" (a walker who stays even with another) is known to be a woman who "accompanies her husband, not smiling at others, who comes directly home not looking for lovers." González Holguín's gloss of "karihuan purini" (literally, I walk with a man) is a more explicit allusion to sexuality, "fornicar la mujer" (a woman who has sexual relations) ([1608] 1952: 527).[6] *Tiyana*, as seen in lines 41 and 52 in the song, also refers to physical location, to sitting down, and to settling down. This verb may refer also to the "calming of passion." Lira's entry, which describes the "force of a stream of water diminishing" (1944: 971), alludes to a possible interpretation of *tiyana* as cooling of ardor. In the song, this sense may be inferred, as the woman singer, when she uses it, is in her house and often sitting in her house; her passion is not described by the active *purina* but the collected passion of *tiyana*.

The overwhelming presence of the verb *shayana* marks all the songs of erotic love. As in those songs of women's strength and women's will (chapter 5), it also is repeated in the love songs. Father

Monteros, collecting songs in the Ecuadoran lowlands in 1942, records a similar use of *shayana* in the song text (my translation):

| | | |
|---|---|---|
| lomo sisa mani-a | | I am a manioc flower, |
| lomo sisa cayari | | call manioc flower. |
| tigrashpa shayani | | Returning [home], I stand, |
| tigra, tigra shayani | | returning, returning, I stand. |
| inti runa cayari | 5 | Call, man of the sun, |
| puca, puca yaycuri | | enter here, red, red |
| yaypushcalla shayani | | in the cut down part of brush, I stand, |
| inti runacituca | | beloved man of the sun. |

(Monteros 1942: 26)

Lira's dictionary gloss of *shayana* alludes to characteristics of "stable personality or sense of self, loyal" (1944: 887), while González Holguín's older dictionary specifies "personal presence" or "stature" ([1608] 1952: 325). An earlier dictionary published by Antonio Ricardo also mentions this meaning and another which refers to the age of sexual encounters in adolescence. A particular type of young woman is mentioned, a *sayacsipsa* (unmarried woman) (*Vocabulario y phrasis* [1586] 1951: 79). There is some reference to a connotation of sexuality in the song in two instances: "armarisha shayasha" (bathing myself, standing) (line 24) and "payñarisha shayasha" (combing [my hair] standing) (line 35). These *shayasha* activities do refer to preparations of a sexual encounter which includes the technique of love potions. This "standing around" is the type associated with "kari apina uras" (the age when one "gets" a man). One singer specifically mentioned standing on top of a large hill, "urku punday shayawnchi" (on the top of a hill we stood), in order to see a lover approach.

In a more general sense, *shayana* refers to a contemplative meditative self which draws inspiration from the vivid imagery of the tropical forest. "Shayarisha iyarisha tiyana" (standing, thinking, act of existence) is one of the most meaningful experiences for a woman; it is a moment when she is gathered up into her own self, summoning her creative energies. It is an individual act, brought about by her contemplation of her life and her spiritual nature or is devoted to thoughts transmitted to her by her own spirit woman vision.

The choice of these verbs describes modes of existence which define the dynamics of a women's self-reflection on her life. *Purina* alludes to the carefree times of sexual encounters, *shayana* describes the contemplative process which remembers and calls forth the repetition of the sexual attraction, and *tiyana* demarcates a space of grounded activity where passion is more restricted, passive, awaiting a lover, as in the house.

However, to fully explicate the song there is one more level of meaning to explore which consists of the physical and spiritual experiencing of existence. The song is not merely about a woman's powers to "call back" her husband or roving children. It also refers to the important number of spirit helpers who guide human activity in the environment of the tropical forest. The music of this song is one of a number of melodies that it is possible to hear in the lowland environment. The powerful water anaconda knows how to sing and to use his own *simayuka*: "The boa, he himself, has his own *simayuka*, then he overpowers Quichua women. When [these] boa spirits rub *simayuka* dust on you, you turn into spirits just like them" ("payguna kakukpi shina tukuna turkarinawn"). The boa transforms himself into a handsome foreign-looking man with white skin and a beard; he stands on the riverbank and calls and sings to *runa* women.

The singer said that when a Quichua woman sings her songs, she is just like the boa spirit who makes women fall in love with him. It is said that he tricks them with his song, and they fall in love with him: "Runara apinara munanchi nin chita llustirina ushanchi, nin" (We want to carry off some Quichua [women], they say. We can unloosen them [unclothe them], they say). The boa spirits think of taking away *runa* women in the same manner that *simayuka* functions: "Iyarisha simayuka kwinta simayuka aysashka *kantan*mi." (Thinking, they drag the women to them by means of song). No matter how far away, even at a great distance, the boa lovers have great power to draw the women to them: "Karulleira api nin apinawn" (Even from far away he picks [them up], they say they pick them up).

Women also have this type of seduction song which they sing, certain that a man will be attracted and desire them: "Chi karira munakpi *canta*kpi kari *enamo*ran kallarin, nin" (When she wants that man when she sings, the man begins to fall in love with her, they say). But it must be this special song, not just any kind of song: "Warmi yanga *kanto*yga yanga *kanta*kpika mana piwas *enamo*rawn" (If a woman sings any old song, when she sings it, no one will fall in love with her).

## The Water Domain: The Symbolism of Bathing

The bathing complex, essential to the song, is one of the favorite spots for engaging in sex. As explained by one singer, the place in a stream or river where the current hits the rocks is a highly regarded domain. Women who bathe in the early morning interact with this foam in the river, for it gives spiritual and physical force/strength: "Chibi shayarisha sambayan tiyawn *urza*ra apinga." This implicit connotation, which cannot be entirely recovered with direct exegesis by the natives, is also found in the myths about the *yaku runa*, the men of the water domain, who are at the same time anacondas and beings with human shapes. These beings reside in the large whirlpools of the rivers (*molino*). In one myth from the lowlands, the boas are said to capture human beings there and live with them forever (Ortiz de Villalba 1976: 90–91).

The bubbles and the foam of the river partake of this sexual meaning, as we saw in the song. There are several studies which argue that foam is a pan-Andean symbol of sexual power. Water which flows through irrigation canals is given an interpretation as a masculine force of fertilization by Billie Jean Isbell (1978: 143). Also, Urton's analysis of *pusuqu* (foam) is revelant for an understanding of the dynamics of seduction. According to his analysis of the Milky Way, the "foam" of the bright stellar clouds in the southern area of the sky results from a collision of two celestial rivers (Urton 1981: 59). This foam (*pusuqu*) is seen as the place of the "union" of the rivers; Viracocha (sea foam), the deity, may represent "the synthesis of opposing motions or objects in the sky and on earth" (ibid.: 204).

For these reasons this ecological area where earth and water forces conjoin (water currents hitting rocks) is seen as a special place. The act of water hitting rocks and splashing has a particular verb, *lluspin* (González Holguín [1608] 1952: 219), which, we may remember, is the verb used to describe the act of escaping or loosening bonds (Lira 1944: 602). In a vivid description of the bathing imagery, the foam is said to "loosen" a woman's bonds (to her lover) so that another desirous lover may have sexual access to the woman: "Yaku puskuyga chimi *enamora*shka *enamora*kpi armanga, nin. Kuti kuti *enamora*nga yaku puskuy armarisha. Puskuwa lluspirin nin paywa *ena*mora*sha simayuka puskuy" (In the river's foam here he wooed her. When he makes love to her she will [want to] bathe, they say. Again and again he/she/they make love, bathing with the foam of the river. With this foam, she is "loosened," they say. Making love with him with *simayuka* and in the foam of the river).

The "unfastening" or "unloosening" may refer to the process of having part of one's identity wander off with a spirit being. Women often refer to a *duyñu* (a spiritual "master") who has power over them and makes them crazy (*loca*) to have sexual intercourse. This "loosening" also may refer to the conception of a child, fathered by the spirit with whom she has intercourse. This child, a *supay wawa*, is an imperfect baby with lots of hair, a cleft pallet, and web feet. When the *runa* woman consents to liaisons with the water spirits, she may not be able to conceive her own (human) children. This is the inference of one man's enraged accusation and the resultant interrogation of his wife: "Kan supay karira tiyashami nin." (Are you with a spirit "master"? he said). Her answer was a firm "No, I don't have one," yet her husband had seen a spirit he thought was her lover in a vision after he took *wanduk*. She took *wanduk* herself "because [she] didn't know for sure" ("mana yachakani"); her spirit lover did not appear ("mana rikurik") in a *wanduk* vision, so that she was convinced that she did not have a lover. Her husband's anger and suspicions were aroused because she had recently experienced the death of her first child. Since women commonly refer to "finding" a certain number of children inside their bodies, usually twelve, if one of these children becomes a *supay wawa* as a result of a liaison with a spirit then she will give birth to fewer human children.

## The Primacy of "Seeing": Andean Realities

Although the verb *rikuna* (to see) is not mentioned in this song, sensorial, visual impressions are the basis for the generation of song texts. Songs are visual impressions of a tropical forest environment where associations create a narrative of personal meaning and serve to organize experience. Visual imagery, as we have seen in previous chapters, is a primary domain of Quechua existence. As we saw in the lengthy poem recited by Manco Capac, seeing and experiencing the presence of the divine being are paramount. This presence did not imply necessarily that the actual physical being of the god(s) become manifest. As we observed in chapter 4, the understanding of the wishes and the future actions of the god(s) might be discerned by seeing specific objects as signs—the entrails of sacrificed animals, the direction in which saliva dripped off fingers, the lay of the coca leaves as they fell in a pattern. A specific meaning could then be extracted from a complex and intricate web of significance and thus a person could expect to understand and know the outcome of an event. The reading of signs transcended ritual events which involved the elite trained for such purposes; the common populace was trained to interpret family matters in their dreams and in their visions as part of daily existence.

Perception also contributed to Andean spatial mapping and categorization. The empire was divided into four distinct regions and local topological direction was oriented to a larger scheme of the entire territory. In the cosmology, domains of significance were described using visual signs. In the case of Santacruz Pachacuti Yamqui's drawing of the temple of Coricancha, the information drawn is greater than that conveyed in the European system of a written narrative text.

Seeing, in its specific literal sense and as a broader semantic referent, is accorded special status in a number of contemporary Quichua songs of the lowlands. One segment of an autobiographical song from the tropical forest is nonsensical when first reading the phrase "aychataska rikusha mikusha purik warmi mani" (I am a woman who's seen, who's eaten [Andean] fish, who has been all over). The parallelism of the placement of "seeing" and "eating" is semantically significant, as we also saw in our discussion of the coupling of *purina* and *tiyana* previously. *Rikusha mikusha* (seeing, eating) coupled reveals an approach to the very nature of existence where sight provides the first confrontation with experience, and the act of eating the heretofore unknown fish from highland lakes enriches the singer's understanding of the world. In fact, she incorporates this new world within her, nurturing her existence. Again, while *purina* may be glossed narrowly as "travel," here the reference is to someone who has lived a rich life, full of many experiences. She has not merely been told what the world is like; instead, she accompanied her husband on foot and has firsthand knowledge of the Andean area.

This same singer, in another song, emphasizes the contrast inherent in the verb form *rikuna* (to see) and *rikurimuna* (to appear). In singing of another trip to Tungurahua Mountain in the highlands, she notes how green it appeared as she looked at it: "virdilla rikurimushka." This verb often is used in contexts of fleeting visions, when the human subject has no controlling mechanism to influence the circumstances. Thus stars coming out at night would be described with this verb, as would physical appearances of human, plant, and animal forms. On the other hand, in González Holguín's seventeenth-century dictionary *ricurimuni* is glossed as "aparecer vision" (when a vision appears) ([1608] 1952: 317). This form in the Peruvian dialect includes an inceptive *ri* which communicates an act in which the subject takes the initiative in carrying out the action (Cusihuamán 1976: 210). Thus *ri* paired with the directional *mu* brings, in this case, the color green revealing itself to the viewer. The passive stance of the seer in this act contrasts markedly with subsequent lines in the same song where the singer describes actively looking at a lake on top of a mountain, bending over to peer down into the water: "Rumi pundamanda kumarisha rikuk warmi mani" (From the top of a boulder, bending over, I am a woman who has seen).

The distinction in the two verb forms does not ascribe greater reality to one over the other. Although González Holguín conveys the "unreality" of this seeing with a gloss containing the semantically loaded *visiones*, in actuality the Quechua speakers do not discriminate in categories of the "real" as opposed to "visions." It is true that syntactically there is acknowledgment of actually being present at an event instead of merely hearing secondhand about it in the use of the verb ending *ska* to denote the latter concept. However, what we nonindigenous people would call "visions" have the force of reality and are described in those terms by Quechua speakers.

The singers are aware, however, that *wanduk* provides an alternate method of "seeing": "Without drinking *wanduk* nothing appears. With it every kind of thing appears, everything shows up." This kind of seeing often includes another soul or spirit being: "When we drink *wanduk* we change into something else and we can see everything. We begin to become like the spirit forces. We don't see with our Christian souls [*yaya dios alma*] but we change into our other spirit souls. Then we see everything." The purpose of this "seeing" is to know, to enlarge one's understanding. Without taking the *wanduk*, this profound seeing is not possible, as is evident in this phrase, "Mana yacharin mana rikurin" (Nothing is fully understood, nothing appears).

When the singer is taught the words of the song in special occasions of drinking *wanduk*, this song shares in the special aura of "seeing" where a person experiences "total knowledge." Signs are revealed in a complete meaning system which allows the seeker of "true seeing" to integrate problematic aspects of life within the focus of the one illustrative scene. The song itself, because of the symbolic layering of images and its transmission by a spirit woman, is an act of metacommunication which defies definition in terms of this world. The words of bathing with *simayuka* become a type of *simayuka* themselves, with a power to draw loved ones back to her. Paralleling the experiencing of knowledge in the vision, the singing of the words reconstructs that all-knowing moment for the singer.

The song itself serves as a vehicle for the transmission of the knowledge through "seeing" its imagery and "hearing" its message. We remember that Sisa specifically dedicated her song to her children with the words "you will have it, lovingly saddened, seeing." In this statement she alludes to a heightened emotion as the children will remember their deceased mother's love for them and they also re-experience the nature of her knowledge, her seeing. Also, by inference of the verb *charina* (to have), they will "possess" her through the lyrics of the song and "see" her in the unfolding of the images.

The nature of memory, the vast domain of seeing, and the stark reality of visions operate to endow communication through song with a privileged function in the society. By means of song, a specialized kind of "thinking," sentiments of love and desire are communicated to a distant receptor. Contemplation, a gathering of forces, is necessary to begin the process: "Iyarisha iyarikpi rikusha *kwinta* iyachin" (Thinking, when you think, just like seeing you are caused to think [of it]). This "thinking" is generated by what one has seen, which is conjured up again to form the dominant imagery of the song: "Rikushkamanda tiyarishka iyarina *mas* yalli rikunga" (You will see better [clearer] in thoughts contemplated, gathered up from what you have seen).

When the seeing of the *wanduk* vision is combined with what is known (or seen) of the intended recipient, then communication to far distant recesses is possible:

Kantakpi shinalleira kariuna uyarinawn *duyño* warmira. Maybi tiyawshas *duyño* warmi yapa iyarin mana karuman purinawn. Uyarin. Mayta tarabana maytas maytas mana cungarin. Chiraygu iyarishkamanda *kantanawn*.

When you sing, in that moment, just like that, the men hear their "real" wife. Wherever they are, they will think a lot about their "real" wife. They won't go far away. They will hear. Wherever they might be working, wherever, wherever [they are] they won't forget. For that reason, women sing about what they have thought [seen] before.

Thus, wherever the men are, they will come back to their "real" wife through the lyric force of the song and the images that are sent.

The song itself is a type of *simayuka* with a metacommunicative function. The words sung by the snake-women serve to bewitch (*upallachina*) the human males with whom they want to make love: "Paygunaga shuk runara *enamora*sha shinalleira *kantan*chi, nin . . . upallachin, nin" (The spirit women when they want to seduce a human male, "we sing just like this," they say . . . "it bewitches [him]," they say). The words, the conveying of the images, are not to be sung in vain. The one woman who is taught the song is empowered to use the words; in the vision she was specifically instructed not to explain the song. Although she may sing the words, she is not supposed to say them or explicate them, as in a long narrative discourse:

"Ama rimangi. Ama *kwintangi*" (Don't say [these words]. Don't tell a story [about this song]). Furthermore, the snake-woman instructed her not to reveal the prohibitions of fasting, not using salt (*sasimi*), and the actual meaning of the words (*shimi*): "Mana kasnay *kwintasha kwinta kantakani ñukalleira*" (Not like this, like telling a detailed story, did I myself ever sing it myself). The learning of the song and the knowledge that it contains confers responsibility on the part of the singer to not be careless with it, for fear of harming others who cannot accept its knowledge.

### *Paktamuna/Shayana:* Presence as Prescience

The power of the thoughts and the words of the song serve to draw back to the singer the person to whom she sings. Often women use the metaphor of fishing with a fishing line, an infrequent method of catching fish in the tropical forest, to describe how a person may be lured back into their power, *anzelushka* (caught on a fishhook). Some refer to song as *simayuka*, ascribing to its lyrics and melody a force of the magical charm which is used to track and pursue game: "Iyarishkami simayuka *kwinta* simayuka aysashka *kantanmi*" (In thinking just like *simayuka*, like *simayuka* pulls an animal in, [they] sing).

It is in regard to this model that the verb *paktamuna* deserves more attention. In a standard gloss common in the tropical forests of Ecuador *paktamuna* means "to arrive"; however, in actual discourse "ña shamun" (he/she is arriving) is more commonly used to indicate the arrival of a person. In the song, the verb recovers some of its more traditional semantic base of equilibrium and balance, as was discussed for the adjective *pactay pactaylla*, "dos cosas iguales parejas" (two equal things) (González Holguín [1608] 1952: 273). In Bolivia, contemporary usage still acknowledges orientation toward balance, of adjustment to create equality, to level off (Lira 1944: 727). We already have seen a variant of this meaning in the songs of the tropical forest in the phrase "mana piwas paktanga" (no one will equal [me]), where the singer boasts that no other woman works as hard as she (the singer) does in her garden plot (chapter 5).

Also, in describing the attributes of a strong wind, Sisa uses *paktamuna* in one more sense which ties it closely to what we would call visionary experiences: "When wind, rain, lots of rain come, trees *kuk-kuk-kuy* [sound], the shamans cause us to dream. Just like that, they come here [*shinay paktamunawn*] and they cause good dreams." So here the arrival is of a different nature than a friend showing up for a visit. In the domain of singing, considering that the song itself is a *simayuka* love device, the one sought after is compelled to arrive in this special manner.

In the highland Quichua dialect of Ecuador, in fact, the verb has a basic meaning of "something that fulfills a basic need and accomplishes a goal that one proposes" (Cordero [1892] 1967: 68). When *paktamuna* is coupled with the verb *shamuna*, it is easier for us to discern its special nature: "*duyño* kari shamusha paktamunga shayarisha iyarisha tiyana" (The "real" [keeper of my essence] man will come, will appear, perfectly ready for what is intended, standing, contemplating, existing). The *paktamunga* and the *shayarisha* described here in song argue for an interpretation of a coming into the presence, of the physical existence of the absent person. While the corporeality of the distant person may prove troublesome for those of us from a modern industrialized society, in the understanding of Quichua speakers this "coming into physical existence," summoned forth by the magic of song, is part of tropical forest reality.[7]

Once again, we turn to González Holguín's definition of the root *sayay* (in Ecuadoran dialects *shayay*) because he explains the physical-spiritual dimensions. Glossed as *estatura* (stature) in many instances, it also can mean the presence of a person, "la presencia personal" (González Holguín [1608] 1952: 325). And, as an outgrowth of the previous situation, *sayay* means "quando aparece en cuerpo visible" (when it appears in a body [one can] see) (ibid.: 627). The flesh-and-bone nature of this appearance is more apparent in the entire passage, which attempts to elucidate the spiritual nature of God and the angels:

> . . . ni ay Diospa sayanin, que no hay en Dios sayay, que es estatura, sino en Christo solo por ser hombre, y en el angel no ay sayanin, sino es quando aparece en cuerpo visible. (Ibid.: 627)

> . . . nor is there presence in God, God does not have *sayay* [bodily presence], which is stature, only Christ because he is a human, neither do angels have *sayay*, except when they appear in human [bodily] form.

For the tropical forest peoples of Ecuador, this explanation might cause some difficulty. As is illustrated by the *ukumbi* snake symbol in the song, things are not always what they appear to be. The harmless *ukumbi* snake is also the fearful water boa, and the boa itself can be a foreign-looking woman with long black hair. Whatever the changing form, it still must be stressed that there is a definite corporeal shape which makes itself known to the singer. The *shayana-*

*paktamuna* concept may well serve to delineate the change from one bodily presence to another. In the Quni Raya myth from Huarochirí (chapter 4), the ragged old beggar who fathered the royal woman's child changed to another form when she ran away in disgust. The Quechua transcription includes the verb *sayarca* in this instance to indicate that when he stood up he transformed himself and was dressed in a shining golden tunic: *"Pachactapas hillarichispa sayarca*, 'mientras hacía relucir su vestidura se paró'" ([His] clothing shining too, he stood [transformed]) (Urioste 1983: 8, 9).

Among the lowland Quichua of Ecuador, a being which "our" world considers a spirit, a vision, may have corporeal presence. Women speak of frightening instances of having sexual relations with boa-men and of bearing their children for them. The description of the act of seduction is done in the concrete imagery of everyday language. Sex is described, when I probed into this, as being "just like with humans, the same." But this erotic union which arouses our curiosity did not elicit a similar response among the singers when I asked, "Does your lover *really* come into your existence?" or "Do you have *real* sex?" or "Was it a man-lover, was it a snake-lover?" In the shifting realities of the tropical forest cosmology, a snake transforms itself into a woman and is also a snake-woman. More important than sexual ecstasy, the songs serve as an explanation of the "forms of life" in that culture.

While the song distills the erotic expression, the companion narrative pinpoints a larger philosophical domain. We see this in the speech of the snake-woman's question, "What in the world are you doing here?" *Yanga*, the evasive answer, "I'm just wandering around," prompts the snake-woman to question further: "Is there something you want to know?" The process of discovery is explored in the switch from singular to plural. "You-all think about it," her command to the singer, attests to Carpenter's (1980) research into the existence of two hearts—a physical center (heart) and a spiritual center (another heart). Self-reflection and interpretation reside in a holistic joining of the dual selves. With the snake-woman's commentary, the woman singer is assured that she will survive her greatest fear that her husband and her children will abandon her, forget her.

"Mana kungariwangi, mana kungariwangi" (Don't forget me), the singer cautions twice in the song. In this act, her own memory of learning the song serves to have others remember her as well. She remembers the song in relation to a specific life crisis, a severe bodily pain, the time she was abandoned by her spouse, a time when she was barren of children. Taking *wanduk*, she sees a vision of her entire life, the world inside and out, and meets up with a special person who befriends her and teaches her a song. The snake-woman, in this specific instance, inspires confidence that the crisis can be rectified, explains the nature of men who wander off and children who grow up. More than that, she reassures with the gift of song, destined for this one woman with this one purpose in mind.

Remembering, for this tropical forest singer, is recreating the visual stimulus which triggers the memory. The image of the snake-woman splashing, bathing, with her children grouped around her visually assures her of the continuity of familial affection. Each layer of the description—the *simayuka*, the foam of the river, deep pools—provides access to remembering and causing others to not forget, to also remember.

Identity is expanded and merged through song; the ambiguity of the person markers allows for a collapsing of rigid boundaries of definition of self, for the (human) woman singer becomes the (spirit snake) woman singer who empowers lover, son, and spirit lover to come into her presence. Time ceases to be measured in the usual categories, for past and present are held close in song. The song, translated accurately, is not a song of "Love Potion Number Nine," full of the ego-centeredness of Western thoughts, rational and scientific attempts to control and dominate one's surroundings. It is much more a song about alignment, of balancing male and female forces, of conjoining what we would call physical and spiritual constructs into one whole.

# 7. Potato as Cultural Metaphor: Acceptance of and Resistance to Difference

THE ANDEAN Indian, accompanied by several of his relatives, carefully mounds up sod around the tender potato plants in his field. The green plants, their sprouting tubers hidden underground, are uniformly spaced in neat rows. This apparent uniformity of the well-spaced plants belies a diversity, noticeable when the plants are uprooted at harvest time; one field may yield as many as forty-six named varieties of the common potato (Brush, Carney, and Huamán 1981: 80). Planting may appear to be random; as many as five small tubers are dropped in a single hole opened by a traditional footplow while at other times only one whole potato is placed in the earth. Actually, however, potatoes are carefully sorted and catalogued months before, during the harvest; the desired varieties are thrown in separate mounds and are stored as seed potatoes high in the rafters of the Andean dwelling.

A more detailed look at one field of potatoes both impresses and confuses us (Figure 27). Each symbol represents a native cultivar of potato which has been selected by the Andean Indian who owns the field. The choice is determined by numerous factors such as the taste and the texture, how well the potato keeps until it can be used, and its potential as a seed potato for next year's crop. The location of this field also is crucial in decisions, for certain lower-altitude cultivars cannot grow higher up. In addition, the family also mentally tracks how many years it is before this field will be fallow, for the potato depletes the soil in several years.

The Andean farmer who dictated the thirty-one names of potatoes depicted in the schema ticked off but a fraction of the four hundred gathered by J. G. Hawkes in 1947. While Hawkes admits that there is some duplication due to regional names used for specific varieties, the extensive list alludes to more than two thousand years (perhaps longer) that the plant has been domesticated in an Andean hearth.[1] The Quechua names for the native cultivars reveal the lore of the

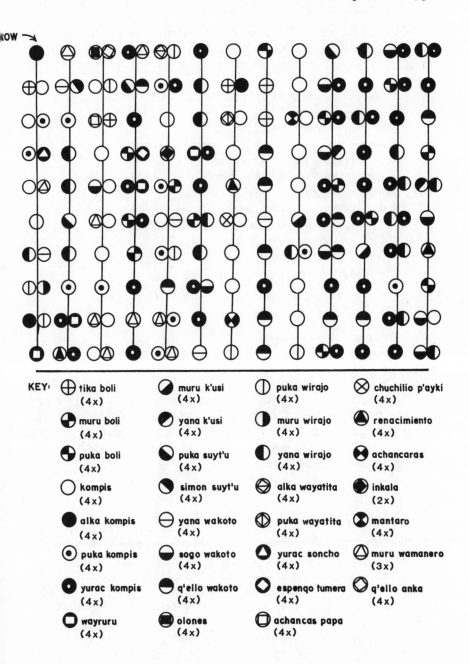

KEY:

| | | | |
|---|---|---|---|
| ⊕ tika boli (4x) | ◖ muru k'usi (4x) | ◑ puka wirajo (4x) | ⊗ chuchilio p'ayki (4x) |
| ⊕ muru boli (4x) | ◗ yana k'usi (4x) | ◐ muru wirajo (4x) | ▲ renacimiento (4x) |
| ⊕ puka boli (4x) | ◣ puka suyt'u (4x) | ◑ yana wirajo (4x) | ⊗ achancaras (4x) |
| ○ kompis (4x) | ◤ simon suyt'u (4x) | ⊖ alka wayatita (4x) | ◉ inkala (2x) |
| ● alka kompis (4x) | ⊖ yana wakoto (4x) | ⊕ puka wayatita (4x) | ⊗ mantaro (4x) |
| ⊙ puka kompis (4x) | ⊖ sogo wakoto (4x) | ◮ yurac soncho (4x) | △ muru wamanero (3x) |
| ● yurac kompis (4x) | ◓ q'ello wakoto (4x) | ○ espenqo tumera (4x) | ◎ q'ello anka (4x) |
| ◻ wayruru (4x) | ⬤ olones (4x) | ▢ achancas papa (4x) | |

*Figure 27.* Native varieties in a potato field, Peru. From Brush, Carney, and Huamán 1981 : 81 (Fig. 2), by permission of Stephen Brush.

Andean people who toil on the moist eastern slopes of the Andes or the high wind-swept *páramo* fields. Each name, as it is pronounced, releases a flood of images, for the wording is descriptive:

> *moro kohui sullu papa:* spotted guinea pig fetus potato
> (Hawkes 1947: 233)
> *kkara papa:* bitter potato (239)
> *yana puma maqui papa:* black puma's paw potato (233)
> *cuchillo paki papa:* the knife-breaker (236)
> *huira ppasña papa:* the fat woman potato (231)
> *runtu papa:* egg potato (232)
> *katari papa:* snake potato (232)
> *chunta papa:* hard wood palm potato (234)
> *ttanta papa:* bread potato (235)
> *aya papa:* ancestor potato (231)
> *chaucha papa:* early potato (242)
> *koyu papa:* potatoes left in the earth at the time of harvest
> (244)
> *kkehuillu:* twisted potato (238)
> *unu papa:* watery potato (239)
> *cachan huacachi papa:* the potato that makes the daughter-in-law cry (231)

The variety of the potato descriptions in both Quechua and Aymara attests to indigenous interest in this tuber as food in the central Andes. In the listing, Andean agriculturalists confirm a tradition of cultivation of this subsistence crop, which often is served for the two Andean meals, breakfast and dinner.[2]

## Potato as Sign

In thinking about the potato, John Murra, in his well-known study "Rite and Crop in the Inca State" (1960), has us perceive the framing devices which shape both European and Amerindian conceptions of cultural categories. He begins with a look at the potato in the six-teenth century, and he cautions us about relying entirely on what we find written in the chronicles and the official reports mailed to Spain; the constant mention of maize and its rituals and the relative silence regarding the potato come about through a selective memory on the part of the Spanish which is influenced by Amerindian atti-tudes regarding both foods. Although Andean peoples relied heavily upon tubers as a staple foodstuff, we have little reference to the po-tato in connection with rituals and ceremonies in the writings of the colonial period. Indigenous peoples in the Incaic territory seemed to prize corn more; corn was the item frequently offered in rituals, corn was the high-status food, and corn was valued because of its superior storage qualities. Much more care was devoted to the growing of corn, which demanded elaborate irrigation systems, terraces, and fertilizer to grow in the protected areas of the Andean terrain (ibid.: 398–407).

The drawings included in the *Nueva corónica* by the Amerindian writer Guaman Poma may indicate a value system at work in the Incaic Empire.[3] The drawings illustrating the ritual and agricultural cycles during one year rarely depict the potato plant (June, December), whereas corn is drawn sprouting and being irrigated, weeded, and watched over (January, March, April, May, September, October, November) (Figure 28). In February, Guaman Poma draws two potato plants crowded into the lefthand corner of the picture, whereas eight plants of corn fill the remainder of the visual space.

Although Guaman Poma rarely illustrates potatoes, he frequently mentions them in the titles of the black and white drawings. He writes, "Zara papa hallmai mita" (Time to mound up earth around the corn and potatoes) in bold letters in his drawing for January, but in fact corn is the only crop illustrated (Guaman Poma [1615] 1980: 1029). In addition, the specific vocabulary naming types of potatoes is entered in his text, although again, more attention is paid to names of corn. Guaman Poma reflects the ideology of the potato as food for every day, for the masses, and not as a special, privileged food such as corn. The devalued status of the potato also is evident in the myths of the Quechua peoples; Murra (1960: 397) calls attention to the figure of Huatyacurí, who is specifically called a "potato eater" in the Quechua narratives of Huarochirí. He is dressed in rags, like a beggar, which indicates his low class position in the society; thus, he eats only potatoes.

The Spaniards who invaded the Americas, battle weary and hungry, often ate the potatoes that they found when they searched the houses of the conquered peoples. The writings about the potato are often positive descriptions; Cieza de León writes one of the earliest descriptions of the potato (1538), comparing it favorably to a tender, cooked chestnut (Salaman [1949] 1985: 102). Many accounts give ample evidence that the new food was eaten by the Spanish, who also treated it like a "truffle" of European origin, valued as a new kind of bread. By the early seventeenth century, Vázquez de Espinosa describes how the potato "is becoming the food of the Spanish no less than of the native" in the diocese of Quito (ibid.: 103).

Chapter 3 of Bernabé Cobo's *Historia del Nuevo Mundo* (History

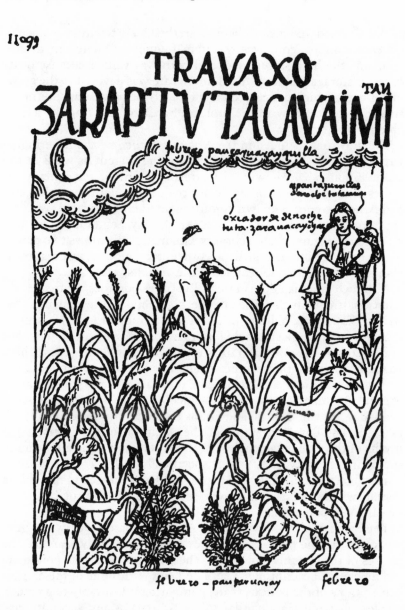

*Figure 28. Travaxo zarap tuta cavai mitan* ("Time to stand watch over the corn all night"). From Guaman Poma [1615] 1980:1032, by permission of Siglo XXI Editores, S.A.

of the New World) ([1653] 1964) describes the appearance of the potato, its ecological niche, as well as the techniques of planting, harvesting, and processing this New World food. He comments on its taste: ". . . son de buen sabor, aunque destas hay una especie que llaman *luqui*, algo amargas, pero buenas para el chuñu" (. . . they have a good taste, although one species of potato that they call *luqui* [is] somewhat bitter, but good for *chuñu*) (ibid.: 168). His description adequately defines the plant but is singularly distant and unemotional when compared to his enthusiastic prose recounting the taste of corn:

> En una ocasión en un pueblo de indios deste reino nos faltó el pan, mandó el cura a las indias que nos hiciesen tortillas de maíz como las solían hacer antiguamente para sus caciques, y hiciéronlas tan regaladas y sabrosas, que parecían fruta de sartén, porque amasaron la harina de *maíz* con huevos y manteca. (Ibid: 161)

> One time while we were in an Indian village there was no bread and the priest told some Indian women to make us some corn tortillas like those that they used to make for the caciques, and they made them so rich and tasty that they were like fruits in the frying pan because they had mixed in eggs and fat with the dough.

Corn is fervently compared to European wheat, God's gift to the Europeans; in fact, Cobo tells us that the two were closely identified in their very nomenclature. Corn was called "trigo de las Indias" (wheat of the Indies) (ibid.: 159) on the Continent. No such comparison is made for the potato; Cobo gives the impression that it is not consumed by Spaniards except as a cure for indigestion (ibid.: 169).

There are other accounts of Spanish resistance to including the potato in their diet. It is said that even when Valdivia's forces were starving during the conquest of Chile and daily measured out a ration of "a few score grains for each man," no one chose to eat potatoes, abundant in the lands. Valdivia, after the smoke of battle cleared away, wrote that he planted corn alongside fields of Old World wheat to feed his men, but he makes no mention of potatoes in a letter to Charles V dated 1551 (Salaman [1949] 1985: 69). As Sauer has noted, "Spanish colonists in the New World did not take readily to native foods if they could provide themselves with the familiar Spanish food items" ([1952] 1975: 152).

The fate of the potato in Europe reflects a similar acceptance and resistance by those people who never ventured overseas. Although one source shows that potatoes were purchased by the Hospital de la Sangre in Sevilla in 1573 (Salaman [1949] 1985: 143), in general there was little mention of its dietary virtues until the eighteenth century. The aversion to the potato stems from its characters: it grew beneath the ground, it was the first edible plant to not be grown from seeds, and it was the first plant to have white or flesh-colored nodules on its underground stems (ibid.: 112). As tubers, potatoes were not highly valued for food. Current wisdom was reflected in the belief that humans are conditioned by what they eat: "Those who eat only the food of savages, the roots, nuts, berries, that which the earth produces, will be like savages" (Pagden 1982: 177). Eating of this food, even to insure survival, was an act of self-defilement, according to values commonly held at the time of the Conquest.[4]

The early botanists recognized that the potato should be included in the nightshade family, Solanaceae, which includes plants such as bitter-sweet, tobacco, jimson weed, belladonna, eggplant, and the tomato. The characteristic flowers of these plants were noted by the herbalists of the sixteenth century, who also identified their poisonous and narcotic properties. However, this same categorization, the Doctrine of Signatures, which identified plants, also prevented the widespread cultivation of the potato. The Doctrine of Signatures, written into the books of the early herbalists, describes the "virtuous properties of plants." This system of classification functions as a belief system of sympathetic magic, the principle that like cures like, so that herbs with yellow sap might cure a "yellow" disease (jaundice). In this system, humans were able to read the healing properties of the plants from their outward appearance: juice of the red beet is good for anemic women, a walnut could strengthen the brain, the apple would improve complexion, and thistles would relieve a stitch in the side (MacPherson 1982: 191–210).

Crops which grow underground are classified as aphrodisiacs in accordance with the Doctrine of Signatures. The meaning of this sign may have come from the Chinese belief that ginseng root was a cure for impotence; it was accepted that another root, the mandrake plant, cured sterility. In the case of the potato, another plant which grew underground, the deeply gnarled skin and shape were easily compared to testicles; the early accounts of the Spanish encountering the new food specifically state "testicles of the earth" (Salaman [1949] 1985: 129). The early herbalists further disseminated this belief in the "lusty" attributes of the potato, although they frequently confused the sweet potato with the white or Peruvian potato. Gaspard Bauhin writes in *The Prodomus* of 1619 that "[people] eat them for exciting Venus, increasing semen" (cited in Salaman

[1949] 1985: 104), and Shakespeare, in *Troilus and Cressida* mentions "the devil luxury, with his fat rump and potato-finger, tickles these together! Fry, lechery, fry!" (cited in ibid.: 425). Although the potato was sought as an aphrodisiac, these beliefs hampered the potato's acceptance as a regular part of the diet. Finally, in the middle of the seventeenth century, its potential as food for the European masses was realized. The Spanish, the first to encounter the potato, sadly were among the last to recognize its nutritional importance (Laufer 1938: 24).

## Classifying Potatoes: Leaf, Tuber, Protein Band, or Texture and Taste

The methodology of the Doctrine of Signatures flourished, disseminating the "virtues and vices" of many different plants in the herbal books of the seventeenth century. Descriptive passages of a plant's botanical characters often were accompanied by illustrations of the flowers, the stem, and the roots. John Gerard, dressed in a ruffled collar of the sixteenth century, holds a potato flower and leaf in a wood cut illustrating his *Herball* ([1597, 1636] 1927). Although he gives the potato importance by holding it in his hand, his accuracy of description can be questioned. In his frontispiece portrait he holds a potato flower with a six-lobed corolla instead of the characteristic five-lobed variety. Furthermore, in his woodcut describing the plant within his book, he does not correctly distinguish the fibrous root structures from the stolons, the underground stems, which bear the potato (Salaman [1949] 1985: 84).

The early depictions in the herbals exhibit a growing European interest in cataloguing variance among plants in a logical, well-ordered system which would eventually lead to the creation of the Linnaean binomial taxonomy in the eighteenth century. Currently, potatoes are classified in the genus *Solanum*, which includes 154 wild tuber-bearing species (Brush, Carney, and Huamán 1981: 72). For the cultivated potato (*Solanum tuberosum*) there are presently three taxonomic systems at work: one used by the Russians, another devised by Dodds, and one more classification by Hawkes. Thus, the number of cultivated species differs considerably from one (Dodds) to as many as twenty (Ugent 1970: 1162). One reason for the discrepancy in systematizing is that, for the cultivated species, it is difficult to perceive distinctions based solely on plant morphology.

To better understand the intricacies of classification, we will look at the triploid cultivated potato *Solanum × chaucha* Juz. et Buk, for scientific botanical classification of this triploid has not been simple in the twentieth century. Triploids are not morphologically distinguishable from tetraploids and diploids, although Hawkes in 1963 claimed that triploids possessed corolla lobes three times broader than others. Russian scientists, following another taxonomic system in 1939, gave taxonomic rank to each minor variant, even though the diagnostic characters used for differentiation were not significant (Jackson, Hawkes, and Rowe 1977: 775–776).

A more recent study by Jackson, Hawkes, and Rowe (1977) attempts to produce a more definitive classificatory system. In a study of twenty triploids, metrical characters usually indicative for the Linnaean system overlapped considerably and made it impossible to differentiate cultivars from these characteristics. Variation in leaflet length/breadth ratios was not great, there was variability in the number of pairs of lateral and interjected leaflets, and none of the floral metrical characters was diagnostic (ibid.: 777–779).

Tuber characters, however, did yield better results. Scientific analysis of the tuber differentiated twenty triploid morphotype potatoes, which are stored in the collection of the International Potato Center in Peru. After listing of the morphotype tuber characters (shape, skin, eyes, sprout, flesh, and pigmentation), the potatoes were analyzed for protein spectra by extracting the sap of the potato, centrifuging it, and then electrophoretically separating the proteins. The resultant bands were then drawn up. In all cases, there were electrophoretic patterns which agreed with morphotype (or tuber) differentiation. The value of protein as a diagnostic tool is argued by Jackson, Hawkes, and Rowe (1977) because, derived directly from DNA, it is representative of genetic identity. However, they caution that it is unwise to base a taxonomic system of triploid cultivars solely upon protein characters. As a supplemental aspect of taxonomic classification, it is only an aid to be used with a taxonomy based on tuber characters: "The value of protein data from electrophoresis lies in the additional taxonomic information which they provide. It would be unwise to erect a system of classification of triploid cultivars based solely on protein characters" (ibid.: 781). Thus, through modern technology, a possible classification system is created which helps to distinguish the different cultivars for triploid potatoes.

The struggle to classify the potato in the twentieth century illustrates a scientific approach based on modern techniques of the centrifuge and microscopes to verify the reality of the many kinds of potatoes. However, although the names of hundreds of potato cultivars had been collected in the Andes, scientists paid scant attention to the Aymara and Quechua nomenclature. The origins of the potato

were obscured as it was relabeled and named for the scientist work-
ing on the analysis or, in the case of the hybrids, named for the site
where it was grown ("State of Maine potato," "Rural New Yorker,"
"Irish Cobbler," "Canadian Purple") (Jabs 1984: 40–41). Recently,
awareness of worldwide dependence on this tuber has led a few sci-
entists back into the potato patch to observe the agricultural pat-
terns and method of selection which the Andean Indian has prac-
ticed for centuries.

One fruitful area of study emerges in a discussion of Amerindian
nomenclature for the potato. Hawkes (1947), after enumerating all
the names, attempted to group them in some order to better under-
stand their meaning. He subdivided them in categories of nouns
(names of human groups, animals, body parts, clothes, plants, tools,
natural phenomena, miscellaneous), as well as adjectives (color,
shape, surface taste, miscellaneous) and classes of potatoes (early,
late, rapidly maturing) (ibid.: 227). His hierarchies only demonstrate
ethnocentric ways of thinking about things, showing us his value
system and our own while he attempts to have us understand the
other categories of Andean peoples.

Weston La Barre's study of Aymara potato names recognizes a
basic dichotomy, stated by the Indians, of *lukki* (bitter, used for
*chuñu*) and *chchoqhe* (potato ready to eat after cooking) (1947: 87).
It turns out that he orients us toward a valid autochthonous classi-
ficatory system which remains a goal for ethnobotanical research to-
day. Stephen Brush's (1980) work with the International Potato Cen-
ter finds a four-level taxonomy described by the natives: folk genus,
species, variety, and subvariety. The species are subdivided accord-
ing to four criteria: "a) cultivation, b) edibility, c) processing, and d)
frost resistance" (ibid.: 41).[5] Thus, for example, the cultivated table
potato, which is steamed, is categorized differently from the bitter
potato, which, when processed, becomes *chuñu*. Furthermore, on
the basis of tuber characters, two of the species contain varieties
which may be characterized by meal color, tuber shape, meal consis-
tency, skin color, and the type of "eye" (ibid.). The naming system
of Andean farmers and chemotaxonomy (based on electrophoresis)
were remarkably consistent: "Like-named tubers from the same
locality were judged to be visually similar and electrophoretically
identical at a fairly high degree (81.2% and 75.8% respectively)"
(ibid.: 44).

Thus, Brush argues for the value of the native powers of classifica-
tion which allow Andean villagers to classify, select, and create ge-
netically diverse potatoes. Inter- and intraploidy hybridization of po-
tatoes is specifically brought about by Andean planting practices,

which appear random but, in fact, are not: "Our research indicates
. . . that selection and distribution of native potato varieties is far
more complex than the random planting of numerous varieties. The
maintenance of these numerous varieties is neither casual or ran-
dom. A regular system of nomenclature, organized in a taxonomic
manner, accompanies this cultivation. Specific cultivars are identi-
fied according to an implicit set of criteria involving tuber and some-
times other characteristics" (Brush, Carney, and Huamán 1981: 85).
Among these "other" are culinary characteristics but also adapta-
tion to local conditions (ibid.). Varietal heterogeneity in the native
fields allows for continued evolution of the potato crop: "The crop
evolution of the cultivated potato is closely linked to the mixture of
species and genotypes which promotes hybridization and crossing
between ploidy levels and among clones" (ibid.: 80). Moreover, the
high variability often increases disease resistance, as different varie-
ties will have different degrees of susceptibility to a fungal pathogen
(Jackson, Hawkes, and Rowe 1980: 107). An entire field will not rot
and die, then, depriving a family of food until the next harvest. Jack-
son's study, like that of Brush, concludes with an appeal for cultural
tolerance: "Undoubtedly, the Indian farmers practice a type of selec-
tion which is related to our own plant breeding work, and there is
probably much that we can learn from the potato farmers of the
Andes" (ibid.: 113).

The potato blight (*Phytophthora infestans*) withered the leaves
and rotted the tubers of the crops in Ireland in 1845, 1846, and 1848
(Slicher Van Bath 1966: 270). The widespread famine produced by
the crop failure led to mass immigration to North America in those
years. The introduction of new genes, resistant to the blight, came
from a wild potato in Chile which was crossed with domestic varie-
ties. In Ireland, farmers depended on a few varieties of potatoes to
feed their families; when the fungus struck the crop, whole fields of
potatoes lay wasted from disease. The method of planting in the
Andes avoids this dependence on only a few varieties.[6] We saw in
the quadrat of the field the numerous varieties mixed in together
to allow survival of some cultivars if others fall victim to disease
(Figure 27).

Instead of promoting a wide range of choice of cultivars, our West-
ern society has cultivated a few specialized potato varieties to pro-
vide greater yield in a mechanized environment. Our choices, ra-
tional ones no doubt, organize the reality of our environment in one
direction, while the Andean example provides an alternative model
for rational choice. It is no accident that forty-odd specific cultivars
of potatoes persist in the Andean fields; the native Amerindians

choose to remember these ancient patterns and escape a total reorganization of their life in the trauma of Conquest.

Wendell Berry assures us that it is fortunate that the Andean farmers persist in their old ways of doing things:

> The prime characteristic of the native, pre-Spanish agriculture
> was its concentration in each individual plant, which accounts
> in large part for the great varietal diversity of the native crops.
> The Spanish agriculture, by contrast, focused not on the indi-
> vidual plant but on the field. It is the difference, still observ-
> able in the present practice of the farmers, between the hoe and
> the plow, between the potato field and the wheat field. (1981: 26)

Berry's trip to the Andes to observe small-scale farming ("agriculture of extraordinary craftsmanship and ecological intelligence") led him quite naturally to question our own agricultural values. He compared "our" way to "theirs":

> Whereas our agriculture is focused almost exclusively on short-
> term production, the traditional Andean agriculture is focused
> on long-term maintenance of the sources of production. The
> themes of our agriculture are volume, speed, man-hour effi-
> ciency. The themes of Andean agriculture are frugality, care,
> security in diversity, ecological sensibility, correctness of scale.
> (Ibid.: 41)

The care with which the Andean Indian has tended the potato over the centuries is testimony to the value of alternate systems of beliefs and practices which may serve to sustain the human population. Scientists are beginning to appreciate a Quechua system of classification of potatoes. The scientific procedure of the protein band system of scientific corroboration, a system highly valued because it is part of the literate, written tradition, now is enriched by equally careful scientific inquiry into the complex judgment about potato propagation made every season by the (often) illiterate descendants of the Incas.

A willingness on the part of Western scientists and nutritionists to look into the properties of *chuñu* in the Andes led to the modern techniques of foodstuff dehydration and gave us food to feed soldiers in World War II; now, it yields food to feed astronauts. The principles of dehydration were long understood by Andean natives, who extracted water by frost-drying their potatoes. Bitter potatoes grown at high altitudes are spread out on the ground so that they will freeze during several nights and thaw during the daytime. This alternation of freezing and thawing causes tuber cells to separate, and the liquid inside is removed easily by trampling. After this process, the potatoes are again spread out to freeze one more night and then allowed to dry, spread out, for another ten to fifteen days (Mamani 1981: 240–241). These potatoes may be stored for years in their dried-out state; in times of drought or potato blight, they are thrown in a cooking pot to nourish the Andean families who planted them (Woolfe 1987: 144–148).

## Translation as a Critique of Western Classification Systems

Hawkes's attempt to categorize the potato names he collected led to a list which revealed more of his thought patterns than those of the Andean peoples who dictated the names to him. Amerindian systems of categorization—taste, ecological niche, tuber color, texture of the meal—are not easily comprehended by most Western researchers, who often see chaos instead of order and patterns. Our own way of perceiving the world can blind us to alternate visions and alternate technologies, for we extrapolate from categories with which we are familiar. Potato planting with a footplow in the Andes seems haphazard until we plot the potato patch and listen to Amerindians describe their own ways of making agricultural decisions.

Jorge Luis Borges leads us to this conclusion in his literary essay about "analytic languages" ("el idioma analítico"). In presenting us with a detailed proclamation from a faraway land, he provokes our laughter just as he challenges our own system of viewing the world:

> On those remote pages it is written that animals are divided
> into (a) those that belong to the Emperor, (b) embalmed ones,
> (c) those that are trained, (d) suckling pigs, (e) mermaids, (f) fabu-
> lous ones, (g) stray dogs, (h) those that are included in this
> classification, (i) those that tremble as if they were mad, (j) in-
> numerable ones, (k) those drawn with a very fine camel's hair
> brush, (l) others, (m) those that have just broken a flower vase,
> (n) those that resemble flies from a distance. (Borges 1974: 708,
> cited in Foucault [1966] 1973: xv)[7]

To best understand the reasoning leading to these divisions, we must separate out our sense of self to enter into a process which strips us of our usual feelings of dominance or superiority. Our logical expectations are suspended because item (*a*), "those that belong to the Emperor," is not followed by item (*b*), "those not belonging to the Emperor." Borges imbues his list with authority; items (*a*) through (*n*) come from a certain *Celestial Emporium of Benevolent Knowledge.* However, our tolerance for this grouping is built upon our enjoyment of the "incommensurate categories," the manner in which contradictions create havoc with our perspective.

In part, our ability to participate in the ironies of these categories depends upon our ability to read them, to return to a written line of mirthful juxtaposition. Are not mermaids (item *e*) fabulous (item *f*)? Or are mermaids (item *e*) animals like items (*d*) and (*g*)? Borges, in writing this list, questions the foundations of Linnaeus's *Systema naturae* (1758) and, ultimately, the very language of scientific discourse. Unable to discern an absolute truth, his postmodernist statement allows us to play with the possibility of knowing set in a framework of a purported manuscript of "benevolent" knowledge.

Whereas for Borges writing provides us with the final devaluation of forms of knowledge, for Walter J. Ong and Jack Goody it is a system which has led to cognitive leaps. The written word, says Ong, relieves the mind of the heavy burden of a "mnemonic load" (1982: 41) and allows access for consultation and further retrieval of material. As Ong suggests, an "utterance" is only remembered if it can be repeated, and oral "facts" are selected for their relevance to what is currently important in a particular society.

Jack Goody (1977) privileges the act of writing primarily for empowering our Western civilization with a device, the syllogism, upon which is based all logical and philosophical discourse. Written systems are essential in formalizing discourse and providing the basic unit of understanding, the syllogism: "The formalisation of propositions, abstracted from the flow of speech and given letters (or numbers) leads to the syllogism. Symbolic logic and algebra, let alone the calculus, are inconceivable without the prior existence of writing. . . . 'Traditional' societies are marked not so much by the absence of reflective thinking as by the absence of the proper tools for constructive rumination" (Goody 1977: 44).

Walter J. Ong, although appreciative of the features of oral societies, also selects the syllogism as the key to understanding forms of knowledge. In furthering his analysis, he cites the examples of A. R. Luria's work with illiterate peasants in the Soviet Union (1931–1932), quoting at length their reactions to formally syllogistic and inferential reasoning. He has us look at several syllogisms used by Luria in this work with the peasants: "Precious metals do not rust. Gold is a precious metal. Does it rust or not?" and "In the Far North, where there is snow, all bears are white. Novaya Zembla is in the Far North and there is always snow there. What color are the bears?"

(cited in Ong 1982: 52–53). These two syllogisms created a lot of difficulty for peasants who did not know the ground rules of academic discourse. They often answered, reshaping the syllogism and changing its abstract character: "They are all precious . . . gold is also precious . . . does it rust or not?" (Luria [1974] 1976: 104). More commonly, they preferred to not venture beyond domains of personal knowledge, as in the answer about white bears in the Far North: "I don't know; I've seen a black bear, I've never seen any others . . . Each locality has its own animals: if it's white, they will be white; if it's yellow, they will be yellow" (ibid.: 109).

On the basis of these answers, Ong concludes that these folk prefer a "person-to-person human lifeworld [rather] than . . . a world of pure abstractions" (1982: 53), where knowledge is inextricably bound to self-reference of social context, familiarity, and operational contexts. An alternate conclusion may be to question the ethnocentric privileging of the syllogism as an accepted model for measuring cognitive powers. "Our" measure of intelligence may not appeal to the logic of oral cultures, which can handle subtle forms of thought found in riddles and puzzles.

Stephen A. Tyler has us focus on the problem of abstract thought in other societies in his chapter devoted to "ordering functions" and vocabulary. He asks himself, not a peasant, the question, "Why is ivy a vine?" and he answers in words which are reminiscent of Luria's subjects: ". . . I do not know *why* an ivy is a vine, only that it is. Now most of our commonplace knowledge is like this; we know certain things go together, but we do not know why. If all cases of inclusion were attributional in our knowledge, we should know why things go together. Since we do not know why, our knowledge of the taxonomic relations of the words of our language is not analytic, even in its origin . . ." (Tyler 1978: 266). After Tyler's statement, we can read Luria's study with a good deal more questioning of our own patterns of analysis. We may even sympathize with this stubborn resistance to explain what a tree is as stated by a peasant in the U.S.S.R.:

> Interviewer:    "Try to explain to me what a tree is."
> Subject:        "Why should I? Everyone knows what a tree is,
>                 they don't need me telling them."
>                                         (Luria [1974] 1976: 86)

Comparison of "our" systems and "theirs" leads Tyler to see similarities, not differences, between technologized and oral societies: "Most biological systematics reflects the same kind of objective classification that we meet with among many primitives" (1978: 270). But as systems and theoretical knowledge grow, these systems are often pursued in themselves: "In a botanical key, for example, we cannot see a direct functional significance in the attributes for describing leaves as alternate or opposed, simple or compound. What does that have to do with the plant as a functionally interdependent system participating in other functionally interdependent systems?" (ibid.: 270). In fact, as we pursue more objective systems of classification, function takes a secondary role and we concentrate more on structuring an elegant analytic model, which is often removed from "the real world."

To eliminate a chaos of information about the world, some principles of classification are necessary. The most basic of these depends on visual images and verbal description, a form of nominalism which classifies experience, but a more complex and varied understanding is necessary to appreciate concepts which serve as a specific means of organizing our world. Therefore, as in the case of the syllogism, we arrive again at the starting point of the analyst and the relative truth of the categories established in one system. A listing of lexemes according to inclusion or distinctive features, therefore, is not of use unless one is aware of the principles for the organization and for the remembrance of the terms. It is of no benefit to gather a listing unless the arrangement of the schemata is apparent. In the case of the potato names gathered by Hawkes and La Barre, although we are amused by the descriptions of the names, we are at the same time confused in our attempts to organize them into meaningful patterns. Our grasp of the cognitive processes involved in the rational choices and selection of potatoes is in no way facilitated by the listing. Faced with the baffling listing of the potato nomenclature, our deductions sound suspiciously like the mutterings of the peasants when presented with a syllogism. Our (dis)organization in terms of color, animal names, or parts of the human body has something in common with the peasant's statements about "yellow bears" and "precious rusting."

Instead, the indigenous selection for Andean potatoes depends upon a multiform grid that includes analysis from many perspectives, as Brush has suggested. His study presents a means of representing this complex network in its broader conceptual framework of socioeconomic factors, cultivation practices, and farmer selection (Figure 29).

This entire complex of factors is implicit in the decisions made by Andean Indians in the planting of their fields. Without benefit of

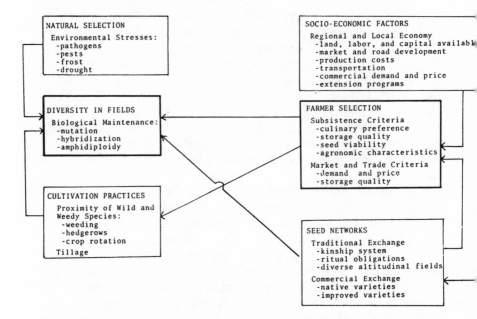

*Figure 29.* Chart: indigenous selection of Andean potatoes. From Brush, Carney, and Huamán 1981 : 85 (Fig. 4), by permission of Stephen Brush.

writing, the Amerindian domesticated the plant in its thousands of cultivars. Only recently have we come to understand the categories of choices for its growth; they are not "prelogical" or "magical belief systems." These agricultural practices have much to teach us about the utilization of our limited resources.

### The Poetry of Potatoes[8]

José María Arguedas, for most of his life, pronounced esthetically beautiful and meaningful the culturally specialized variants of language that he found in Quechua. For Arguedas, a non-Indian who nevertheless grew up speaking Quechua as his first language, no language could equal the emotive power of Quechua:[9]

> No encontré ninguna poesía que expresara mejor mis sentimientos que la poesía de las canciones quechuas. Los que hablamos este idioma sabemos que el kechwa supera al castellano en la expressión de algunos sentimientos que son las más característicos del corazón indigena: la ternura, el cariño, el amor a la naturaleza. (Arguedas 1938: 16)

I never found any poetry that could better express my feelings than the poetry of the Quechua songs. Those of us who speak this language are aware that Quechua is more expressive than Spanish in [conveying] feelings that are characteristic of the Quechua soul [heart]: tenderness, affection, and love of nature.

With the same fervor, Arguedas defended a Quechua way of life and knowledge of agriculture which differed in expression from scientific formulas and synthetic fertilizers. One of his poems written in Quechua highlights these contrasts between the Western conceptions of the world as opposed to those of the Quechua. Arguedas's "Huk Doctorkunaman Qayay" (A calling out to some doctors) celebrates the knowledge in the Andes accumulated over the centuries, while he also mentions the racial prejudice which the Andean Indian encounters:[10]

Manas imatapas yachaniñachu atrasus kayky; huk umawansi umaykuta kutichinqaku. (Dicen que ya no sabemos nada, que somos el atraso, que nos han de cambiar la cabeza por otra mejor.) (Arguedas 1973: 50–51)

They say that we don't know anything, that we are backwardness itself, that they will exchange our heads for better ones. (My translation of the Quechua)

Yet Arguedas builds a poetic argument for the value of Andean ways of knowing; he urges the scientists and learned doctors to adjust their telescopes, clean off their glasses, and look at the many varieties of Andean crops which flower and grow:

Pichqa pachak hukman papakunam waytachkan chay ñawikipa mana aypanan qori tuta, qollqi punchao allpapa. Chaymi ñutquy, chaymi sonqoy. (Quinientas flores de papas distintas crecen en los balcones de los abismos que tus ojos no alcanzan, sobre la tierra en que la noche y el oro, la plata y el día se mezclan. Esas quinientas flores son mis sesos, mi carne.) (Ibid.: 50, 51, 53)

Five hundred kinds of potatoes grow where your eyes don't reach, in the golden night, the silver day, of the land. That's where my brains are, that's where my heart is. (My translation of the Quechua)[11]

Arguedas's message bears repeating in academic circles today. Mauricio Mamani continues to remind us that the Andean Indians are specialists in their own manner and in their own right:

Los diferentes colores de flor indican las diferentes variadades de papa
y el agricultor serrano es el único especialista que reconoce cada una
de ellas y puede explicarnos las características de cada variedad desde
que brota de la tierra, hasta que se cumple con su ciclo vital. (Mamani
1981: 236)

The different colors of the potato flower indicate different
kinds of potatoes, and the Andean farmer is the only specialist
who recognizes each one of them. [Only he] can explain the
characters of each variety from the moment it pushes up
through the earth right up to when its life cycle has finished.

The Quechua texts translated in this book describe a means of link-
ing our rational, analytical world with one which is phrased in other
metaphors, other ideologies. The structuring of the Quechua songs
calls for our active reading and participation to understand them;
barely detectable changes in verb forms often provide considerable
pleasure to Quechua speakers who value such lyrical nuance. We
have to be taught to perceive both the consistencies in the structure
of the form (style and genre within a collective tradition) and the
variation inevitable in the individual working out of the poetic
message.

We do not enter easily into the poetry of potatoes, as is evident
in the reading of a song from the Cuzco region of Peru sung by
Maximiliano Cruz Ch'uktaya:[12]

### 1

| | |
|---|---|
| Q'uñi uquchapi | In the deep [earth] of Quñi, |
| papacha tarpusqay | the potatoes [I] planted, |
| wiñashanmanraqchu | are they growing yet? |
| icha manaraqchu | Are they [I wonder]? |
| rurushanmanraqchu | 5 Are the [tiny] potatoes forming? |
| icha manaraqchu. | Are they [I wonder]? |

### 2

| | |
|---|---|
| Papa tarpusqayta | Of the potato[es] [I] planted, |
| tapurikushyani | I ask a question, humbly, |
| papa tarpusqayta | of the potato[es] [I] planted. |
| tapupayashyani | 10 I ask a question, carefully, |
| | respectfully, |
| ruruchanraykullas | "are there some [tiny] potatoes |
| | [fruits] yet?" |

| | | |
|---|---|---|
| raphichanraykullas. | | "Are there some leaves bursting forth yet?" |
| **3** | | |
| Yuyashankiraqchu | | Do you still remember? |
| icha manañachu | | Do you? [I wonder?] |
| makiwan, chakiwan | 15 | How, with our hands and feet |
| tarpuyunqanchista | | we planted? |
| ñuqa niñuchay | | My little boss-man, |
| yuyashallanima | | I still remember |
| ñuqa niñuchay | | my little boss-man. |
| yuyakushanimá | 20 | I still remember |
| makiwan, chakiwan | | how, with our hands and feet, |
| tarpuyusqanchista. | | we planted. |
| **4** | | |
| Qusñipata patapiri | | In the high plains of Quñipata |
| phuyullas puñushan | | the clouds are sleeping. |
| chayta qhawarispas | 25 | When I see that |
| yawarta waqani | | I sob [cry bloody tears]. |
| chayta yuyarispas | | When I remember that |
| yawarta waqani. | | I sob [cry bloody tears]. |
| HAWACHAN | | HAWACHAN |
| Ptiaq chay, maytaq chay | 30 | Who? Where? |
| q'usñipatamanta waqyamuwan. | | From Qusñipata is crying out to me[?] |
| | | (Cruz Ch'uktaya 1987: 63) |

The repetition in the lines of the song is readily apparent to a reader, even to someone who does not speak the Quechua language. The individual suffixes—*ri, ku, paya, ra,* and *yku*—all convey a Quechua esthetics for infinite variation within the verb phrase which complicates the meaning with nuance. For instance, in the second verse, the Quechua poet speaks directly to the potato plant he covered with earth awhile ago. In an intimate relationship with the potato plant, he questions, "Does it have potatoes [growing] yet?" and "Does it have leaves bursting out yet?":

| | |
|---|---|
| Papa tarpusqayta | Of the potato[es] [I] planted, |
| tapurikushyani | I ask a question, humbly, |
| papa tarpusqayta | of the potato[es] [I] planted. |

| | |
|---|---|
| tapupayashyani | I ask a question, carefully, respectfully, |
| ruruchanraykullas | "are there some [tiny] potatoes [fruits] yet?" |
| raphichanraykullas. | "Are there some leaves bursting forth yet?" |

The individual suffixes mark the intense emotionality, which colors the questioning and the wondering. The verb *tapuy* in the second line bears the weight of the linguistic forms *ri* and *ku*, which indicate, respectively, an inceptive (a beginning of an action) with supplicative overtones (Parker 1969: 66), while *ku* explicates a more characteristic action (ibid.: 71–72). The fourth line, a repetition of this verb "to question," includes *paya*, which particularizes the emerging dialogue between the planter and the plant; the action is done repetitively, but carefully and attentively (ibid.: 65–66). The Spanish translation which accompanies the Quechua verses in the anthology slights these gradations in meaning and purifies the forms; the elimination of the subtle variation negates the very differences which should be emphasized to a reader from another poetic tradition. More difficult to convey is the parallelism of the dominant verb forms *tapuy* (to ask a question) and *tarpuy* (to plant); the translation to English allows for no phonemic similarity between planting and questioning.

The planting and the questioning are the very structure of the song; these verbs are repeated in later verses, a reverie of other times when potatoes were sown by hand and using the footplow (verse 3). The "icha manañachu" (lines 4, 6, 14), a dubitative, leads naturally to the rhetorical questions at the close of the song: "Pitaq chay?" (Who is that?), "Maytaq chay?" (Where is that from?). The mention of potatoes is not centered entirely in the descriptions of agriculture. The final reference to the clouds, to the sobbing, to the site of Quñispata in the landscape may enclose a veiled reference to the Machukuna ancestors, who are thought of in terms of potatoes and territorial space. Catherine Allen notes the importance between these ancestral grandparents and potatoes in the current agricultural practices in Sonqo, near Cuzco:

> Left to themselves on these moonlit nights, the Machukuna congregate and hold work parties to cultivate their potato fields. These fields are "just where ours are"—and yet they are not the same fields. The two sets of fields (those of the Machukuna and the Runakuna) are nevertheless related, for the

Machukuna's nocturnal labors result in the fertility and pro-
ductivity of the fields men work in daylight. . . . Every com-
munity has "its" Machukuna, who are considered an intrinsic
part of its territory and crucial to its well-being. (Allen 1986: 4)

From the innuendo of modal suffixes in Quechua, we turn to an-
other potato poem where our Western expectations of poetics are
both met and violated:[13]

### In Praise of the Potato

Potato, sojourner north, first sprung
from the flanks of volcanos, plainspoken kin
to bright chili and deadly nightshade,
sleek eggplant and hairy tobacco,

we could live on you alone if we had to,
and scorched-earth marauders never bothered you much.

I love you because your body's a stem,
your eyes sprout, and you're not in the Bible,

and if we did not eat your strength,
you'd drive it up, into a flower.

(Williams 1987: 74)

The structure of the paired verse lines leads us to expect a syntactic
parallelism often associated with the Bible; in the Psalms, for in-
stance. The title, "In Praise of the Potato," in fact also heightens our
expectations of a reverent hymn to the potato nourishing our exis-
tence. Yet the eventual disclaimer, "You're not in the Bible," dashes
these associations, as does the more colloquial, informal diction
found in the use of "you'd" and "you're" and "your body's a stem."
The core of the imagery resides in the taxonomy which is laid out
in lines 3 and 4; each member of the Solanaceae family is emblazoned
in our memory with a mention of its distinctive attribute, very simi-
lar to the "lost baby" song of Saraguro (chapter 4). The third line rev-
els in an intangible sensuousness ("bright" and "deadly"), while the
line which follows offers palpable reality ("sleek" and "hairy"). The
taxonomic rhythms are echoed in the botanical accuracy of the final
verses, where the poet carefully alerts us to the peculiarities of the
potato, which possesses underground stems from which springs the
tuber. These tubers, as the poet suggests, send out their own roots
which would push upward, eventually transformed into flowers.
The symbolism of the esthetic, symbolized flower lingers in the
poem and dissolves our (human) destructive tendencies shown in

both eating the fruit of the plant and also waging war ("scorched-earth marauders").

Translation of this poem into Quechua would cause some cross-cultural dissonance, according to the Quechua patterns we have analyzed. The didactic underpinnings (of plant origins and human treachery) would fade into more speculative interpretations of the "real" world: this all would come about in a reshaping of the verbal concepts, of less drive and strength and more orientation toward a balancing of forces.

The history of European interest and Andean Indian interest in the potato reveals some misconceptions and beliefs about the plant through the centuries. In our discussion of "translating" values across cultures, we have come to see the difficulties of rendering acceptable rewordings from one culture to another. The lowly potato serves as a sign, albeit a more tangible one, of the problem of cross-cultural interpretation. The potato was not readily adopted as an edible substance because of a European belief system which labeled it negatively for centuries after the Conquest. Now, the potato serves as a major staple food in over 130 countries and scientists turn to Andean farmers to understand some of its secrets which are not found in chemical analyses. The story of the potato is one of increasing tolerance; the Old World overcame its prejudice against the "lusty" tuber, consumed vast tons of potatoes, and, because of the potato's starchy nutrients, experienced enormous population growth. Only the daily toil of the Andean Indians, carefully hoeing and mounding soil around the young plants, has preserved and perpetuated the thousands of varieties which still grow in the Andes today.

Discussion of the preservation of Andean ways of life must also include a recognition of the changes taking place in Peru and in the highlands. As Peruvians shift from a "regional dish to a national menu," potatoes are spurned in favor of imported foodstuffs, wheat (for bread) and rice. This food preference does not utilize the ecological resources of Peru which for centuries have been exploited successfully by extensive kin networks in the highland and lowland zones (Murra 1960). As Peruvians begin to demand more rice, bread, and noodles in their diet, the country becomes more dependent on imports which, generally, are grown in countries situated in temperate zones. One researcher favors a return to the consumption of tubers (potato, *oca, olluco*) and highland cereals (soft wheat, soft maize, *quinua, canahua*) (Figure 30). This return to basics would be more nutritional and also raise the incomes of the marginalized highland peasantry: ". . . the agricultural resources of the highlands cannot

*Figure 30.* Harvesting grain with a communal labor force at the foot of Chimborazo Mountain, Colta-Monjas, Ecuador.

be of concern only because they may serve to augment the quantity of food available to the nation, but also because they are the livelihood of a population (close to 25 percent of the poorest families in the country) whose opportunity to improve their economic standards depends on better exploitation of those resources" (Caballero 1984: 16).

For these Andean farmers the potato is not a macrometaphor but a reality, a necessary means of sustaining their existence. "We have much to learn from them," the scientific team of Jackson, Hawkes, and Rowe (1980) proclaimed after studying Amerindian agricultural practices. However, our learning from these Andean peoples should not stop after we take notes on their erosion techniques, the genetics of their potatoes, and labor-intensive farming. As we write about them, we must also do our best to write down their very own words, in a language which is not our own. The interpretation of these Andean thoughts, the process of translation, of poetry and of potatoes, must be one which conveys the notion of their separate reality, which makes us appreciate and value our significant differences.

# Notes

## Introduction

1. *Quichua*, in this passage and those which follow, refers to the dialects spoken in Ecuador. The spelling *Quechua* designates the dialects spoken in Peru; this term also refers to the language in general as a pan-Andean phenomenon.

## 1. The Dimensions of Quechua Language and Culture

1. This picture was taken in 1974 at the traffic circle near the Quito airport, Ecuador.

2. For the most thorough discussion of the history of the Otavalan weavers, consult Salomon (1973, 1986). In matters of ethnicity, Weinstock (1970), Walter (1981), and Parsons (1945) are useful sources. Meisch (1987) carefully describes Otavalan weaving techniques and Otavalan costume.

3. An illustration of this theme is found in Robert F. Berkhofer, Jr.'s book *The White Man's Indian* (1979). Plate 11, "Pollution: It's a Crying Shame" (1972) is a poster featuring a Cherokee who prominently displays one long braid and sheds a tear because of ecological destruction.

4. I am grateful to Paula Matthews for bringing this pamphlet, an advertisement published by Jordan Marsh in April 1982, to my attention. I appreciate Jordan Marsh's permission to reproduce the photograph and captions for the discussion of ethnicity and cultural difference.

5. Quichua is the spelling used by Santo Tomás ([1560] 1951) and the publications of the Lima Council (1584–1585); however, Alonso de la Huerta uses Quechua in 1616 (Cerrón Palomino 1987: 32).

6. Recent study of Quechua poetics by Mannheim, Husson, Pease, Beyersdorff, and Schechter suggests a revision of Lara's pioneering research. These scholars are less concerned with genre than in understanding the generating principles of Quechua lyric.

7. This song was taped during the harvest of grain in the community of Colta-Monjas near Riobamba, Ecuador. I am grateful to an indigenous leader, Juan Remache, for his assistance in taping this song and many others in 1975.

8. This message is foremost in the writings of the Quechua linguist Rodolfo Cerrón Palomino (1981, 1987).

9. Monica Barnes (1987) has also cited this passage in her study of the early catechisms and confession manuals. I have benefited from her interest in this theme and her sharing of the facsimiles during my fellowship period at Cornell University.

## 2. Translation and the Problematics of Cultural Categories

1. Antonello Gerbi ([1975] 1985: 340–346) reviews the ideological concerns which led to the creation of the *Requerimiento*, a document which Gerbi calls "incomprehensible." Gerbi also summarizes critical opinions regarding the document.

2. The many eyewitness accounts of the events at Cajamarca are listed in Hemming (1970: 550, note to p. 41). As Hemming states, it appears that Valverde did not read the complete text of the *Requirement*, although he did speak about Christianity.

3. Vicente L. Rafael's chapter, "The Politics of Translation" (pp. 23–55) in *Contracting Colonialism* (1988), is an excellent source for understanding the relationship between language and colonial politics. I am indebted to John Ackerman for guiding me to this source.

4. Excellent discussions of Iberian language policies in the New World are found in Heath (1976) and Burrus (1979). For Peru, studies by Mannheim (1984) and Heath and Laprade (1982) are useful analyses; Hartmann (1977) carefully researches policy regarding Quichua in Ecuador. MacCormick (1985) touches upon the theme in her insightful study of conversion in the Andes.

5. Rojas Rojas also treats this theme in his book *Expansión del quechua* (1980).

6. In 1980, Enrique Urbano's study of the Trinity showed that the terminology Father, Son, and Holy Ghost has been "retranslated" and now refers to spatial epochs which represent the remote past, the more recent past and present, and reference to the future. "God the Father" as spoken of by indigenous peoples demarcates a time when the moon governed, a long time ago. Clearly distinct from this time period is the "God the Son" time marker, which refers to the Incas and the arrival of the Spanish, as well as references to the present time. There is no continuity from one time to another, for a cataclysm, or *pachacuti*, terminates each epoch; therefore, the notion of a Father-Son relationship is different from the human family imagery implicit in the Christian framework (Urbano 1980: 112–113).

7. The contemporary usage of the designation *espíritu* by Quechua speakers does not refer to one compartmentalization of a three-headed Trinity. Instead, this word defines a time period, the future, distinct from other epochs and extending to the year 2000 (Urbano 1980: 113). Thus, in the case of the Trinity, Andean people have appropriated this imported concept and semantically restricted its designations to conform to their own purposes.

8. Jákfalvi-Leiva's (1984) monograph on the Inca Garcilaso well analyzes this theme and that of translation in greater detail.

9. Lotman's model of world view and conceptualization of value is well argued by Rolena Adorno (1981). López-Baralt (1982) also relies on the Lotman model.

## 3. Script and Sketch

1. This scene is described by Wachtel ([1971] 1977: 22).

2. Also see ibid.

3. Todorov ([1987] 1985: 80) mentions a similar incident involving a letter and some fruit as found in Peter Martyr.

4. This phrase is omitted in the reproduction of the drawing of the Coricancha (Santacruz Pachacuti Yamqui [1613] 1927: 158), yet it appears in Figure 11 at the peak of the drawing. I am indebted to Bruce Mannheim for lending me a microfilm version of the original manuscript. R. T. Zuidema informs me that there is mention of a *pachaunanchac* ("[relojes para que] no perdiesen la cuenta de estos meses y los tiempos que habia de sembrar y hacer las fiestas") ([clocks] to not lose track of these months and the time to plant and to have celebrations), in Betanzos ([1551] 1968: 56).

## 4. Cultural Translation of the Andean Oral Tradition

1. This same feature of excluding nonspeakers of one's language is noted for the Amuesha by Smith (1982: 84).

2. In addition to the original Quechua found in the 1927 manuscript of Santacruz Pachacuti Yamqui ([1613] 1927: 148–149), this text exists in several emended versions which aid our reading. I prefer the modern text and translation published by José María Arguedas (1955), although I also consult the versions written by Mossi in Lafone Quevedo (1950: 306–307) and Bendezú (1977). Lines 28–32 are well translated in Mannheim's (1986a) manuscript. After completing my own study of this *oración*, I was informed of the publication of Jan Szemínski's (1985) article; his transcription of the passage in the manuscript is also useful.

3. Mannheim (1987b) also defines this usage of *sqa*. Allen (1986) describes the categories of a "true story/event" as opposed to a "mythical" one. As she points out, the two terms often overlap when the Quechua speakers define them; however, the basic distinction frequently is marked in Quechua syntax.

4. Although Todorov is discussing Aztec culture in this passage, the distinction he makes between European modes of thought and indigenous modes is provocative in our study.

5. I am indebted to Frank Salomon for drawing my attention to these structural parallels and the many layers of meaning of *tío pullo* as well as its topographic significance (line 62, Saraguro song).

6. This song was sung by an elderly Quechua-speaking woman in Sara-

guro, Ecuador, 1975. Louisa Stark first told me about this song; she and Pieter Muysken also loaned me versions.

7. The exact location of Tiupulillu is near Tulcán, according to information in the volume on Ecuador, *Gazateer* no. 36, p. 176: 0425/78-38w.

8. Schechter (1983) gives further details regarding the child's wake in Ecuador and other countries of Latin America.

## 6. The Metaphysics of Sex

1. For additional information regarding the use of amulets, see Haley and Grollig (1976), Mariscotti de Görlitz (1978), and Girault (1984).

2. Seitz (1982) limits her study of communicative acts to only one sense of the verb.

3. For a description of the preparation of datura, see Whitten (1976: 98–100).

4. This song was taped in the environs of Arajuno, Ecuador, in 1975.

5. See Macdonald (1979) for male perspectives on *simayuka* and the hunting complex in the lowland regions of Ecuador.

6. The ambivalent attitudes toward *puricc* are examined by Delgado Vivanco (1942), who states that the "foreigner" represents the opposite of all that the *ayllu* stands for in continuing cultural traditions. Yet the *puricc* also is very much sought out as a mate to introduce new customs.

7. For an alternate version of the metacommunicative act of lowland songs, see Seitz (1981b, 1982).

## 7. Potato as Cultural Metaphor

1. A conservative figure of 400 B.C. is utilized by Ugent (1970) for the domestication of the potato; other researchers allude to "thousands of years of cultivation."

2. There are other sources for potato nomenclature in Sánchez Farfán (1979) and Vargas (1936).

3. Rolena Adorno very astutely investigates Guaman Poma's illustrations as a visual myth, "a system of signs that communicates on more than one level . . . the first system [is] the set of pictorial signs that constitutes the immediate substance of the particular representation, and the second level system [is] the syntagmatic combination of those elements in space" (1979: 31).

4. The potato was identified as a root in *Gerard's Herball* ([1597, 1636] 1927) and therefore was ascribed the negative attributes. Kahn (1984: 94) also comments on the conception of root crops in the United States: "Emerson, Thoreau, and their fellow Transcendentalists, for instance, would have no truck with food that grew below ground."

5. Potato nomenclature analyzed by Sánchez Farfán (1979) reveals additional classificatory categories of food, food processing (*chuñu*), storage qualities, size, shape of tuber, texture, and meal consistency.

6. Jabs (1984) promotes the concept of genetic diversity; many crops are

grown from standardized, hybridized seeds so that a fungus can destroy millions of one plant in one season. Gene pools of seeds, such as the National Seed Storage Laboratory in Colorado, stockpile seeds that may be used to create new cultivars. In Peru, the International Potato Center maintains an inventory of 13,000 varieties of potatoes native to South America, stored as both true seeds and tubers (Woods and Martin 1987).

7. The original Spanish text: "En sus remotas páginas está escrito que los animales se dividen en (a) pertenecientes al Emperador, (b) embalsamados, (c) amaestrados, (d) lechones, (e) sirenas, (f) fabulosos, (g) perros sueltos, (h) incluidos en esta clasificación, (i) que se agitan como locos, (j) innumerables, (k) dibujados con un pincel finísimo de pelo de camello, (l) etcétera, (m) que acaban de romper el jarrón, (n) que de lejos parecen moscas" (Borges 1974: 708).

8. This subheading and the analysis are inspired by Paul Friedrich's comments on the "poetry of peppers" and many other provocative thoughts in his *The Language Parallax* (1986).

9. For further analysis of the Quechua themes in Arguedas's work, see Escobar (1984) and Harrison (1983).

10. John V. Murra's (1978) introduction to *Deep Rivers* gives further analysis of Arguedas's social consciousness.

11. Frances Horning Barraclough's English translation (1978: xiii), based on Arguedas's Spanish version of this poem, differs from my English translation derived from the Quechua.

12. I am indebted to Christine Franquemont for bringing this song to my attention and to Billie Jean Isbell for lending me the anthology. The poem appears in the anthology *Urqukunapa Yawarnin/La sangre de los Cerros* (Montoya, Montoya, and Montoya 1987). It was collected by Leo Casas, transcribed by Yanet Oroz, and offered to the anthologists by William Rowe.

13. I am grateful to Rolena Adorno for sending me a copy of this poem after reading an earlier version of this chapter. I acknowledge David Williams's kind permission to include the poem in this book.

# Bibliography

Acosta, José de. [1588] 1954. *De procuranda indorum salute o predicación del evangelio en las Indias.* In *Obras del P. José de Acosta,* ed. Francisco Mateos, pp. 389–609. Biblioteca de Autores Españoles, vol. 73. Madrid: Atlas.

———. [1590] 1954. *Historia natural y moral de las Indias.* In *Obras del P. José de Acosta,* ed. Francisco Mateos, pp. 3–389. Biblioteca de Autores Españoles, vol. 73. Madrid: Atlas.

Adorno, Rolena. 1974. "The 'Nueva Corónica y Buen Gobierno' of Don Felipe Guaman Poma de Ayala: A Lost Chapter in the History of Latin American Letters." Ph.D. dissertation, Cornell University.

———. 1979. "Icon and Idea: A Symbolic Reading of the Visual Text of Guaman Poma." *Indian Historian* 12, no. 3: 27–50.

———. 1981. "On Pictorial Language and the Typology of Culture in a New World Chronicle." *Semiotica* 36, nos. 1–2: 51–106.

———, ed. 1982. *From Oral to Written Expression: Native Andean Chronicles of the Early Colonial Period.* Syracuse: Maxwell School of Citizenship and Public Affairs, Syracuse University.

———. 1986a. *Guaman Poma: Writing and Resistance in Colonial Peru.* Austin: University of Texas Press.

———. 1986b. "Visual Mediation in the Transition from Oral to Written Expression." *New Scholar* 10, nos. 1–2: 181–196.

Albó, Xavier. 1979. "The Future of Oppressed Languages in the Andes." In *Peasants, Primitives, and Proletariats: The Struggle for Identity in Latin America,* ed. David L. Browman and Ronald A. Schwartz, pp. 267–289. New York: Mouton.

Allen, Catherine. 1986. "Time, Place and Narrative in an Andean Community." Paper presented at the Latin American Studies Association Meeting, Boston.

———. 1988. *The Hold Life Has: Coca and Cultural Identity in an Andean Community.* Washington, D.C.: Smithsonian Institution Press.

Almeida, Ileana, and Julieta Haidar. 1979. "Hacia un estudio semántico del quichua ecuatoriano." In *Lengua y cultura en el Ecuador,* pp. 327–342. Otavalo: Instituto Otavaleño de Antropología.

Arguedas, José María. 1938. *Canto kechwa con un ensayo sobre la capacidad de creación artística del pueblo indio y mestizo.* Lima: Bustamante y Ballivián.
———. 1955. "Los himnos quechuas católicos cuzqueños de J. M. B. Farfán y Jorge A. Lira." *Folklore americano* 3: 121–232.
———. 1972. "Huk Docturkunaman Qayay." In *Temblar/Katatay*, pp. 50–57. Lima: Institución Nacional de la Cultura.
Armas Medina, Fernando de. 1953. *Cristianización del Perú (1532–1600).* Seville: Escuela de Estudios Hispano-Americanos de Sevilla.
Asad, Talal. 1986. "The Concept of Cultural Translation in British Social Anthropology." In *Writing Culture: The Poetics and Politics of Ethnography*, ed. James Clifford and George E. Marcus, pp. 141–165. Berkeley: University of California Press.
Ascher, Marcia, and Robert Ascher. 1981. *Code of the Quipu: A Study in Media, Mathematics, and Culture.* Ann Arbor: University of Michigan Press.
Ballón Aguirre, Enrique. 1986. "Política linguopedagógica peruana." *Revista Andina* 4, no. 2 (December): 479–499.
Barnes, Monica. 1987. "The *Doctrina Christiana* (Lima Catechism) of 1584, and the *Confessionario* (Confessional Manual), and *Tercero Cathecismo* (Book of Sermons) of 1585: Their Influence upon the Development of Andean Catholicism." Paper presented at the V International Symposium on Latin American Indian Literatures, Ithaca, N.Y.
Barrionuevo, Alfonsina. 1973. *Sirvinakuy: El matrimonio de prueba.* Lima: Iberia.
[Barrios de] Chungara, Domitila. 1980. *La mujer y la organización.* Cuzco: Centro Las Casas.
Barthel, Thomas S. 1971. "Viraco chas Prunkgewand." *Tribus* 20 (November): 63–125.
Barthes, Roland. 1977. "Rhetoric of the Image." In *Image/Music/Text*, selected and trans. Stephen Heath, pp. 32–52. New York: Hill and Wang.
Bassnett-McGuire, Susan. 1980. *Translation Studies.* London: Methuen.
Beauvoir, Simone de. 1952. *The Second Sex.* New York: Knopf.
Bendezú Aybar, Edmundo. 1977. "El mito de Wiraqocha en un himno de Sallqamaywa." *Runa* 1 (March): 22–23.
———, ed. 1980. *Literatura quechua.* Caracas: Biblioteca Ayacucho.
Benjamin, Walter. [1955] 1969. "The Task of the Translator." In *Illuminations*, ed. Hannah Arendt, trans. Harry Zohn, pp. 69–83. New York: Schocken Books.
Berkhofer, Jr., Robert F. 1979. *The White Man's Indian: Images of the American Indian from Columbus to the Present.* New York: Vintage Books.
Berry, Wendell. 1981. "An Agricultural Journey in Peru (1979)." In *The Gift of Good Land: Further Essays Cultural and Agricultural*, pp. 3–47. San Francisco: North Point Press.
Betanzos, Juan de. [1551] 1968. *Suma y narración de los Incas.* In *Crónicas peruanas de interés indígena*, ed. Francisco Esteve Barba, pp. 1–150. Madrid.

Beyersdorff, Margot. 1986. "Fray Martín de Murúa y el 'cantar' histórico inka." *Revista Andina* 4, no. 2 (December): 501–521.

Bierhorst, John. 1983. "American Indian Verbal Art and the Role of the Literary Critic." In *Smoothing the Ground: Essays on Native American Oral Literature*, ed. Brian Swann, pp. 78–87. Berkeley: University of California Press.

Bills, Garland D., Bernardo Vallejo C., and Rudolph C. Troike. 1969. *An Introduction to Spoken Bolivian Quechua*. Austin: University of Texas Press.

Bolton, Ralph, and Charlene Bolton. 1975. *Conflictos en la familia andina*, trans. Jorge A. Flores Ochoa and Yemira D. Nájar Vizcarra. Cuzco: Centro de Estudios Andinos.

Borges, Jorge Luis. 1974. "El idioma analítico de John Wilkins." In *Otras inquisiciones, Obras completas (1923–1972)*, ed. Carlos V. Frias, pp. 706–709. Buenos Aires: Emecé.

Bourque, Susan C., and Kay Barbara Warren. 1981. *Women of the Andes: Patriarchy and Social Change in Two Peruvian Towns*. Ann Arbor: University of Michigan Press.

Brandi, John, ed. 1976. *Chimborazo: Life on the Haciendas of Highland Ecuador*, trans. Michael Scott and Mal Warwick. Rooseveltown, N.Y.: Akwesasne Notes.

Brower, Reuben A., ed. 1959. *On Translation*. Cambridge: Harvard University Press.

Brown, Michael F., and Margaret L. Van Bolt. 1980. "Aguaruna Gardening Magic in the Alto Río Mayo, Peru." *Ethnology* 19, no. 2 (April): 169–191.

———. 1984. "The Role of Words in Aguaruna Hunting Magic." *American Ethnologist*: 545–558.

Brush, Stephen B. 1977. *Mountain, Field, and Family: The Economy and Human Ecology of an Andean Valley*. Philadelphia: University of Pennsylvania Press.

———. 1980. "Potato Taxonomies in Andean Agriculture." In *Indigenous Knowledge Systems and Development*, ed. David W. Brokensha, D. M. Warren, and Oswald Werner, pp. 37–47. Landham, Md.: University Press of America.

Brush, Stephen B., Heath J. Carney, and Zósimo Huamán. 1981. "Dynamics of Andean Potato Agriculture." *Economic Botany* 35, no. 1: 70–88.

Burrus, Ernest J. 1979. "The Language Problem in Spain's Overseas Dominions." *Neue Zeitschrift für Missionswissenschaft* 35, pt. 3: 161–171.

Caballero, José María. 1984. "Agriculture and the Peasantry under Industrialization Pressures: Lessons from the Peruvian Experience." *Latin American Research Review* 19, no. 2: 3–43.

Cabello Balboa, Miguel. [1586] 1951. *Miscelánea antártica: Una historia del Perú antiguo*. Lima: Universidad Nacional Mayor de San Marcos, Instituto de Etnología.

Carneiro, Robert L. 1983. "The Cultivation of Manioc among the Kuikuru of the Upper Xingú." In *Adaptive Responses of Native Amazonians*, ed. Raymond B. Hames and William T. Vickers, pp. 65–113. New York: Academic Press.

Carpenter, Lawrence K. 1980. "A Quichua Postulate and the Implications for Development." Paper presented at the Annual Meeting of the American Anthropological Association, Washington, D.C.

Castro Pozo, Hildebrando. [1924] 1979. *Nuestra comunidad indígena.* Lima: Perugraph Editores.

Catford, J. C. 1965. *A Linguistic Theory of Translation: An Essay in Applied Linguistics.* London: Oxford.

Cayón Armelia, Edgardo. 1971. "El hombre y los animales en la cultura quechua." *Allpanchis Phuturinga* 3: 135–162.

Cereceda, Verónica. 1978. "Sémiologie des tissus andins: Les talegas d'Isluga." *Annales: Economies, Sociétés, Civilisations* 33, nos. 5–6 (September–December): 1017–1037.

Cerrón Palomino, Rodolfo. 1981. "En torno a la elaboración del quechua." Ms.

———. 1987. *Lingüística quechua.* Cuzco: Centro de Estudios Rurales Andinos Bartolomé de las Casas.

Chang-Rodríguez, Raquel. 1982. "Writing as Resistance: Peruvian History and the *Relación* of Titu Cusi Yupanqui." In *From Oral to Written Expression: Native Andean Chronicles of the Early Colonial Period,* ed. Rolena Adorno, pp. 41–64. Syracuse: Maxwell School of Citizenship and Public Affairs, Syracuse University.

Chuquín, Carmen. 1977. "Tiupullu." Ms. for Latin American Studies Course 345. Urbana: University of Illinois.

Cobo, P. Bernabé. [1653] 1964. *Historia del Nuevo Mundo.* In *Obras de P. Bernabé Cobo,* vol. 1, ed. P. Francisco Mateos. Biblioteca de Autores Españoles, vol. 91. Madrid: Atlas.

———. 1979. *History of the Inca Empire: An Account of the Indians' Customs and Their Origin Together with a Treatise on Inca Legends, History, and Social Institutions,* trans. and ed. Roland Hamilton. Austin: University of Texas Press.

Cole, Peter. 1982. *Imbabura Quechua.* Lingua Descriptive Studies 5. Amsterdam: North-Holland Publishing Company.

Condori Mamani, Gregorio. 1977. *Autobiografía,* ed. Ricardo Valderrama Fernández and Carmen Escalante Gutiérrez. Cuzco: Centro de Estudios Rurales Bartolomé de las Casas.

*Confessionario para los curas de indios.* [1585] 1985. *Corpus Hispanorum de Pace,* vol. 26-2, pp. 189–333. Madrid: Consejo Superior de Investigaciones Científicas.

Conrad, Geoffrey W., and Arthur A. Demarest. 1984. *Religion and Empire: The Dynamics of Aztec and Inca Expansionism.* London: Cambridge University Press.

Cordero, Luis. [1892] 1967. *Diccionario Quichua-Español/Diccionario Español-Quichua. Anales de la Universidad de Cuenca* 23, no. 4 (October–December).

Corominas, Juan. 1954. *Diccionario crítico etimológico de la lengua castellana.* 4 vols. Bern: Editorial Francke.

Costales Samaniego, Alfredo and Piedad. 1968. "El Quishihuar o el árbol de Dios, II." *Llacta* 12, no. 24 (March).

Crick, Malcolm. 1976. *Explorations in Language and Meaning: Towards a Semantic Anthropology*. London: Malaby Press.

Cruz Ch'uktaya, Maximiliano. 1987. "Papa tarpuy." In *La sangre de los cerros, Urqukunapa yawarnin: Antología de la poesía quechua que se canta en el Perú*, ed. Rodrigo Montoya, Edwin Montoya, and Luis Montoya, pp. 63–64. Lima: Centro Peruano de Estudios Sociales, Mosca Azul, Universidad Nacional Mayor de San Marcos.

Cusihuamán G., Antonio. 1976. *Gramática Quechua, Cuzco-Callao*. Lima: Ministerio de Educación/Instituto de Estudios Peruanos.

Delgado Vivanco, Edmundo. 1942. "El forasterito en el folklore." *Waman Puma* 2, nos. 11–14 (August–November): 25–30.

Demarest, Arthur A. 1981. *Viracocha, the Nature and Antiquity of the Andean High God*. Cambridge: Peabody Museum Press.

Derrida, Jacques. 1985. "Des tours de Babel," trans. Joseph F. Graham. In *Difference in Translation*, ed. Joseph F. Graham, pp. 165–209. Ithaca: Cornell University Press.

Dobash, Russell P., and R. Emerson Dobash. 1981. "Community Response to Violence against Wives: Charivari, Abstract Justice and Patriarchy." *Social Problems* 28, no. 5 (June): 563–581.

Dobkin de Ríos, Marlene. 1972. *Visionary Vine: Psychedelic Healing in the Peruvian Amazon*. San Francisco: Chandler.

———. 1978. "A Psi Approach to Love Magic, Witchcraft and Psychedelics in the Peruvian Amazon." *Phoenix: New Directions in the Study of Man* 2, no. 1 (Summer): 22–27.

———. 1984. *Hallucinogens: Cross-Cultural Perspectives*. Albuquerque: University of New Mexico Press.

*Doctrina christiana y catecismo para instrucción de indios*. [1584] 1985. *Corpus Hispanorum de Pace*, vol. 26-2, pp. 5–187. Madrid: Consejo Superior de Investigaciones Científicas.

Dumézil, Georges. 1955. "Catégories et vocabulaire des échanges de services chez les Indiens Quechua: *Ayni* et *mink'a*." *Journal de la Société des Américanistes de Paris* n.s. 44: 3–16.

Duviols, Pierre. 1977a. *La destrucción de las religiones andinas (Conquista y Colonia)*, trans. Albor Maruenda. Mexico City: Universidad Nacional Autónoma de México.

———. 1977b. "Los nombres quechua de Viracocha, supuesto 'Dios Creador' de los evangelizadores." *Allpanchis phuturinqa* 10: 53–64.

———. 1978. "*Camaquen, upani*: Un concept animiste des anciens péruviens." In *Amerikanistische Studien: Festschrift für Hermann Trimborn*, ed. Roswith Hartmann and Udo Oberem, pp. 132–144. St. Augustin: Anthropos Institute.

Earls, John, and Irene Silverblatt. 1976. "La realidad física y social en la cosmología andina." In *Proceedings, Forty-Second International Congress of Americanists*, pp. 299–325. Paris.

*Ecuador*. 1957. *Gazeteer*, no. 36. Washington, D.C.: Office of Geography, Department of the Interior.

Escobar, Alberto. 1972. "Lenguaje e historia en los *Comentarios Reales*." In *Lenguaje y discriminación social en América Latina*, pp. 145–176. Lima: Milla Batres.

———. 1984. *Arguedas o la utopía de la lengua*. Lima: Instituto de Estudios Peruanos.

Farfán, J. M. B. 1945. "Sipas-Tarina o ciertas formas de cortejar a la mujer quechua." *Revista del Museo Nacional* 14: 139–143.

Flores Ochoa, Jorge A. 1978. "Classification et dénomination des camélidés sud-américains." *Annales: Economies, Sociétés, Civilisations* 33, nos. 5–6 (September–December): 1006–1016.

Foletti-Castegnaro, Alessandra. 1985. *Tradición oral de los quichuas amazónicos del Aguarico y San Miguel*. Quito: Ediciones Abya-Yala.

Forman, Sylvia Helen. 1972. "Law and Conflict in Rural Highland Ecuador." Ph.D. dissertation, University of California, Berkeley.

Foucault, Michel. [1966] 1973. *The Order of Things: An Archeology of the Human Sciences*. New York: Vintage Press.

Frawley, William, ed. 1984. "Prolegomenon to a Theory of Translation." In *Translation: Literary, Linguistic, and Philosophical Perspectives*, pp. 159–179. London: Associated University Presses.

Friedrich, Paul. 1986. *The Language Parallax: Linguistic Relativism and Poetic Indeterminacy*. Austin: University of Texas Press.

Garcilaso de la Vega, El Inca. [1609, 1617] 1963. *Los comentarios reales de los Incas*. In *Obras completas del Inca Garcilaso de la Vega*, ed. P. Carmelo Sáenz de Santa María, S.I. Biblioteca de Autores Españoles, vols. 133, 134, 135. Madrid: Atlas.

———. [1609, 1617] 1966. *Royal Commentaries of the Incas and General History of Peru*, trans. Harold V. Livermore. 2 vols. Austin: University of Texas Press.

*Gerard's Herball*. [1597, 1636] 1927. Ed. Marcus Woodward. London: Gerald Howe.

Gerbi, Antonello. [1975] 1985. *Nature in the New World: From Christopher Columbus to Gonzalo Fernández de Oviedo*, trans. Jeremy Moyle. Pittsburgh: University of Pittsburgh Press.

Gibson, Charles, ed. 1968. *The Spanish Tradition in America*. New York: Harper and Row.

Girault, Louis. 1984. *Kallawaya: Guérisseurs itinérants des Andes, recherches sur les pratiques medicinales et magiques*. Paris: Editions de l'Orstom, Institut Français de Recherche Scientifique pour le Développement en Coopération.

Gisbert, Teresa. 1980. *Iconografía y mitos indígenas en el arte*. La Paz: Editorial Gisbert & Cía.

Golte, Jürgen. 1973. "El concepto de *sonqo* en el *runa simi* del siglo XVI." *Indiana* 1: 213–218.

González Holguín, Diego. [1608] 1952. *Vocabulario de la lengua general de todo el Perú llamada lengua quichua o del Inca*, ed. Raúl Porras Barre-nechea. Lima: Universidad Nacional Mayor de San Marcos.

Goody, Jack, ed. 1968. *Literacy in Traditional Societies.* Cambridge: Cambridge University Press.

———. 1977. *The Domestication of the Savage Mind.* Cambridge: Cambridge University Press.

Greenblatt, Stephen J. 1976. "Learning to Curse: Aspects of Linguistic Colonialism in the Sixteenth Century." In *First Images of America*, ed. Fredi Chiappelli, pp. 561–581. Berkeley: University of California Press.

Guaman Poma de Ayala, Felipe. [1615] 1936. *Nueva corónica y buen gobierno (Codex péruvien illustré). Travaux et Mémoires de L'Institut d'Ethnologie*, vol. 23. Repr. Paris: L'Institut d'Ethnologie, 1968.

———. [1615] 1980. *El primer nueva corónica y buen gobierno*, ed. John V. Murra and Rolena Adorno. Quechua translations by Jorge L. Urioste. 3 vols. Mexico: Siglo XXI.

Guevara, Darío. 1972. *El castellano y el quichua en el Ecuador.* Quito: Editorial de la Casa de la Cultura.

Guiraud, Pierre. 1975. *Semiology.* Trans. George Gross. Boston: Routledge and Kegan Paul.

Hadingham, Evan. 1987. *Lines to the Mountain Gods: Nazca and the Mysteries of Peru.* Norman: University of Oklahoma Press.

Haley, Harold B., and Francis X. Grollig, S.J. 1976. "Amulets in the Lake Titicaca Basin." *International Congress of Americanists Proceedings* 3: 172–183.

Hanke, Lewis. 1938. "The 'Requerimiento' and Its Interpreters." *Revista de historia de América* 1: 25–34.

———. 1949. *The Spanish Struggle for Justice in the Conquest of America.* Philadelphia: University of Pennsylvania Press.

Hardman, M. J., ed. 1981. *The Aymara Language in its Social and Cultural Context: A Collection of Essays on Aspects of Aymara Language and Culture.* Gainesville: University Presses of Florida.

Harris, Olivia. 1978. "Complementarity and Conflict: An Andean View of Women and Men." In *Sex and Age as Principles of Social Differentiation*, ed. J. S. La Fontaine, pp. 21–40. New York: Academic Press.

———. 1980. "The Power of Signs: Gender, Culture and the Wild in the Bolivian Andes." In *Nature, Culture and Gender*, ed. Carol P. MacCormack and Marilyn Strathern, pp. 70–95. Cambridge: University of Cambridge Press.

Harrison [Macdonald], Regina Lee. 1979a. "Andean Indigenous Expression: A Textual and Cultural Study of Hispanic-American and Quichua Poetry in Ecuador." Ph.D. dissertation, University of Illinois, Urbana.

———. 1979b. "Women's Voices on the Wind: Cultural Continuity in Quichua Lyrics." Paper read at the 78th annual meeting of the American Anthropological Association, December 1, 1979.

———. 1981. "The Quechua Oral Tradition: From Waman Puma to Contemporary Ecuador." *Review* 28: 19–22.

————. 1982. "Modes of Discourse: *Relación de antigüedades deste reyno del Pirú* by Joan de Santacruz Pachacuti Yamqui Salcamaygua." In *From Oral to Written Expression: Native Andean Chronicles of the Early Colonial Period*, ed. Rolena Adorno, pp. 65–100. Syracuse: Maxwell School of Citizenship and Public Affairs, Syracuse University.

————. 1983. "José María Arguedas: El substrato quechua." *Revista iberoamericana* 49, no. 122 (January–March): 111–133.

Hartmann, Roswith. 1977. "Apuntes históricos sobre la cátedra del quechua en Quito (siglos XVI y XVII)." *Boletín de la Academia Nacional de Historia* 59, nos. 127–128: 20–41.

Hawkes, J. G. 1947. "On the Origin and Meaning of South American Indian Potato Names." *Linnean Society of London Botanical Journal* 53: 205–250.

Heath, Shirley B. 1976. "Colonial Language Status Achievement: Mexico, Peru, and the United States." In *Language in Society*, ed. Albert Verdoodt and Rolf Kjolseth, pp. 49–91. Louvain: Peeters.

Heath, Shirley Brice, and Richard Laprade. 1982. In *Language Spread: Studies in Diffusion and Social Change*, ed. Robert L. Cooper, pp. 118–147. Bloomington: Indiana University Press.

Helps, Sir Arthur. 1900. *The Spanish Conquest in America*, vol. 1. London: John Lane.

Hemming, John. 1970. *The Conquest of the Incas*. New York: Harcourt Brace Jovanovich.

Herrero, Joaquín, and Federico Sánchez de Lozada. 1983. *Diccionario quechua: Estructura semántica del quechua cochabambino contemporáneo*. Cochabamba, Bolivia: Editorial C. E. F. Co.

Hocking, George M. 1977. "The Doctrine of Signatures." *Quarterly Journal of Crude Drug Research* 15: 198–200.

Hopkins, Diane. 1982. "Juego de enemigos." *Allpanchis phuturinqa* 17, no. 2: 167–189.

Howard, Rosaleen. 1980. "Turkey Buzzard Tales of the Ecuadorean Quichua." In *Folklore Studies in the Twentieth Century: Proceedings of the Centenary Conference of the Folklore Society*, ed. Venetia J. Newall, pp. 240–247. Great Britain: St. Edmundsbury Press.

Howard-Malverde, Rosaleen. 1981. *Dioses y diablos: Tradición oral de Cañar, Ecuador*. Amerindia, Special no. 1.

————. 1984. "*Dyablu*: Its Meanings in Cañar Quichua Oral Narrative." *Amerindia* 9: 49–78.

Husson, Jean-Philippe. 1985. *La Poesie quechua dans la chronique de Felipe Waman Puma de Ayala: De l'art lyrique de cour et danses populaires*. Paris: L'Harmattan.

Isbell, Billie Jean. 1976. "La otra mitad esencial: Un estudio de complementariedad sexual andina." *Estudios andinos* 12: 37–56.

————. 1978. *To Defend Ourselves: Ecology and Ritual in an Andean Village*. Austin: University of Texas Press.

Isbell, Billie Jean, and Fredy Amilcar Roncalla Fernández. 1977. "The Ontogenesis of Metaphor: Riddle Games among Quechua Speakers Seen as

Cognitive Discovery Procedures." *Journal of Latin American Lore* 3, no. 1: 19–49.

Jabs, Carolyn. 1984. *The Heirloom Gardener.* San Francisco: Sierra Club Books.

Jackson, M. T., J. G. Hawkes, and P. R. Rowe. 1977. "The Nature of *Solanum* × *Chaucha* Juz. et Buk., a Triploid Cultivated Potato of the South American Andes." *Euphytica* 26: 775–783.

———. 1980. "An Ethnobotanical Field Study of Primitive Potato Varieties in Peru." *Euphytica* 29: 107–113.

Jákfalvi-Leiva, Susana. 1984. *Traducción, escritura y violencia colonizadora: Un estudio de la obra del Inca Garcilaso.* Syracuse, N.Y.: Maxwell School of Citizenship and Public Affairs, Syracuse University.

Jakobson, Roman. 1971a. "On Linguistic Aspects of Translation." In *Word and Language*, vol. 2 of *Selected Writings*, pp. 260–266. The Hague: Mouton.

———. 1971b. "Quest for the Essence of Language." In *Word and Language*, vol. 2 of *Selected Writings*, pp. 345–359. The Hague: Mouton.

———. 1971c. "Shifters, Verbal Categories, and the Russian Verb." In *Word and Language*, vol. 2 of *Selected Writings*, pp. 130–147. The Hague: Mouton.

Jara, Fausto. 1982. *Taruca: Ecuador quichuacunapac rimashca rimaicuna/ La venada: Literatura oral quichua del Ecuador*, trans. Fausto Jara J. and Ruth Moya. Quito: Instituto Geográfico Militar.

Jara, Victoria de la. 1974. *Los nuevos fundamentos para el estudio integral de la escritura peruana.* Lima: INIDE.

Kahn, E. J., Jr. 1984. "Potatoes: Man Is What He Eats." In *The Staffs of Life*, pp. 85–110. Boston: Little, Brown, and Company.

Kauffmann Doig, Federico. 1978. "Los retratos de la capaccuna de Guamán Poma y el problema de los *tocapo*." In *Amerikanistische Studien: Festschrift für Hermann Trimborn*, ed. Roswith Hartmann and Udo Oberem, pp. 298–308. St. Augustin: Anthropos Institute.

Kelly, L. G. 1979. *The True Interpreter: A History of Translation Theory and Practice in the West.* New York: St. Martin's Press.

Kendall, Ann. 1973. *Everyday Life of the Incas.* London: B. T. Batsford.

La Barre, Weston. 1947. "Potato Taxonomy among the Aymara Indians of Bolivia." *Acta Americana* 5: 83–103.

Lafone Quevedo, Samuel A. 1950. "El culto de Tonapa." In *Tres relaciones de antigüedades peruanas*, ed. Marcos Jiménez de la Espada, pp. 287–353. Asunción: Guaraní.

Lakoff, George. 1987. *Women, Fire, and Dangerous Things: What Categories Reveal about the Mind.* Chicago: University of Chicago Press.

Lakoff, George, and Mark Johnson. 1980. *Metaphors We Live By.* Chicago: University of Chicago Press.

Lara, Jesús. [1947] 1979. *La poesía quechua.* Mexico City: Fondo de Cultura Económica.

Larson, Mildred L. 1984. *Meaning-Based Translation: A Guide to Cross-Language Equivalence.* New York: University Press of America.

Laufer, Berthold. 1938. *The American Plant Migration: Part I: The Potato.* Field Museum of Natural History Anthropological Series, vol. 28, no. 1.

Leach, Edmund. 1976. *Culture and Communication: The Logic by Which Symbols Are Connected.* Cambridge, England: Cambridge University Press.

Leacock, Eleanor, and June Nash. 1977. "Ideologies of Sex: Archetypes and Stereotypes." *Annals of the New York Academy of Sciences* 285: 618–645.

Lehmann-Nitsche, R. 1928. "Coricancha: El templo del sol en el Cuzco y las imágenes de su altar mayor." *Revista del Museo de la Plata* 31, no. 3a.

Leonardi, P. José. 1966. *Lengua quichua: Dialecto del Napo, Ecuador, Gramática y diccionario.* Quito: Editora Fénix.

Lévi-Strauss, Claude. 1969. *The Raw and the Cooked: Introduction to a Science of Mythology,* trans. John and Doreen Weightman. New York: Harper.

Lewis, Philip E. 1985. "The Measure of Translation Effects." In *Difference in Translation,* ed. Joseph F. Graham, pp. 31–63. Ithaca: Cornell University Press.

Lira, Jorge A. 1944. *Diccionario kkechuwa-español.* Tucumán: Universidad Nacional de Tucumán, Instituto de Historia, Lingüística y Folklore.

Lockhart, James. 1968. *Spanish Peru 1532–1560: A Colonial Society.* Madison: University of Wisconsin Press.

———. 1972. *The Men of Cajamarca: A Social and Biographical Study of the First Conquerors of Peru.* Austin: University of Texas Press.

López-Baralt, Mercedes. 1979a. "Guaman Poma de Ayala y el arte de la memoria en una crónica ilustrada del siglo XVII." *Cuadernos americanos* 38, no. 3 (May–June): 119–151.

———. 1979b. "Millenarism as Liminality: The Andean Myth of Inkarrí." *Point of Contact* 6 (Spring): 65–82.

———. 1980. "Notas sobre problemas interpretativos ligados a la traducción: El caso de la literatura oral amerindia." *Sin nombre* 10, no. 4: 49–70.

———. 1982. "La crónica de indias como texto cultural: Articulación de los códigos icónico y lingüístico en los dibujos de la *Nueva corónica* de Guamán Poma." *Revista iberoamericana* 43, nos. 120–121: 461–531.

Lotman, Juri M. 1975. "On the Metalanguage of a Typological Description of Culture." *Semiotica* 14, no. 2: 97–123.

Luria, A. R. [1974] 1976. *Cognitive Development: Its Cultural and Social Foundations,* trans. Martin Lopez-Morillas and Lynn Solotaroff. Cambridge: Harvard University Press.

MacCormack, Carol P. 1980. "Nature, Culture and Gender: A Critique." In *Nature, Culture and Gender,* ed. Carol P. MacCormack and Marilyn Strathern, pp. 1–25. Cambridge: University of Cambridge Press.

MacCormick, Sabine. 1985. "'The Heart Has Its Reasons': Predicaments of Missionary Christianity in Early Colonial Peru." *Hispanic American Historical Review* 65, no. 3: 443–466.

Macdonald, Regina Lee Harrison. See Harrison [Macdonald], Regina Lee.

Macdonald, Theodore, Jr. 1979. "Processes of Change in Amazonian Ecuador: Quijos Quichua Indians Become Cattlemen." Ph.D. dissertation, University of Illinois, Urbana.

MacPherson, Peter. 1982. "The Doctrine of Signatures." *Glasgow Naturalist* 20, pt. 3: 191–210.

Mamani, Mauricio. 1981. "El chuño: Preparación, uso, almacenamiento." In *La tecnología en el mundo andino: Runakunap kawsayninkupaq rurasqankunaqa*, vol. 1, ed. Heather Lechtman and Ana María Soldi, pp. 235–247. Mexico City: Universidad Nacional Autónoma de México.

Mannheim, Bruce. 1984. "*Una nación acorralada:* Southern Peruvian Quechua Language Planning and Politics in Historical Perspective." *Language in Society* 13: 291–301.

———. 1986a. "Semantic Coupling in Quechua Verse." Ms.

———. 1986b. "Popular Song and Popular Grammar, Poetry and Metalanguage." *Word* 37, nos. 1–2 (April–August): 45–75.

———. 1986c. "The Language of Reciprocity in Southern Peruvian Quechua." *Anthropological Linguistics* (Fall): 267–273.

———. 1987a. "Couplets and Oblique Contexts: The Social Organization of a Folksong." *Text* 7, no. 3: 265–288.

———. 1987b. "A Semiotic of Andean Dreams." In *Dreaming: Anthropological and Psychological Interpretations*, ed. Barbara Tedlock, pp. 132–153. Cambridge: Cambridge University Press.

Mariscotti de Görlitz, Ana María. 1978. "Pachamama Santa Tierra: Contribución al estudio de la religión autóctona en los Andes centro-meridionales." *Indiana* 8, supplement.

Maynard, Eileen. 1966. "Indian-Mestizo Relations." In *The Indians of Colta: Essays on the Colta Lake Zone*, ed. Eileen Maynard, pp. 1–115. Ithaca, N.Y.: Cornell University Department of Anthropology.

Means, Philip Ainsworth. 1928. *Biblioteca Andina, Part One. The Chroniclers*, pp. 271–525. Transactions of the Connecticut Academy of Arts and Sciences, 29.

Meisch, Lynn. 1987. *Otavalo: Weaving, Costume and the Market*. Quito: Ediciones Libri Mundi.

Menéndez Pidal, Ramón. 1958. "El lenguaje del siglo XVI." In *La lengua de Cristóbal Colón*, pp. 47–84. Madrid: Espasa-Calpe.

Millones, Luis. 1978. *Los dioses de Santa Cruz: Comentarios a la crónica de Juan de Santa Cruz Pachacuti*. Lima: PUCP, CISEPA.

Millones, Luis, Virgilio Galdo G., and Anne Marie Dussault. 1981. "Reflexiones en torno al romance en la sociedad indígena: Seis relatos de amor." *Revista de crítica literaria latinoamericana* 8, no. 14: 7–29.

Miracle, Andrew W., Jr., and Juan de Dios Yapita Moya. 1981. "Time and Space in Aymara." In *The Aymara Language in Its Social and Cultural Context: A Collection of Essays on Aspects of Aymara Language and Culture*, ed. M. J. Hardman, pp. 33–57. Gainesville: University of Florida Press.

Montaluisa, Luis O. 1980. "Historia de la escritura del quichua." *Revista de la Universidad Católica* 8, no. 28 (November): 121–145.

Montell, Gosta. 1929. *Dress and Ornaments in Ancient Peru: Archaeological and Historical Studies*. Göteborg.

Monteros, P. Raimundo M. 1942. *Música autóctona del oriente ecuatoriano.* Quito: Imprenta del Ministerio de Gobierno.

Montoya, Rodrigo. 1980. "Comunidades campesinas: Historia y clase." *Sociedad y política* 3, no. 9: 29–40.

Montoya, Rodrigo, Edwin Montoya, and Luis Montoya, eds. 1987. *La sangre de los cerros, urqukunapa yawarnin: Antología de la poesía que se canta en el Perú.* Lima: Centro Peruano de Estudios Sociales, Mosca Azul, Universidad Nacional Mayor de San Marcos.

Mugica, P. Camilo. 1979. *Aprenda el quichua: Gramática y vocabularios.* Quito, Ecuador: Imprenta del Colegio Técnico "Don Bosco."

Müller, Rolf. 1972. *Sonne, Mond und Sterne über dem Reich der Inka.* Berlin: Springer-Verlag.

Muñoz Bernard, C. 1976. "Cuestiones y vitalizas: Apuntes etnográficos sobre la medicina popular en la sierra oriental del Cañar, Ecuador." *Bulletin de L'Institut Français d'Etudes Andines* 5, nos. 3–4: 49–72.

Murra, John V. 1960. "Rite and Crop in the Inca State." In *Culture in History: Essays in Honor of Paul Radin,* ed. Stanley Diamond, pp. 393–408. New York: Columbia University Press.

———. 1978. "Introduction." In *Deep Rivers,* by José María Arguedas, trans. Frances Horning Barraclough, pp. ix–xv. Austin: University of Texas Press.

Muysken, Pieter Cornelis. 1977. *Syntactic Developments in the Verb Phrase of Ecuadorian Quechua.* Lisse: Peter de Ridder Press.

Nebrija, Antonio de. [1492] 1926. *Gramática de la lengua castellana,* ed. Ig. González Llubera. London: Oxford.

Nida, Eugene A. 1959. "Principles of Translation as Exemplified by Bible Translating." In *On Translation,* ed. Reuben A. Brower, pp. 11–32. Cambridge: Harvard University Press.

———. 1964. *Toward a Science of Translating.* Leiden: J. Brill.

Nuñez del Prado Béjar, Daisy Irene. 1972. "La reciprocidad como ethos en la cultura indígena." B.A. thesis, Universidad Nacional de San Antonio Abad, Cuzco.

Oberem, Udo. 1980. *Los Quijos: Historia de la transculturación de un grupo indígena en el oriente ecuatoriano.* Otavalo: Instituto Otavalo de Antropología.

Ong, Walter J. 1982. *Orality and Literacy: The Technologizing of the Word.* New York: Methuen and Co.

Orr, Carolyn, and Betsy Wrisley. 1965. *Vocabulario quichua del oriente del Ecuador.* Quito, Ecuador: Instituto Lingüístico de Verano.

Orr D., Carolina, and Juan E. Hudelson, eds. 1971. *Cuillurguna: Cuentos de los quichuas del oriente ecuatoriano.* Quito: Houser Ltd.

Ortiz, Alejandro. 1982. "Moya: Espacio, tiempo y sexo en un pueblo andino." *Allpanchis* 17, no. 2: 189–209.

Ortíz de Villalba, Juan Santos. 1976. *Sacha pacha: El mundo de la selva.* Quito, Ecuador: Imprenta del Colegio Técnico "Don Bosco."

Ortiz Rescaniere, Alejandro. 1973. *De Adaneva a Inkarrí: Una visión indígena del Perú.* Lima: Retablo de Papel.

————. 1980. *Huarochirí, 400 años después.* Lima: Pontificia Universidad Católica del Perú.

Ortner, Sherry B. 1974. "Is Female to Male as Nature Is to Culture?" In *Woman, Culture, and Society,* ed. Michelle Zimbalist Rosaldo and Louise Lamphere, pp. 67–89. Stanford, Calif.: Stanford University Press.

Ossio, Juan. 1977. "Myth and History: The Seventeenth Century Chronicle of Guamán Poma de Ayala." In *Text and Context,* ed. Ravindra K. Jain, pp. 51–95. Philadelphia: Institute for Study of Human Issues.

Osuna Ruiz, Rafael. 1968. *Introducción a la lírica prehispánica.* Maracaíbo: Universidad de Zulia.

*Oxford English Dictionary, a Supplement.* 1976. Vol. 2, ed. R. W. Burchfield, pp. 777–778. Oxford: Clarendon Press.

Pagden, Anthony. 1982. *The Fall of Natural Man: The American Indian and the Origins of Comparative Ethnology.* Cambridge: Cambridge University Press.

Parker, Gary John. 1969. *Ayacucho Grammar and Dictionary.* The Hague: Mouton.

Parsons, Elsie Clews. 1945. *Peguche: Canton of Otavalo, Province of Imbabura, Ecuador: A Study of Andean Indians.* Chicago: University of Chicago Press.

Pease, Franklin G. Y. 1983. "Notas sobre literatura incaica." *Historia y cultura* 16: 95–112.

"Peru: *k'ausak'rak'mi kani.*" 1975. *Latin America* 9, no. 22 (June): 175.

Platt, Tristan. 1976. *Espejos y maíz: Temas de estructura simbólica andina.* Cuadernos de Investigación CIPCA, no. 10. La Paz: Centro de Investigación y Promoción del Campesinado.

Polo de Ondegardo, Juan. [1561–1571] 1917. "Instrucción contra las ceremonias y ritos que usan los indios conforme al tiempo de su infidelidad." In *Colección de libros y documentos referentes a la historia del Perú,* series 1, no. 3, pp. 189–203.

Porras Barrenechea, Raúl. 1952. "Prólogo." In *Vocabulario de la lengua general de todo el Peru llamada quichua o del Inca,* Diego González Holguín, ed. Raúl Porras Barrenechea, pp. v–xliv. Lima: Imprenta Santa María.

————. 1962. *Los cronistas del Peru (1528–1650).* Lima: San Martí.

Posner, Michael I. 1973. *Cognition.* Glenview, Ill.: Scott Foresman and Company.

Prescott, Suzanne, and Carolyn Letko. 1977. "Battered Women: A Social Psychological Perspective." In *Battered Women: A Psychosociological Study of Domestic Violence,* ed. María Roy, pp. 72–96. New York: Van Nostrand Reinhold Co.

Quine, Willard V. 1959. "Meaning and Translation." In *On Translation,* ed. Reuben A. Brower, pp. 148–173. Cambridge: Harvard University Press.

Rafael, Vicente L. 1988. *Contracting Colonialism: Translation and Christian Conversion in Tagalog Society under Early Spanish Rule.* Ithaca: Cornell University Press.

Real Academia Española. [1732] 1969. *Diccionario de autoridades.* Ed. facsimile. Madrid: Gredos.

*Recopilación de leyes de los reynos de las Indias.* [1550] 1943. Madrid: Consejo de la Hispanidad.

Renart, Juan Guillermo. 1980. "Mitificación y desmitificación de animales en la poesía folklórica quechua de contenido social." *Ottawa Hispánica* 2: 51–71.

Revilla, Arcenio, and Ana B. de Revilla. 1965. "Appendix I: The Hacienda Colta Monjas." In *Indians in Misery: A Preliminary Report on the Colta Lake Zone, Chimborazo, Ecuador*, ed. Eileen Maynard, pp. 95–130. Ithaca, N.Y.: Department of Anthropology, Cornell University.

Rojas Rojas, Ibico. 1980. *Expansión del quechua: Primeros contactos con el castellano.* Lima: Signo.

Rosaldo, Michelle Z. 1980. *Knowledge and Passion: Ilongot Notions of Self and Social Life.* London: Cambridge University Press.

Ross, Ellen M. 1963. *Introduction to Ecuador Highland Quichua or Quichua in Ten Easy Lessons.* Quito: Instituto Lingüístico de Verano.

———. 1980. *Quichua-English/English-Quichua Dictionary*, ed. Louisa R. Stark. Madison, Wis.: Foundation for Inter-Andean Development.

Rostworowski de Diez Canseco, María. 1983. *Estructuras andinas del poder: Ideología religiosa y política.* Lima: Instituto de Estudios Peruanos.

Rougemont, Denis de. [1940] 1974. *Love in the Western World*, trans. Montgomery Belgion. New York: Harper Colophon Books.

Rowe, John Howland. 1946. "Inca Culture at the Time of the Spanish Conquest." In *The Andean Civilizations*, vol. 2 of *The Handbook of South American Indians*, ed. Julian H. Steward, pp. 183–330. Washington, D.C.: Bureau of American Ethnology.

———. 1953. "Eleven Inca Prayers from the Zithuwa Ritual." *Kroeber Anthropological Society Papers* 8–9: 82–99.

———. 1960. "The Origins of Creator Worship among the Incas." In *Culture in History: Essays in Honor of Paul Radin*, ed. Stanley Diamond, pp. 408–429. New York: Columbia University Press.

———. 1967. "Colonial Portraits of Inca Nobles." In *The Civilizations of Ancient America: Selected Papers of the XXIXth International Congress of Americanists*, ed. Sol Tax, pp. 258–271. New York: Cooper Square.

Salaman, Redcliffe N. [1949] 1985. *The History and Social Influence of the Potato.* Cambridge: Cambridge University Press.

Salmond, Anne. 1982. "Theoretical Landscapes on Cross-Cultural Conceptions of Knowledge." In *Semantic Anthropology*, ed. David Parkin, pp. 65–89. New York: Academic Press.

Salomon, Frank. 1973. "Weavers of Otavalo." In *Peoples and Cultures of South America*, ed. Daniel Gross, pp. 460–493. New York: Doubleday/Natural History Press.

———. 1982. "Chronicles of the Impossible: Notes on Three Peruvian Indigenous Historians." In *From Oral to Written Expression: Native Andean Chronicles of the Early Colonial Period*, ed. Rolena Adorno, pp. 9–39. Syracuse: Maxwell School of Citizenship and Public Affairs.

———. 1986. *Native Lords of Quito in the Age of the Incas: The Political*

*Economy of North Andean Chiefdoms.* Cambridge: Cambridge University Press.

Sánchez Farfán, Jorge. 1979. "Papas y hombres." *Antropología andina* 3: 51–71.

Sáncho, Pe[d]ro. [1543] 1988. *La relación de Pero Sancho,* ed. Luis R. Arocena. Buenos Aires: Ultra.

Santacruz Pachacuti Yamqui Salcamaygua, Joan de. [1613] 1927. *Relación de antigüedades deste reyno del Pirú.* In Colección de libros y documentos referentes a la historia del Perú, vol. 9, ed. Horacio A. Urteaga, pp. 125–235. Lima: San Martí.

———. [1613] 1928. *An Account of the Antiquities of Peru,* trans. and ed. Philip Ainsworth Means. In *Biblioteca Andina, Part One. The Chronicles,* pp. 67–120. Transactions of the Connecticut Academy of Arts and Sciences 29.

Santo Tomás, Domingo de. [1560] 1951. *Lexicon o vocabulario de la lengua general del Peru.* Lima: Universidad Nacional Mayor de San Marcos, Instituto de Historia.

Sauer, Carl O. [1952] 1975. *Seeds, Spades, Hearths, and Herds.* Cambridge: M.I.T. Press.

Schechter, John M. 1979. "The Inca *Cantar Histórico:* A Lexico-historical Elaboration on Two Cultural Themes." *Ethnomusicology* 23, no. 2 (May): 191–204.

———. 1980. "El cantar histórico incaico." *Revista músical chilena* 34, no. 151: 38–60.

———. 1983. "*Corona y baile:* Music in a Child's Wake of Ecuador and Hispanic South America, Past and Present." *Latin American Music Review* 4, no. 1: 1–80.

Schmitz, H. Walter. 1977. "Interethnic Relations in Saraguro (Ecuador) from the Point of View of an Anthropology of Communication." *Sociologus* 27, no. 1: 64–85.

Seitz, Barbara. 1981a. "'Power' Songs of the *Sacha Huarmi* (Jungle Woman) as Transformational Communication Acts." In *Discourse in Ethnomusicology II: A Tribute to Alan P. Merriam,* ed. Caroline Card et al., pp. 153–172. Bloomington, Ind.: Ethnomusicology Publications Group, Indiana University.

———. 1981b. "Quichua Songs to Sadden the Heart: Music in a Communication Event." *Latin American Music Review* 2, no. 2 (Fall/Winter): 223–252.

———. 1982. "'Llaquichina' Songs of the 'Sacha Huarmi' (Jungle Woman) and Their Role in Transformational Communication Events in the Ecuadorian Oriente." Ph.D. dissertation, University of Indiana, Bloomington.

Sharon, Douglas. 1978. *Wizard of the Four Winds: A Shaman's Story.* New York: Free Press.

Silverblatt, Irene. 1978. "Andean Women in the Inca Empire." *Feminist Studies* 4, no. 3 (October): 37–62.

———. 1980. "The universe has turned inside out . . . There is no justice for

us here: Andean Women under Spanish Rule." In *Women and Coloniza-tion: Anthropological Perspectives*, ed. Mona Etienne and Eleanor Lea-cock, pp. 149–185. South Hadley, Mass.: Bergin and Garvey.
———. 1982. "Dioses y diablos: Idolatrías y evangelización." *Allpanchis phuturinqa* 16, no. 19: 31–49.
———. 1987. *Moon, Sun, and Witches: Gender Ideologies and Class in Inca and Colonial Peru*. Princeton, N.J.: Princeton University Press.
Skar, Sarah Lund. 1979. "The Use of the Public/Private Framework in the Analysis of Egalitarian Societies: The Case of a Quechua Community in Highland Peru." *Women's Studies International Quarterly* 2, no. 4: 449–460.
Slicher Van Bath, B. H. 1963. *The Agrarian History of Western Europe A.D. 500–1850*, trans. Olive Ordish. London: Edward Arnold.
Smith, Richard Chase. 1982. *The Dialectics of Domination in Peru: Native Communities and the Myth of the Vast Amazonian Emptiness*. Cultural Survival Occasional Papers, 8 (October). Cambridge, Mass.: Cultural Survival.
Stark, Louisa R. 1975. *Apuntes sobre la gramática quichua de la sierra ecuatoriana*. Otavalo, Ecuador: Instituto Inter-Andino de Desarrollo.
Stark, Louisa R., Lawrence K. Carpenter, Miguel Andrango Concha, and Carlos A. Conterón Córdova. 1973. *El Quichua de Imbabura: Una gramá-tica pedagógica*. Otavalo, Ecuador: Instituto Inter-Andino de Desarrollo.
Stark, Louisa R., and Pieter Muysken. 1977. *Diccionario español-quichua/quichua-español*. Quito, Ecuador: Publicaciones de los Museos del Banco Central del Ecuador.
Stern, Steve J. 1982. *Peru's Indian Peoples and the Challenge of Spanish Conquest: Huamanga to 1640*. Madison: University of Wisconsin Press.
Stevens, Evelyn P. 1973. "*Marianismo*: The Other Face of *Machismo* in Latin America." In *Female and Male in Latin America: Essays*, ed. Ann Pescatello, pp. 89–103. Pittsburgh: University of Pittsburgh Press.
Swann, Brian, ed. 1983. *Smoothing the Ground: Essays on Native Ameri-can Oral Literature*. Berkeley: University of California Press.
Szemínski, Jan. 1982–1984. "Las generaciones del mundo según don Felipe Guaman Poma de Ayala." *Estudios latinoamericanos* 9: 89–123.
———. 1985. "De la imagen de Wiraqucan según las oraciones recogidas por Joan de Santa Cruz Pachacuti Yamqui Salcamaygua." *Histórica* 9, no. 2: 247–263.
Tambiah, S. J. 1968. "The Magical Power of Words." *Man* n.s. 3, no. 2: 175–208.
Taussig, Michael T. 1980a. *The Devil and Commodity Fetishism in South America*. Chapel Hill: University of North Carolina Press.
———. 1980b. "Folk Healing and the Structure of Conquest in Southwest Colombia." *Journal of Latin American Lore* 6, no. 2: 217–278.
Taylor, Anne Christine, and Ernesto Chau. 1983. "Jivaroan Magical Songs: Achuar Anent of Connubial Love." *Amerindia* 8: 87–127.
Taylor, Gerald. 1974–1976. "*Camay, camac* et *camasca* dans le manuscrit

quechua de Huarochirí." *Journal de la Société des Américanistes* 63: 231–244.

———, ed. 1980a. *Rites et traditions de Huarochirí: Manuscrit quechua du début du 17e siécle.* Paris: Editions L'Harmattan.

———. 1980b. "Supay." *Amerindia* 5: 47–65.

Tedlock, Dennis. 1983. *The Spoken Word and the Work of Interpretation.* Philadelphia: University of Pennsylvania Press.

*Tercer Concilio Limense (1582–1583).* [1582–1583] 1982. Ed. Enrique T. Bartra, S.J. Lima: Facultad Pontificia y Civil de Teología de Lima.

*Tercero cathecismo y exposición de la doctrina christiana por sermones.* [1585] 1985. *Corpus Hispanorum de Pace,* vol. 26-2, pp. 333–777. Madrid: Consejo Superior de Investigaciones Científicas.

Theroux, Paul. 1979. *The Old Patagonian Express: By Train through the Americas.* Boston: Houghton Mifflin Company.

Titu Cusi Yupanqui, Diego de Castro. [1570] 1973. *Relación de la conquista del Peru.* Lima: Biblioteca Universitaria.

"Tiupullu." 1957. In *Ecuador, Gazateer no. 36,* p. 176. Washington, D.C.: Office of Geography, Department of the Interior.

Todorov, Tzvetan. [1982] 1987. *The Conquest of America: The Question of the Other.* Trans. Richard Howard. New York: Harper.

Torero Fernández de Córdova, Alfredo. 1974. *El quechua y la historia social andina.* Lima: Universidad Ricardo Palma.

Torres Rubio, P. Diego de. [1603] [1700] 1963. *Arte de la lengua quichua, con las adiciones que hizó P. Juan de Figueredo,* ed. Luis A. Pardo. Cuzco: Pardo.

Trimborn, Hernan. 1953. "El motivo explanatorio en los mitos de Huarochirí." *Letras* 4–9: 135–146.

Turino, Thomas. 1983. "The Charango and the *Sirena:* Music, Magic, and the Power of Love." *Latin American Music Review* 4, no. 1: 81–119.

Tyler, Stephen A. 1978. *The Said and Unsaid: Mind, Meaning, and Culture.* New York: Academic Press.

Ugent, Donald. 1970. "The Potato." *Science* 170, no. 3963 (December): 1161–1166.

Uhle, Max. 1968. *Vom Kondor und vom Fuchs.* Berlin: Verlag Gebr. Mann.

Urbain, Jean-Didier. 1980. "Le Système Quechua de l'échange: Développements métaphoriques et adaptation d'un 'vocabulaire de base.'" *L'homme* 20, no. 1: 71–90.

Urbano, Henrique-Osvaldo. 1980. "Dios Yaya, Dios Churi y Dios Espíritu: Modelos trinitarios y arqueología mental en los Andes." *Journal of Latin American Lore* 6, no. 1: 111–127.

Urioste, George. 1981. "The Spanish and Quechua Voices of Waman Puma." *Review* 28: 16–19.

———, ed. 1983. *Hijos de Pariya Qaqa: La tradición oral de Waru Chiri (Mitología, ritual y costumbres).* 2 vols. Syracuse, N.Y.: Maxwell School of Citizenship and Public Affairs.

Urton, Gary. 1981. *At the Crossroads of the Earth and the Sky: An Andean Cosmology.* Austin: University of Texas Press.

Varese, Stéfano. 1982. "Restoring Multiplicity: Indianities and the Civilizing Project in Latin America." *Latin American Perspectives* 9, no. 2 (Spring): 29–41.

Vargas, Carlos. 1936. "El *solanum tuberosum* a través del desenvolvimiento de las actividades humanas." *Revista del Museo Nacional* 5, no. 2: 193–248.

*Vocabulario y phrasis en la lengua general de los indios de Perú, llamada Quichua.* [1586] 1951. Ed. Guillermo Escobar Risco. Lima, Peru: Instituto de Historia de la Facultad de Letras, Universidad Nacional Mayor de San Marcos.

Voloshinov, V. N. 1971. "Reported Speech." In *Readings in Russian Poetics: Formalist and Structuralist Views,* ed. Ladislav Matejka and Krystyna Pomorska, pp. 149–175. Cambridge, Mass.: M.I.T. Press.

Wachtel, Nathan. 1973. *Sociedad e ideología: Ensayos de historia y antropología andinas.* Lima: Instituto de Estudios Peruanos.

———. [1971] 1977. *The Vision of the Vanquished: The Spanish Conquest of Peru through Indian Eyes, 1530–1570,* trans. Ben and Siân Reynolds. New York: Barnes and Noble.

Walter, Lynn. 1981. "Otavaleño Development, Ethnicity, and National Integration." *América indígena* 41, no. 2 (April–June): 319–337.

Weinstock, Steven. 1970. "Ethnic Conceptions and Relations of Otavalo Indian Migrants in Quito, Ecuador." *Anuario indigenista* 30 (December): 157–167.

Whitten, Norman. 1976. *Sacha Runa: Ethnicity and Adaptation of Ecuadorian Jungle Quichua.* Urbana: University of Illinois Press.

———. 1978. "Ecological Imagery and Cultural Adaptability: The Canelos Quichua of Eastern Ecuador." *American Anthropologist* 80: 836–859.

Williams, David. 1987. "In Praise of the Potato." *Atlantic Monthly* (March): 74.

Wölck, Wolfgang. 1973. "Attitudes towards Spanish and Quechua in Bilingual Peru." In *Language Attitudes: Current Trends and Prospects,* ed. Roger Shuy and Ralph W. Fosold, pp. 129–147. Washington, D.C.: Georgetown University Press.

Wolf, Eric R. 1959. *Sons of the Shaking Earth.* Chicago: University of Chicago Press.

Woods, Michael, and Mark Martin. 1987. "Potatoes from True Seed." *The World and I* (June): 176–183.

Woolfe, Jennifer A. 1987. *The Potato in the Human Diet.* New York: Cambridge University Press.

Yaranga Valderrama, Abdón. 1979. "La divinidad *Illapa* en la región andina." *América indígena* 39, no. 4: 697–720.

Zárate, Agustín de. [1555] 1862. *Historia del descubrimiento y conquista del Perú.* In *Historiadores primitivos de Indias,* vol. 2, ed. Enrique de Vedia, pp. 459–563. Biblioteca de Autores Españoles. Madrid: Rivadeneyra.

Zubritski, Yu A. 1977. "Motivos políticos en la poesía quechua." *Latin American Research Review* 12, no. 2: 161–170.

————. 1979. *Los Incas—Quechuas*, trans. Vidal Vidal Villanueva. Moscow: Editorial Progreso.

Zuidema, R. Tom. N.d.a. "The Andean Myth of Hatyacuri and Its Bororo and Kayapo Parallels." Ms.

————. N.d.b. "Organizing Space for Computing the Calendar: Sun, Moon, Pleiades, Stars in Inca Astronomy." Ms.

————. 1977. "The Inca Calendar." In *Native American Astronomy*, ed. Anthony F. Aveni, pp. 219–259. Austin: University of Texas Press.

————. 1978a. "Jerarquía y espacio en la organización social incaica." *Estudios andinos* 8, no. 14: 1–28.

————. 1978b. "Mito, rito, calendario y geografía en el antiguo Perú." *Actes du XLIIe Congrès International des Americanistes*, vol. 4, pp. 347–357. Paris.

————. 1979. "El ushnu." *Revista de la Universidad Complutense* 28, no. 117: 317–362.

————. 1982. "Bureaucracy and Systematic Knowledge in Andean Civilization." In *The Inca and Aztec States 1400–1800: Anthropology and History*, ed. George A. Collier, Renato I. Rosaldo, and John D. Wirth, pp. 419–459. New York: Academic Press.

Zuidema, R. T., and U. Quispe. 1973. "A Visit to God: The Account and Interpretation of a Religious Experience in the Peruvian Community of Choque-Huarcaya." In *Peoples and Cultures of Native South America*, ed. Daniel R. Gross, pp. 358–377. New York: Doubleday/Natural History Press.

# Index

abandonment, fear of, as theme of love songs, 148–152, 157, 166–167, 168–169, 171

*achupalla* (pineapple plant): symbolism of, 108

Acosta, José de, 36, 43

advertisements, cultural stereotypes of Indians in, 9–14, 197n.3, 197n.4

agricultural practices: disadvantages for women, 134; importance of reading signs, 95; land ownership, 121–122; *paju* ceremony, 137; schedule for planting in cosmological ideogram, 70; symbols related to, in Manco Capac's poem, 98; women's work in the tropical forest environment, 138–139

Aldana, Hernando de, 40

Allen, Catherine, 192

Almagro, 41

alternative realities, 30–31, 184–188

*amaru.* See snakes

Anchicocha (mountainous region), 105; representing *tinkuy*, 103

Andean Indians: and Amerindian vs. Christian concepts, 25–28; cultivation of potatoes by, 180–184, 187–188; cultural stereotypes of, 9–13, 197nn.3–4; distinctive dress of, 10, 11, 13; and nomenclature for potatoes, 172, 174, 180–182, 200n.5

animal symbolism: in myth of Quni Raya, 102–105; in song of lost baby, 107–111. See also snakes

aphrodisiacs: potatoes as, 178–179; in writings of Santacruz Pachacuti Yamqui, 145. See also love potions

Arguedas, José María, 92, 188–189

Asad, Talal, 29

Atahualpa (Inca leader): consultation of, with oracle, 100; "listening" to book, 55–56; murder of, 33–34, 40–43, 198n.2

Avila, Francisco de, 66, 102

*ayahuaska*, 148. See also hallucinogens

*ayllu* (localized kindred or larger localized group, self-defined), 46, 49, 94, 134–135

Aymara Indians, 100, 180–181

Aymara language, 19, 51–52

*ayni* (reciprocal labor, in kind), 52, 53–54

Aztec culture, 199n.4

baby. See *wawa*

Ballón Aguirre, Enrique, 28

barbarian, Greek concept of, 35–36

Barrios de Chungara, Domitila, 117, 143

Barthel, Thomas, 60

Barthes, Roland, 9, 12

bathing. See rivers, bathing, and foam

Bauhin, Gaspard, 178

Beauvoir, Simone de, 115; *The Second Sex*, 114

Bendezú Aybar, Edmundo, 92, 96

Benjamin, Walter, 28

Berry, Wendell, 183

bestiality, Catholic abhorrence of, 27–28

boa spirits, 162–163, 169, 170. See also snakes

Bolton, Ralph and Charlene, 128

Borges, Jorge Luis, 184, 185

Brush, Stephen, 53, 179, 181, 182, 187